Scientific Parenting

Scientific Parenting

What Science Reveals
About Parental Influence

———●━━━━━━━━━━━━━━━━●———

Dr. Nicole Letourneau
with Justin Joschko

DUNDURN
TORONTO

Editor: Allison Hirst
Design: Jesse Hooper
Printer: Webcom

Library and Archives Canada Cataloguing in Publication

Letourneau, Nicole, author
        Scientific parenting : what science reveals about parental
influence / by Dr. Nicole Letourneau, with Justin Joschko.

Includes bibliographical references and index.
Issued in print and electronic formats.
ISBN 978-1-4597-1008-5 (pbk.).--ISBN 978-1-4597-1009-2 (pdf).--ISBN 978-1-4597-1010-8 (epub)

        1. Child development. 2. Parenting. 3. Parent and child. I. Joschko, Justin, author II. Title.

HQ767.9.L42 2013   305.231   C2013-900892-6
                                           C2013-900893-4

1   2   3   4   5   17   16   15   14   13

Conseil des Arts
du Canada

Canada Council
for the Arts

Canada

ONTARIO ARTS COUNCIL
CONSEIL DES ARTS DE L'ONTARIO

We acknowledge the support of the **Canada Council for the Arts** and the **Ontario Arts Council** for our publishing program. We also acknowledge the financial support of the **Government of Canada** through the **Canada Book Fund** and **Livres Canada Books**, and the **Government of Ontario** through the **Ontario Book Publishing Tax Credit** and the **Ontario Media Development Corporation**.

Care has been taken to trace the ownership of copyright material used in this book. The author and the publisher welcome any information enabling them to rectify any references or credits in subsequent editions.

J. Kirk Howard, President

Printed and bound in Canada.

VISIT US AT
Dundurn.com | @dundurnpress | Facebook.com/dundurnpress | Pinterest.com/dundurnpress

Dundurn
3 Church Street, Suite 500
Toronto, Ontario, Canada
M5E 1M2

Gazelle Book Services Limited
White Cross Mills
High Town, Lancaster, England
L41 4XS

Dundurn
2250 Military Road
Tonawanda, NY
U.S.A. 14150

Contents

Preface

You've heard the expression before, I'm sure: when all you have is a hammer, everything looks like a nail.

I've always been fascinated by parenting, how it works and, perhaps even more so, how it doesn't. I remember as a child listening in on my parents' conversations with family and friends, gathering gossip on the problems festering beneath the surface of my neighbourhood. So-and-so's an alcoholic. So-and-so can't control her weight. So-and-so dropped out of school. So-and-so has "some problems upstairs." The problems upstairs intrigued me most of all. It was a mysterious, vaguely menacing term, hinting at something deeper and more complex than drinking or obesity or illness — something in which all those other problems were hopelessly entangled.

I watched and I listened, and as I grew, I continued to wonder about where these social problems originated. We can discuss history, systemic poverty, and cultures of oppression, but I found these provide explanations rather than answers — it's a subtle difference between those two, but key. Explanations tell us why something is wrong; answers tell us how to fix it.

We can't change our pasts, but we can change our futures. And, to polish a tarnished cliché, the future lies in the hands of our children. I'd spent my entire life spotting nails; parenting, I discovered, was my hammer.

My interest in parenting followed me to graduate school, where I began to study the science underlying child development. The broad trends, I found, were obvious — abuse begets abuse, addiction begets addiction, troubled homes breed troubled youths. It's in the specifics that things get complicated. Because some kids break free from the cycle of addiction, poverty, and violence. There is something special about these children, but what exactly that might be is difficult to quantify. We call it resilience, but what do we mean by that, really? And why do some children have it when others clearly don't? Intelligence is one answer. Epigenetics, a fascinating new science, offers another. But more than anything else, it seems that relationships make the difference. Kindness, support, and love lay a foundation solid enough to weather the harshest storms. And it need not come from home (though of course that helps); teachers, coaches, grandparents, and neighbours can all act as vital lifelines to children in need.

There's no one "right" way to parent a child. Truly gifted parents don't have access to a special guidebook or subscribe to any one theory of child-rearing. They simply become the people their children need them to be. They learn. They listen. They adapt. They push when they need to and hold back when they can. They evolve as their children do, developing new solutions to new problems.

There are no easy answers. This book was not intended to preach about how to parent, but to teach about why parenting matters. Parents know, deep down, that theirs is the most important job in the world. This book tells them why. It should be the book you turn to when you are feeling guilty about not spending enough time at work. The time you spend with your children is time well spent.

The studies and experiments we explore pull back the curtain on the mysteries of early childhood, allowing us a glimpse at the amazingly complex mechanisms at play during a child's first critical years of life. The study of child development is not a homogenous field. It draws conclusions from many different disciplines within medicine, nursing, psychology, sociology, biology, and even chemistry. It trawls the very fringe of scientific inquiry, exploring the findings excavated from the depths of science's latest theories. It traces conditions as diverse as heart disease, depression, cancer, ADHD, diabetes, alcoholism, aggression, and asthma to their roots in early childhood. It strives to learn exactly what babies need to reach their potential, and examines the consequences when these needs aren't met. My goal is to gather this information and present it in an accessible, engaging way.

Some may call this another "blame the mother" book. I don't see it that way. It's true that mothers shoulder a disproportionate amount of the responsibility of child-rearing, and catch flak for their failures while their successes yield them little credit. The media seems to fixate on the monstrous, caricaturized figure of the Bad Mother, but I truly believe that all parents try to do their best. And in the most egregious cases of bad parenting, namely abuse, culpability becomes a capricious, shifting thing. Do we blame the mother alone? Where was the father in all this? And what about the neighbours, who watched scenes of abuse unfold and said nothing? Or the ER nurse who asked too few questions? Where were the police? And where did these abusive behaviours come from in the first place? Do we blame the grandparents? Did someone abuse them? How far back do we go? How can you spot the genesis of a cycle of abuse? A circle has no beginning.

Blame is unproductive. We are a society, and we succeed or fail as one. The brighter and better and more innovative we raise the next generation to be, the better all of our lives become.

Parents need support, and providing it can only benefit all of us. And our efforts now will pay dividends generation down the line. As leading attachment theorist Pat Crittenden said, we are raising the next generation of parents.

Parenting is my hammer. And that's fine. Even the simplest of tools can build structures of great and lasting beauty.

Introduction

The Rise and Fall of the Resilient Child

―――――――――●―――――――――

*"The best way to not get your heart broken
is to pretend you don't have one."*

— CHARLIE SHEEN

Chapter 1

Resilience at What Cost?

Sophie sits on the floor by the foot of her bed. She is eight years old. Her mother tucked her in moments ago, but she's up again already, knees drawn to her chest, rocking silently back and forth. The sound of her parents fighting echoes from a vent across the room. She places a pillow over the vent and weighs it down with a stack of old books, but her contraption only muffles the sound; no matter what she does, the voices always worm through. She can't sleep when her parents fight, and they often fight late and long. The Walkman she once used to drown out their voices no longer works — the batteries are dead, and she's afraid to ask her father for new ones. He rarely hits her, but he can say mean things when he's in a bad mood, and his bad moods have become more and more common since he lost his job. Her mother is a safer choice, but she doesn't control any of the household money, what little of it there is. Eventually a plate shatters, a few more harsh words are exchanged, and the back door slams. Sophie hears her mother collapse in her favourite armchair, its worn springs creaking beneath her weight, and sob quietly. This could go on for some time, but it's a gentler sound than the fighting, and Sophie can, at least, sleep through it.

The next day Sophie comes downstairs to a big breakfast. Her plate brims with two eggs — sunny side up, just the way she likes them — four strips of bacon, and two slices of diagonally cut toast shimmering with butter. Beads of condensation collect on the side of her orange juice. Sophie's mother putters around the kitchen, smiling brightly and humming some long, meandering melody. The performance is well-intentioned but not terribly effective; her smile fails to reach her tired, red-rimmed eyes. Sophie offers her an equally forced smile in return. She knows her mother tries her best, and wants more than anything to please her. Things go best, she's learned, when her parents are happy, and they're happiest when she's quiet and well-behaved.

As Sophie eases the front door shut behind her, the anxiety balled up in her chest dissipates. She spends the short bus ride to her elementary school hoisting up a smile and pushing unpleasant thoughts of the night before as far back as she can, where they collect like gloomy refuse in the basement of her mind.

School is a welcome respite from the tension of her home life. Sophie excels in her studies, chats with her friends, and though she is sometimes teased for her ratty clothes and scuffed, over-sized sneakers — hand-me-downs from an older cousin — she's never really been bullied.

At the end of the school day Sophie's teacher hands out parent notices. Her class is going to a museum next Friday and in order to attend Sophie needs 10 dollars to cover the cost of admission. On her way out of the building Sophie pauses by a waste basket and, with a sigh, tosses the pink paper away. She knows better than to ask her parents for money.

As Sophie grows, she learns more and better ways to avoid conflict with her family. She joins the school soccer team and the drama club, and plays at her friends' houses. At 14, she starts her first part-time job. She uses her newfound cash to buy a CD player with which to drown out her parents' squabbles. Her cousin, with whom she is fairly close, has an apartment downtown, and when problems at home escalate Sophie sometimes stays with her. She sees her friends often, though always at their houses or around town. No one hangs out at her place. She has never offered and her friends know enough not to suggest it.

In high school, Sophie starts talking back to her parents and staying out later and later. Occasionally one of her friends gets a hold of a bottle of gin or wine and together they drink it greedily. Sophie becomes known as a partier. Some nights, when the desire overtakes her, she drinks with the urgency of a drowning woman, filling her belly and struggling madly against a riptide of drunkenness. After such binges, she feels ashamed. Memories of her father's drunkenness, his reeling and aggression and clownish behaviour, flood her mind. Disgust fills her mouth with its bitter taste and she fears and loathes with equal measure the thought that she may be like him. To compensate, she throws herself into her studies, spending long hours at the library and enrolling in as many extracurricular activities as she can handle.

At 18, Sophie graduates, applies for student loans, and moves away to attend university. Bills are a constant struggle, and she has to work two jobs while studying full-time, but she stays afloat by earning scholarships that take her, fully funded, through to graduate school. She earns her Masters of Education and lands a job as a teacher. She is a warm, talented, and outgoing educator, and her students love her.

Sophie is "resilient." She is the American Dream made manifest, a testament to the ability of talent and drive to overcome the most seemingly insurmountable odds. Hers is a story from which we as a society draw immeasurable comfort. We love meritocracy. We love to be the authors of our own destinies, to believe the outcomes of our lives are governed by our actions, and not by the indifferent hands of chance. This belief populates our modern stories and our most enduring fables, from Harry Potter to Cinderella to Oliver Twist. We embrace underdogs, cheering their successes, lamenting their failures, and assuring ourselves that their virtues, and not their social standing, are the basis on which they will ultimately be judged. It is a pleasant thought, and, better still, not solely the product of Hollywood fantasy.

For more than 30 years, researchers Emmy Werner and Ruth Smith chronicled the lives of 505 children from the Hawaiian island of Kauai. Beginning in 1955, the children were interviewed at multiple stages from infancy to adulthood. In the early years, their parents were interviewed as well. Participants answered a range of questions about their home lives, worries, memories of childhood, and plans for the future. Approximately one-third of the children involved in the study were considered to be from vulnerable homes, meaning they grew up in families suffering from chronic poverty, marital discord, a disorganized family structure (their mother or father leaving for prolonged periods, etc.), and/or substance abuse problems. Some of these children were beaten, berated, and belittled by their parents.

Unfortunately, these adverse environments often took their toll. Two out of three children in the vulnerable group developed serious learning or behaviour problems by 10 years old, and accumulated a record of delinquencies and mental health problems by age 18. A sad statistic, but one with a silver lining: though two out of every three children succumbed to the negative aspects of their environments, one out of three flourished in the face of these challenges. Like Sophie, they adapted to their environments and developed ways to thrive despite being denied the picture-perfect family life to which every child should, and in a better world would, be entitled.

A child's resilience can be the product of many factors. There is no golden attribute that, if possessed, can protect every child from the emotional fallout of a tumultuous or abusive childhood. But many small things can, together, make a big difference in children's capacity to shield themselves from the consequences of an ailing home life. Werner and Smith noted three clusters of factors commonly possessed by resilient children: 1) a robust intelligence coupled with other attributes generally correlated to success, such as toughness, drive, and a sociable temperament; 2) strong ties with a non-parental guardian figure, such as a teacher, older sibling, or other relative; 3) some kind of external support system, be it school or church or an organized sports team, that offered the child a sense of purpose and achievement. Not every resilient child will necessarily meet all three categories, but each one improves her chances.

Consider Sophie from our story at the start of this chapter. She was certainly a bright, well-liked, and driven child. She had a network of friends that she could rely on for support, and an older cousin who provided her with a much-needed emotional outlet and a safe space. Her job, her schoolwork, and her extra-curricular interests gave her a sense of agency and independence from her parents. And her mother tried her best under difficult circumstances.

If one of these three supports had been taken from her — if she'd been less bright, or if her friends had shunned her, or if she'd not been allowed to take a part-time job or join clubs at school — would she have fallen, or could she have balanced effectively on the remaining two? It's impossible to say for sure, though her access to all three forms of support certainly helped her. The more legs a person stands on, the harder they are to topple.

The Dark Side of Resilience

Sophie loves being a teacher. Her days are full and gratifying; it's the evenings that get to her. When she is home at night, a low and looming anxiety wells up in her chest. She thinks about commitments she's made throughout the day, promises to co-workers, students, and parents, some of which she's not sure she can fulfill. Saying no does not come naturally to Sophie; in the moment it can be almost impossible for her to do so. The urge to please is simply too overwhelming to deny.

Though most nights she comes home exhausted, Sophie finds it difficult to sleep without music playing, and the smallest creak or groan makes her jump. She often has a glass of wine with dinner to calm her nerves, and sometimes the glass becomes a bottle. Sometimes her teenage thirst for oblivion returns to her and one bottle becomes two. Her doctor complains about her blood pressure, and though Sophie is active and eats well, she can't seem to make it go down.

Dating is a bewildering and painful affair. She wavers between promiscuity and guilt-fueled promises of celibacy. She has trouble trusting men, and after a few dates, all of which end in sex, she inevitably pushes them away. The cycle continues until she meets David, a kind, patient man she can't help but trust. Fighting her subconscious spasms of panic in the face of commitment, she continues to see him. His relaxed, easy-going nature sooths her, and he eventually earns her trust. Over time, her panic withdraws, and she finds herself less and less in thrall to it.

Sophie and David move in together. She is reluctant to get too serious, but David makes her happy and she feels more at ease with him than she has ever felt with anyone. They buy a house, get married, and after a couple of years of trying, have a baby girl. They name her Elizabeth. Hers was a difficult birth, requiring a Caesarean section, but both Sophie and Elizabeth pull through well. David rises to the occasion, taking on the bulk of the household chores, feeding and changing Elizabeth, and catering to Sophie's every whim during her recovery. In spite of this treatment and her erstwhile excitement about being a mother, Sophie doesn't feel the rush of love and affection for Elizabeth that she'd expected. The whole experience seems anticlimactic, tedious, and regrettable. Horrified by these feelings, she blames the painkillers the doctor prescribed her, and assures herself that, once she heals, the sense of loving fulfillment all mothers must feel will come.

But they don't. Even after she recovers, Sophie continues to feel nothing but resentment toward Elizabeth, sadness at her situation, and a kind of terrible emptiness sucking at her insides, a black hole into which every good thought, every positive emotion, every ounce of optimism disappears. She performs her motherly duties — feeding Elizabeth when she's hungry, changing her diaper, bathing her — but does so either begrudgingly, greeting Elizabeth's every gurgled entreaty with a grumble or exasperated sigh, or numbly, performing her duties with the perfunctory, emotionless bearing of an automaton. She feels old beyond her years and robbed of any pleasure her life once contained.

Elizabeth is a beautiful baby, with soft, round cheeks and eyes of a deep, shimmering blue that beckon for attention. With her father, Elizabeth is all coos and smiles, but with Sophie, she is strangely listless and withdrawn. Playtime, to Sophie, is a frustrating experience, another duty doled out by despotic parenting experts. Try as she might, she can't understand what Elizabeth wants or likes as easily as her husband can. If infants speak a language of giggles and cries, then David is fluent while Sophie can barely speak a word. And this language barrier works two ways. Elizabeth, faced with her mother's garbled missives and begrudging attention, grows fussy and uncooperative. Sophie reacts to her daughter's petulance by becoming increasingly frustrated and exhausted. The two of them enter a vicious circle of resentment and hostility.

Whatever she tries, Sophie cannot seem to understand her daughter's needs. Her resentment turns to desperation, which turns to fear. It seems as if Elizabeth never stops crying, and nothing Sophie does can placate her. Sophie feels like a hapless peasant press-ganged into service by a tiny tyrannical captain whose language she doesn't even speak.

Farther down beneath Sophie's resentment and anger and fear festers a profound sense of guilt and inadequacy. She knew raising a child would be hard work, but she'd always been told that the rewards reaped far outweighed the effort sown. Instead, she feels as if she's laboured over salted earth, her sweat and tears yielding nothing but a few scraggily weeds.

During the first few months of Elizabeth's life, David stays home as much as possible. However, their tenuous finances eventually catch up with them, giving him no choice but to return to work full-time. He is reluctant to do so, considering his wife's deteriorating emotional state, but they simply cannot afford to have him home any longer.

With David gone for long hours, Sophie's old fears begin to resurface. Her family live in another city and she can't turn to them for support. She feels utterly alone. Her insomnia returns. When David leaves for work in the morning, the sound of the door closing behind him slides like an ice pick into her heart. The walls of her house seem to contract. The air stiffens and she finds it hard to breathe. David senses his wife's anxiety, but he's powerless to do anything about it. He has to work, and every month his hours get longer and longer.

One day, while Sophie is preparing lunch, Elizabeth pinches her finger in a kitchen cupboard. She wails uncontrollably. Sophie picks her up, perfunctorily caressing her back and telling her everything's okay in a voice that seems unsure and a little annoyed. Unappeased, Elizabeth continues to cry. Sophie feels her chest tighten. Elizabeth's cries punch through her like a power drill, boring into the shell in which her fear and dread and pain had throbbed and festered, waiting for release. Their prison punctured, the bilious thoughts pour out, sweeping her away in a flood of self-loathing. She only just manages to set Elizabeth down safely before she collapses, knees drawn up to her chest, face contorted into a rictus of misery. She rocks silently back and forth to the sound of Elizabeth's wailing. David finds her hours later when he returns home from work, still rocking, her eyes red and swollen.

Sophie seeks professional help. She is — belatedly — diagnosed with postpartum depression, an insidious and all-too-common condition affecting mothers (and, less frequently, fathers) during the first year of their child's life. Through counselling and the support of her husband, Sophie manages to overcome her depression and eventually bond with Elizabeth. Thawed by therapy support, and introspection, Sophie's heart finally melts in response to Elizabeth's blue eyes, chubby fists, giggles, and first words. However, the scars of her childhood pain remain with her always and she worries about how she will cope if she has a second baby.

Such is the dark underbelly of resilience. Some children can escape abusive homes and lead successful, happy, productive lives, but few, if any, can ever completely escape their early childhood experiences. Werner and Smith, while commenting on the remarkable tenacity of some of their study's participants, noted that resilient individuals often remain socially withdrawn. They struggle with depression or anxiety or bad relationships and fight an endless uphill battle with the ghosts of their pasts.

A troubled childhood pursues us indefinitely. It affects our relationships with our family, our co-workers, our spouses, and our children. It impacts our health, both emotional and physical, in a number of ways; studies have linked disadvantaged upbringing to conditions as diverse as obesity, heart disease, aggression, depression, substance abuse, and schizophrenia. It causes tremendous suffering, much of it silent, ignored, or denied. It is, above all, highly individual. No one can predict precisely how someone with a difficult home life will cope. Given sufficient data, we can speculate about a given child's probability of developing a behaviour disorder, or getting pregnant at 15, or becoming an alcoholic. But prediction on its own does not mean prevention. Telling Sophie that her emotional outcome is among the highest percentile of success, considering her family's behaviour and socioeconomic status, will do nothing to help loosen the icy fist clenched around her guts every time she faces stress, nor will it see her through long nights spent lying awake in bed and staring at the ceiling, cocooned by the radio, overwhelmed by her fears and a suffocating sense of personal failure. Statistics are public knowledge, but Sophie's private, inner pain remains her own.

Even those statistics, blunted and impersonal as they are, make for troubling reading. As science continues to unravel the mysteries of human development, the importance of a nurturing, supportive environment has become increasingly clear. In the January 2012 issue of *Pediatrics*, the American Academy of Pediatrics released a report urging healthcare professionals and policymakers to address the threat of toxic stress — the presence of severe and chronic stress in infancy and early childhood — on health and development. Their technical report, drawing from disciplines as varied as genomics, developmental psychology, epidemiology, sociology, and economics, highlights the influence of early environments on how children develop. They provide evidence linking a number of adverse conditions — including heart disease, depression, liver cancer, autoimmune disorders, and asthma — to toxic stress. Similar reports have been made across the scientific community. Even a trait as seemingly deep-rooted in our genes as height can be affected by childhood stress! There is no longer any doubt that poverty, discrimination, and maltreatment greatly increase a child's chances of becoming overly aggressive, engaging in criminal activity, being dangerously promiscuous, or suffering from ADHD, depression, and a host of other symptoms.

Though some of the examples in this book are extreme, the findings we discuss are by no means limited to the abusive and impoverished households banished to the fringes of our society. They affect all of us. Mercifully, Sophie's home life is not the norm. But the fallout of her childhood — the anxiety, the post-partum depression, the compulsive people-pleasing — affects a distressing number of people every day. Parenting is not a binary of good and bad, but a complex network of actions and reactions, emotions and behaviours and relationships that play off one another to produce a unique individual. It is not our aim to judge or reinforce barriers between good and bad parenting, but to help parents understand how their genes, attitude, behaviours, diet, and home life influence the way their child fits into the world. In so doing, we hope to show you how parenting really is the most important job you will ever do. Your efforts shape an individual and help set the course of their lives. The lives of these many individuals combined affect and, indeed, reflect all of society.

To do this, we've cast a wide net, trawling the seas of biology, genomics, medicine, nursing, sociology, epigenetics, and psychology for the freshest and most illuminating research these fields can offer. Not content with the flotsam that washes up on the media's well-trodden shores, we've dredged the murky depths of academic discourse, diving into laboratories and textbooks for treasures hidden from the light of day. We've snared some good theories in our efforts, wondrous bejewelled ones, slimy ones still wriggling in the hands of those who first discovered them. This book is an exhibit of our findings, each display neatly labelled so as to explain what we found and why it matters.

Is this a parenting book? Yes and no. It's about parenting, surely, though it's also about being parented, the biological and behavioural mechanisms whirring beneath the surface of a growing child. Parents will find it interesting and enlightening (we hope), but the scientific findings we discuss apply to every-body. We all come from families, after all. Some are wonderful and supportive and kind, others cold and formal and detached, still others abusive and neglectful and downright cruel. But every one of them, for better or worse, made us who we are today. This book explains how they did so.

Raising a child is not like building a bookshelf; one cannot simply by a kit from IKEA, follow a few simple instructions, and end up with something identical to the picture on the package. Not every household is allocated the same tools, or even the same building materials. Every child fits together a different way, and what reinforces one child's development may undermine the integrity of another. Quite unlike carpentry, child-rearing is messy, organic, and occasionally unpredictable. Thankfully, it's also a lot more forgiving. One false cut or misread measurement won't ruin the finished product.

Because of this, we cannot provide a set of easy-to-follow instructions. We have no grand comprehensive Parenting Strategy guaranteed to produce a perfect, even-tempered, kind, loving, intelligent, talented, chubby-cheeked child. What we *can* offer is a thorough and accessible explanation of the latest scientific findings on how children develop, why they behave in certain ways, and how this information can inform the way you parent.

In short, this book is not about the "what" of parenting — what lessons to teach your child, what demeanour to adopt when interacting them, what programs to enroll them in — but the "why" and "how." Why do some children stop crying the instant their mothers pick them up while others seem inconsolable? Why do identical twins raised in the same environment grow into unique individuals with distinct personalities? How does neglect in infancy link to heart disease or addiction in adulthood?

Parenting is not something to fear. Our ancestors have been doing it for eons. If survival is our measure of success, then we have been very successful. But if success means something more, we need to consider how children succeed in today's context. Parenting is an intricate and sublime process, a ballet of genetic and environmental influences, a kaleidoscope of factors converging into a single harmonious entity. In short, it is something worth learning about.

The anecdotes found throughout the book, we should note, are fictional.[1] They don't represent the experiences of any one real person or family, but are cobbled together from 20 years of professional experience. Their purpose is to illustrate, through narrative, the theories this book discusses, to pin a human face to the numbers and definitions and conclusions of scientific studies. Sophie may not exist, but I (Nicole) can assure you that people like her do.

Lastly, while this book was written with the average reader in mind, it will occasionally deal with fairly complex scientific concepts. Our goal is to explain these ideas in an enlightening and accessible way so that you can really understand "why" parenting is so important. Readers interested in exploring epigenetics and gene-by-environment interaction in greater detail can avail themselves of our bibliography.

Section 1

Nature vs. Nurture?

"A child is born with the potential ability to learn Chinese or Swahili, play a kazoo, climb a tree, make a strudel or a birdhouse, take pleasure in finding the coordinates of a star. Genetic inheritance determines a child's abilities and weaknesses. But those who raise a child call forth from that matrix the traits and talents they consider important."

— EMILIE BUCHWALD

Chapter 2

The Other Hundred Years' War

Thomas emerges from behind the curtain. His young face is anxious but composed. The stage light gleams off the filigreed tuning keys of the classical guitar hanging from a strap across his shoulders. He shields his eyes from the spotlight and scans the crowd until his eyes settle on a familiar face. He heads toward the stage's lone stool and sets his sheet music — two pages of Bach's *Jesu Joy of Man's Desiring* — on the metal stand perched nearby. He takes a seat. The audience applauds politely. Thomas smiles, offers them an appreciative wave, and begins to play. The fingers of his left hand jump effortlessly from fret to fret, string to string, moving with the grace and dexterity of practiced gymnasts. Notes flow from Thomas's guitar in a melodious stream, filling the room from wall to wall with sumptuous harmonies.

Thomas's mother watches from the front row, beaming. When the performance ends she applauds a little louder than the rest, though she's careful to keep her exuberance in check; she promised Thomas that she wouldn't embarrass him. As the boy bows and leaves the stage, a woman beside Thomas's mother leans in to her.

"Was that your son?" the woman asks.

"Why yes, it was," Thomas's mother replies.

"He looks just like you. And he plays beautifully."

Thomas's mother blushes. "Thanks. He gets that from his father."

The woman gives a knowing smile. "Good genes."

Thomas's mother nods. "It's certainly not from my side. None of us can carry a tune."

"It's the same with my Amelia. They all have beautiful voices on her father's side. She's lucky she got that from him and not me."

A hush settles over the crowd. From behind the curtain emerges a young girl in a pleated dress. Thomas's mother notes the reaction of the woman she'd been speaking to — the alert posture, the wide, nervous eyes, the anticipatory lean forward — and figures the girl on stage must be Amelia.

Amelia holds no instrument. Her hands fidget, eager for something to do. She holds them together in front of her and steps toward the mike, her eyes nervously scanning the crowd. Her mother waves but Amelia doesn't seem to notice.

There is a moment where Thomas's mother thinks the poor girl is going to faint. Amelia sways slightly on her feet, her face wide and pale. But then her mouth opens and the audience lets out a collective gasp. From Amelia's parted lips leap notes of startling operatic grandeur. Her voice is so rich and strong it seems to force the audience back several inches. They stare in awe of the enormous sound issuing from such a tiny, fragile-looking vessel. The melody soars, circling the audience like a majestic bird of prey. As her final note echoes off the back wall, the audience applauds, Amelia's mother loudest of all. Amelia scurries offstage. Thomas's mother gives Amelia's mother an impressed look.

"Wow."

Amelia's mother shrugs, slightly embarrassed. "That's all her father's doing. It's in his blood."

The Fallacy of Nature vs. Nurture

Good genes. It's in his blood. I get that from my mother. These easy, off-the-cuff statements mask a long and bitter history of feuding, contention, and one-upmanship. The 20th century has been subject to a long and heated debate over what force makes humans develop the way they do. This hundred years' war has pitted scientist against scientist, causing our keenest minds to fortify themselves inside bunkers of rigid, absolutist doctrine. The combatants have varied over the years, but each has aligned himself with one of two camps: nature or nurture. Nature surmises that human traits are the result of our genome: 46 long and elaborate strands of deoxyribonucleic acid, each comprised of a double-helix pattern woven around histone proteins and shaped into a hyper-concentrated figure called a chromosome. Nurture, meanwhile, attests that our traits arise from exterior influences: the food we eat, the language we speak, the parenting style under which we are reared, and so forth.

Over the years, both nature and nurture have gained and lost prestige with the scientific community and the public. In the early days of the 20th century, a group of scientists called eugenicists made a convincing case for the supremacy of genes, surmising that a person's physical stature, mental faculties, and even criminality were the product of his genetic makeup.[2] Humanity, they argued, stemmed from multiple bloodlines, and purifying our gene pools through selective breeding would result in a better, smarter, stronger human race. Criminals and the mentally ill were discouraged from having children, as it was believed their negative traits would muddy the gene pool. Eugenics, infected as it was by a number of unsettling racist overtones, reached a deplorable climax in Nazi Germany as the ideological drive behind Hitler's Final Solution.

The aftermath of the Second World War dealt a fatal blow to the ugly science, and a grievous — though not quite deadly —

wound to the concept of genetic predestination. Eager to distance themselves from the horrors of Nazism, some scientists promptly embraced eugenics' polar opposite: behaviourism. The discipline, which had existed as a philosophy for centuries and was forged into its modern form by Ivan Pavlov at the start of the 20th century, was championed by noted psychologist B.F. Skinner, whose "radical behaviourism" proposed that human beings were little more than highly complex machines programmed by a series of external stimuli. As supporters of nature worked desperately to scrub the swastika-shaped stains from their banner, Skinner waved the nurture flag proudly.

Behaviourism was later eclipsed by the cognitive sciences, which adopted the same "mind is machine" metaphor, but drew the opposite conclusion. The mind was indeed a machine, they argued, and human behaviour was preprogrammed into it by genes.[3]

Though nature and nurture each retain a small collection of loyalists, the battle has, in recent years, become more of an illusion than reality. Modern academic opinion has, for the most part, ceded the importance of both factors. This is not to say that there is unanimous approval of a single theory. However, the developmental sciences have undergone a paradigm shift. The question is no longer whether nature trumps nurture or vice versa; rather, it is how the two variables interact to produce a unique individual.

Family Resemblance

Newspaper headlines regularly trumpet the discovery of the gene for this or that, hinting to the average reader that, with just a little more research, everything from obesity to alcoholism will be miraculously cured by the tweak of a few key nucleotides. Sadly, this is not the case. A closer reading of such articles reveals a more mundane truth. The so-called "gene for drug use" or "gene for aggression" or "gene for the obsessive collection of

Elvis memorabilia"[4] does not apply a fatalistic tag to the individual, dooming them to a life of addiction or anger or hording ceramic figurines of the King. It can, at best, only predict one's susceptibility to this kind of behaviour. And even then, there are other factors to consider.

The idea purported by the phrase "gene for X" is that a brief series of nucleotides — the tiny molecules that comprise DNA's four-letter alphabet — commands an organism to develop a certain trait. By deleting this sequence or changing the order of the letters, one could remove the aberrant trait or replace it with something more desirable. This concept raises suspicions to a number of observers outside of the scientific field. "This may be true for something relatively straightforward, like eye colour or height," they might say, "but surely complex psychological traits like greed or anger cannot be the result of a single poorly worded genetic phrase." A well-reasoned argument, but it is only half right. In truth, even those seemingly simple physiological traits arise from both environmental and genetic influences.

Certainly, some traits seem more genetically determined than others. When we see several generations of a single family gathered together, we often notice certain similarities between its members. Perhaps a majority of them have the same freckled skin. Or the same green eyes. Or the same stubby fingers. Maybe we spot a family resemblance in their high cheekbones or aquiline noses. Or we note that none of the adults are shorter than five foot eleven. However, even a brief observation will turn up differences as well. The grandfather sits at the kitchen table and delivers an impassioned argument to his youngest daughter, who responds in kind. Meanwhile, her older sister and her mother sit two chairs down, fidgeting awkwardly with the cutlery and sharing nervous glances, uneasy about the heated tone the conversation has taken. Among the youngest generation, a boy of about six dives off the couch and onto an easy chair while a girl, two years his senior, whines at him to stop before he hurts himself. Another girl, this one only four, stands in the corner and scribbles on the wallpaper with a crayon while her cousin, also four, watches her nervously, wondering whether or not he should tell the adults.

Were an outside observer asked to label which of the family's traits were genetically determined, they would without hesitation point out the green eyes, the freckles, and height. More astute individuals would likely also mention the nose or the cheekbones or the stubby fingers. But most would hesitate to attribute a genetic link to the argumentative dispositions of the father and daughter, or the awkward brooding of the mother-daughter combo two seats down, or the devil-may-care bravado of the couch-leaper and the wall-scribbler. We tend to see these behaviours as less genetically motivated than something like eye colour. After all, one cannot educate a child taller or discipline green eyes brown. However, to divide traits into genetically determined and environmentally determined compartments is to misunderstand how genes work.

Consider hair colour, a trait that, on the surface, seems to be determined solely by a person's genes. A child's hair is seldom a colour that does not have some familial precedent. By contrast, the influence of the environment on one's hair colour seems nonexistent. Blonde Nordic children adopted by Chinese families do not spontaneously develop black hair. However, this does not mean genes alone are responsible for a person's hair colour. After all, genes can really only do one thing: instruct cells, by way of an interpreter called RNA, to create a series of amino acids, which then link together to form proteins. Now, this one function is extremely, unbelievably important. Proteins are the body's proletariat, the workers who carry out the myriad tasks which allow us, the society in which they dwell, to function. But genes cannot, on their own, dictate the colour of a person's hair. Hair colour is determined by melanin, which is the end product of the amino acid tyrosine. Now, genes do code for tyrosine, hence the genetic influence. However, in hair, the degree of melanin accumulation is decided in part by the concentration of copper in the cells producing that hair. When that cell has more copper, the hair is darker. Should the intake of copper be reduced to below a certain threshold, hair generated by the same follicle will be lighter than it was previously, when copper supplies were plentiful.

Similar factors are responsible for every human trait imaginable. The reason height seems to be determined solely by genetics is that, thankfully, just about everyone in the first world receives the base nutritional intake necessary for those genes to take effect. Likewise, most people get enough copper in their diet, as it can be found in a wide number of dietary staples, including fish, whole grains, nuts, potatoes, leafy greens, dried fruit, cocoa, black pepper, and yeast. Because it is almost universally consumed in sufficient quantities, copper's contribution to hair colour goes largely unnoticed. Somewhat paradoxically, the ubiquity of its influences renders them invisible. Such is the case with thousands of environmental factors we take for granted. It isn't until a radical change in the environment depletes once-plentiful resources that we realize how much those resources contributed to our development. In the words of Joni Mitchell, you don't know what you've got 'til it's gone.

A dramatic example of this occurred in Europe in October of 1944. The tides of war had turned on the Germans, who found their once seemingly invincible army forced back on all sides. Allied forces had reclaimed the southern part of the Netherlands, but the Germans maintained control of the rest. In an attempt to demoralize the Dutch, who had been emboldened by the partial liberation of their country and threatened a violent uprising, the Germans placed an embargo on all food supplies heading into the country and flooded the surrounding fields, spoiling the season's harvest. To make matters worse,

November proved the start of a very harsh winter. The Dutch canals were frozen solid, thwarting Allied attempts to ship in supplies by barge. Thus began the Dutch Hunger Winter, a devastating famine that lasted into the spring of 1945 and was responsible for 18,000 deaths by illness and starvation. Though the tragedy of the famine was harsh and immediately felt, the full brunt of its impact did not appear until long after the embargo was lifted and food supplies returned.

Almost immediately after it ended, researchers saw in the Hunger Winter the potential for a large-scale natural experiment. A population of well-fed people with documented medical histories had undergone severe malnutrition for a precisely delineated amount of time, and then quickly reverted to a normal diet. Over the following decades, researchers studied the medical records of individuals who had gestated (were growing in their mothers' uteruses) during the famine, noting any statistical abnormalities between them and other Dutch nationals who had not been so affected. The results were fascinating. Children whose mothers had been malnourished during the first trimester of their pregnancy were unusually likely to suffer from spina bifida,[5] cerebral palsy, and other conditions of the central nervous system. Additionally, girls from that cohort were twice as likely as the general population to develop schizophrenia. Clearly, malnutrition during those first few months of development impinges on the brain's ability to properly develop.

However, perhaps the most surprising finding involved men born to mothers who had been malnourished during the first two trimesters of their pregnancy. A 1976 study found that these men, now in their thirties, were significantly more likely to be obese than other men of their age and background whose mothers had not experienced the Hunger Winter. Further studies, though performed on rats instead of people, have helped us to understand the mechanism behind this strange phenomenon.

Mothers' malnutrition during the first two trimesters of pregnancy leads to unusually high insulin levels in male fetuses during the third trimester, which can affect the development of the fetus' brain. We don't yet know for sure why this occurs, and why it doesn't affect females, but it does make sense from an evolutionary standpoint. Mothers experiencing famine could be hormonally conditioning their children's metabolism to most effectively function in an environment where sources of nutrition are scarce. If a child is born into an environment plagued by famine, the ability to readily store fat would be a significant advantage. However, once the boys were born and the problem of food scarcity was solved, they nevertheless retained their prenatal conditioning despite the fact that their evolutionary advantage had become a disadvantage.

The Hunger Winter provides a good example of how environmental influences on development can easily remain buried beneath the surface of human development, only to be unearthed generations later by a dramatic change in the landscape. Had the Hunger Winter not occurred, we may never have learned that the prenatal environment can affect an individual's propensity to store fat, and the men studied would likely have developed a body type similar to those of their relatives (though, as always, diet and exercise would have played an important part).

Admittedly, the Hunger Winter is an extreme example. Under normal circumstances, attributing environmental influence to height or hair colour may seem unnecessarily pedantic. After all, if the environmental factor contributing to a trait's development is present everywhere on Earth, isn't it fair to say that said trait is genetically determined? If someone's genetic makeup dictates they will have green eyes, they're almost certainly going to get them, whether they live on the streets of inner-city Baltimore or in a mansion in Beverly Hills. Likewise, for certain conditions, a single aberrant gene really is the root cause. One could reasonably argue that calling CFTR[6] "the gene for cystic fibrosis" is accurate shorthand, as cystic fibrosis occurs when an individual inherits two mutated versions of that specific gene. The environment in which the affected child is raised will not alter how the gene behaves.

Nevertheless, relying on terms like "the gene for X" can be dangerously reductive, as it blinkers our thinking and encourages limited, simplistic approaches to complex problems.

Let's consider the scene that began this chapter. Remember Thomas? Was his facility with the guitar purely the result of his genes? It would be difficult to argue that environmental influence didn't play some part. No one picks up an instrument and plays Bach on the first try. It takes hours and hours of practice to develop the requisite agility, finger strength, and muscle memory. Despite what anyone with particularly accomplished parents may hope, skills and knowledge do not come prepackaged inside our chromosomes. Bodybuilders do not sire toned, muscular children, nor do the offspring of computer programmers enter the world knowing how to code in C++. Every generation must develop these skills from scratch.

Okay, so Thomas's talent was tempered by hours of dedicated study. But what about Amelia? An instrument may require extensive experience to be played competently, but some people are blessed with a natural singing voice. Amelia's father, we are told, is an excellent singer, and so too are most of his immediate family. It stands to reason that their musical aptitude was passed down through the generations. Thomas had to work to develop his skills, but Amelia was simply fortunate enough to inherit a gift. Right?

Genetically speaking, it is possible that Amelia was born with certain traits advantageous to a burgeoning singer. If her father's family has truly abounded with talented vocalists throughout the generations, then perhaps their genes code for better-than-average lung capacity, a strong diaphragm, or exceptionally dexterous vocal cords, and these predispositions are what drew her ancestors to singing in the first place. This could be the case, but to assume it must be — and to cite Amelia's proclivities as the only evidence — is tremendously naive. It is equally possible, perhaps even probable, that Amelia possesses no physiological advantage as a singer whatsoever. Half her genes come from her mother, after all, who readily admits that her whole family is tin-eared and musically inept. This is not to say that Amelia's talent wasn't inherited, only that we mustn't limit our idea of inheritance to a transaction involving a few dozen molecules.

If Amelia is from a musical home, she probably grew up with music as an important part of her life. We can assume the record player was running often, and that her father regularly sang around the house. In this case, her musical education began before she was even born.

Children develop an aural connection with the outside world as early as six months after conception. Researchers recruited a group of pregnant women and had them read one of two stories — *The Cat in the Hat* or *The King, the Mice, and the Cheese* — aloud twice a day from the time they were seven months pregnant until the day they gave birth. Two days after they were born, the children of these mothers were tested to see which story they preferred, using a fairly ingenious device that measured how often they sucked on a pacifier. Sucking is a reflex ingrained in children from birth, and one of the few motions over which infants have conscious (or close to conscious) control. By adjusting the speed of their sucking, the babies could choose whether they heard a recording of *The Cat in the Hat* or *The King, the Mice, and the Cheese*. Infants consistently preferred to hear recordings of whichever story their mothers had read aloud while they were in the womb. More fascinating still, researchers achieved the same result even if the recording was not of the child's mother reading, but a total stranger.

This means the children were not simply responding to the unique vocal register of their mothers, but to the specific cadence of the story itself.

Conceivably, then, if Amelia's father played a variety of music around the house during her gestation, she would have become familiar with the notions of melody, harmony, and counterpoint before she had even drawn her first breath. This is not to say she would have been composing symphonies in her crib, but repeated listening would have attuned her ear to the pitches and intervals common in Western music. Perhaps just as importantly, she would have developed a positive association with the songs she heard in utero, making it that much more likely she would take to music as a child.

As Amelia grew, her musical upbringing would have continued to influence her behaviour. There would have been musical scores lying around for her to ponder, tapes and CDs for her to listen to, and instruments for her to tinker with. And even if her father was not the type of man to force his child to follow in his footsteps, he would almost certainly have encouraged any interest in music that Amelia displayed. After all, what parent wouldn't want their child to feel passionate about the same things they do?

We inherit more from our parents than our chromosomes. They are the ones who teach us, feed us, scold us when we misbehave, and console us when we scrape our knees or embarrass ourselves at school. They are responsible for cultivating the environments in which we are raised. We are as much the beneficiaries of their affluence (or lack thereof), their dispositions, and their teachings as we are of their genes.

Of course, none of Amelia's hypothetical early training can guarantee that she will become a musical prodigy. Innate ability does exist, and there are limits to the extent that environmental factors can sculpt an individual. They can chisel out a form, but the genetic material from which the subject is carved will inevitably factor into the final outcome of the sculpture. What's more, unlike a sculpture, humans are not passive subjects prostrate before the whims of their environment. They have the power to change their surroundings, either through the ingenuity of invention or by simply deciding to live in, speak to, and engage with the places, people, and pursuits that most interest them. A child's natural talents influence his behaviour, which in turn influences the environmental factors he will encounter. Children generally like to do what they're good at, and the more they do it, the better at it they get. It is in these instances where the nature versus nurture divide seems truly absurd. Without an inherent knack for music or chess or skateboarding, a child will be less inclined to dedicate the time necessary to improve, but if they never dedicate the time in the first place, they won't improve no matter how innately talented they are.

Chapter 3
The Usual Suspects

●━━━━━━━━━━━━━━━━━━━━━━━━━●

It's after midnight. The investigators hunker over a desk loaded with papers, coffee mugs, and stacks of manila folders. Their eyes, red and stinging from the room's fluorescent lights and the lateness of the hour, pore over the contents of a folder labelled "7-repeat," a member of the prominent DRD4 family with a nasty reputation. It's a repeat offender, convicted on charges of aggravated ADHD and second-degree substance dependence. One of the investigators points to a line in the report. The other jots down the info in a notepad. Their efforts haven't been in vain. They can pin the suspect to 18 victims in their sample alone.

They parse the data, make sure there isn't some variable skulking behind the scenes, setting 7-repeat up as a fall guy. Nothing turns up. The case looks promising. With a satisfied nod, the investigators write up a warrant for further scrutiny. The charge: aiding and abetting the development of depression in susceptible children. A serious offence.

The human genome is a vast and labyrinthine network of codependent variables, dozens of which can be responsible for a single, seemingly simple trait. Nevertheless, researchers studying the effects of gene-by-environment interactions on childhood development seem to come across the same few subjects over and over again. These "usual suspects" are not the sole focus of this book — we will discuss other genes as well, along with studies that don't focus on any one gene in particular — but their names will be mentioned frequently over the following chapters, so it is perhaps worth getting to know them. However, before we do that, we should first take a moment to discuss what exactly a gene is.

What Is a Gene?

It is outside the scope of this book to chronicle every gene responsible for moderating a person's susceptibility to adverse conditions. Such a list would be far too extensive for our purposes, nor could its contents be truly exhaustive. The human genome contains a complex interplay of genetic and epigenetic variables (more on epigenetics in a later chapter), and our understanding of how it works is still far from comprehensive. The common notion that one gene is responsible for one trait is at best overly simplistic, and at worst completely false. Even the most simplistic traits are determined by multiple genes, and a single gene can be responsible for multiple traits.[7]

Perhaps part of the problem stems from the word *gene* itself. Despite the fact that just about everyone has heard of them, few people could accurately tell you exactly what genes are. This confusion extends into the scientific community, where the precise definition of the word *gene* remains fluid, as new discoveries continue to roil the already murky waters of our understanding. You might be wondering how this could be. We've cloned cats and sheep. We've made great strides in the field of genetic therapy. We've mapped the human genome. How could we have done all that without even knowing what a gene is?

The reason is that genes are more of a theoretical construction than a physical thing. They are a method of categorizing data in a manner satisfying to the human mind. But they do not, strictly speaking, exist.

When we discuss DNA, the molecules that make up the abstract concepts we refer to as genes, we are on firmer ground. The essential buildings blocks of genetics are nucleotides, tiny molecules comprised of a sugar, a phosphate, and a nucleobase. The bases determine the character of the nucleotide. They come in four varieties: adenine, thymine, cytosine, and guanine. Nucleotides are commonly referred to by whatever base they possess or, when documented in sequence, by each base's first initial (*A, T, C,* and *G*, respectively).

The sugar of one nucleotide bonds readily with the phosphate of another, allowing nucleotides to form chains millions of units long called polymers. Each polymer links up with a sympathetic partner running parallel, and together the two molecules entwine, forming the iconic double helix as depicted on the front of biology textbooks the world over. Unlike the sugar–phosphate bonds of each individual polymer, which can occur regardless of which bases the adjacent nucleotides possess, the bonds between the two polymers are highly specific. Each nucleotide has only one compatible molecule: adenine links with thymine, and cytosine with guanine. As a result, each polymer forms a perfect template for its partner — by observing the nucleotide sequence of one strand, one could assemble a flawless replica of the other. This attribute is the backbone of genetic inheritance.

Nucleotides are the letters with which the sweeping epic of the human genome is written, and their alphabet, at a mere four characters, is mercifully small. However, just as an Anglophone could not pick up a book written in Swedish and read it simply by identifying the consonants and vowels, understanding the alphabet of DNA means little without an adequate grasp of its lexicon and grammar.

The nucleotide letters form "words" called codons, which in the language of DNA are all three letters long. Each codon represents an amino acid. When placed in sequence, they instruct the cells they inhabit to construct a series of amino acids called a polypeptide chain. The beginning and end of each chain is determined by special "start" and "stop" codons. These codons do not represent an amino acid. They are not words, but punctuation. With them, codon sequences form the genetic equivalent of sentences.

The common definition of a gene is a unit of inheritance that codes for a protein. If a gene is a group of nucleotides that codes for a protein, and a protein is a series of polypeptides linked together into a single unique shape, then, for the purposes of our metaphor, a gene is a set of one or more codon sequences, or a genetic paragraph. On the surface, the analogy seems apt. However, this straightforward definition has, in recent years, come up against significant scientific scrutiny. Unlike actual text, genes are not grouped neatly along a unidirectional, linear sequence, wherein the parameters between one gene and the next can clearly be set. Rather, a single gene sprawls across a great swath of DNA, and the sequences that code for a protein (called exons) are interspersed with long stretches called introns that code for nothing at all. Deemed "junk DNA" due to their apparent lack of function, introns must be transcribed into RNA and removed before the exons can be spliced together and sent outside the nucleus to be translated into amino acids. In literary terms, this would be the equivalent of garbage text *banana judge effervescing creamsicles* breaking up an otherwise *philosophy the grandeur at sideways* intelligible sentence. It is not, to our eyes, the most efficient way of doing things.[8]

Complicating matters further, a phenomenon called alternative splicing allows a single gene to code for more than one protein. During the splicing stage of gene transcription, where the selected passage of DNA has been transcribed into RNA and the introns are being removed, portions of the exon are occasionally omitted, creating an RNA sequence that will only code for some of the amino acids prescribed by the gene. This will change the character of the polypeptide chain and, ultimately, the protein. Though it may seem like an error in the transcription process, alternative splicing is a normal part of gene expression. In humans, approximately 95 percent of genes with more than one exon sequence are alternatively spliced, greatly increasing the amount of polypeptide chains for which the human genome can code.

As if things weren't ill-defined enough, genes cannot even be read without the intervention of other genes. Proteins bond to groups of nucleotides called promoter sequences, which, true to their name, promote the transcription of the gene with which they are affiliated. Often, promoter sequences are found adjacent to the gene they promote, but recent research has shown this is not necessarily the case. Promoters can occur hundreds of thousands of base pairs away from the target gene, or even on a different chromosome altogether. What's more, genes themselves can be cobbled together from the exons of other genes, some of which may come from two or more different chromosomes.

So, with all this in mind, what exactly is a gene? The term "unit of heredity," though falling out of favour in some circles, is still fairly accurate. But unlike other units of measure — inches, litres, grams, and so forth — genes are not tied to any sort of physical constant. They can be dozens or hundreds or thousands of base pairs long. They can exist across great stretches of DNA, or even across chromosomes. They can reconfigure to different lengths and code for different end products through alternate splicing. They are defined, in short, not by any precise physical characteristic beyond their approximate molecular makeup (all contain sugars, phosphates, and nucleotides), but by what they do: code for an RNA chain.[9]

The genes we will discuss over the course of this book have each been labelled "the gene" for a plethora of adverse conditions, from alcoholism to heart disease to adultery. These hyperbolic claims are usually the result of errors in translation between scientists and the public, not a deliberate misrepresentation of the facts. "Gene for cheating found" simply makes for a better headline than "scientists discover three-way causal relationship between gene, environmental influences, and an increased predisposition toward adultery." In truth, the genes accused of causing these conditions aren't "causing" anything. They are, at most, permitting them to happen. How? That's not an easy question to answer, in part because we don't yet know precisely how these genes influence our behavioural development. However, on a purely chemical level, we have a good understanding of their purpose.

The Science of Feeling Good

The name Dopamine Receptor D4 (or DRD4) refers to both a gene and the protein-based product for which it codes,[10] called a receptor. A receptor is a protein product that facilitates communication between cells. A multitude of receptors exist within the human body, each attuned to one specific molecule. In this case, the dopamine receptor binds with — as one might suspect — dopamine. Along with serotonin (which we will get to shortly), dopamine is a neurotransmitter responsible for the *sense of pleasure* humans derive from sex, drugs, music, sunsets, ice cream sundaes, roller coasters, warm baths, books, and any other wonderful thing you care to name.

Before we continue, perhaps we should all take a minute to thank dopamine, because it's almost impossible to name an activity humans engage in that this chemical does not facilitate. We are, after all, continually driven by our desire for some pleasurable reward, be it in the short term (eating at a nice restaurant, watching a funny movie) or long term (exercising to feel healthier, working long hours for financial gain and/or personal satisfaction). Thanks, dopamine!

Along with its duties in the reward centre of the brain, dopamine plays an important role in cognition, voluntary movement, sleep, attention, and memory. It is a truly versatile molecule, but its ability to induce pleasure is the attribute for which, arguably, it is most famous.

The human body contains more than one kind of dopamine receptor. There are five types known at present, labelled D1 through D5. Current research has indicated the possible presence of dopamine receptors D6 and D7 as well, although the results remain inconclusive. Our focus is on receptor D4. In order to understand why, we must elucidate on an important element of heredity called an allele.

Alleles and Polymorphisms

Perhaps, while sitting in biology class or watching the news or scanning an article in a popular science magazine, you have come across these two seemingly contradictory facts: a) chimpanzees and humans share approximately 98 percent of their genes,[11] and b) children share 50 percent of their genes with their mother and the other half with their father. Both of these facts are true. Ostensibly this suggests that, genetically speaking, you are much more closely related to the chimp you saw gallivanting about the zoo as a child than you are to either one of your parents. I hope you approach this conjecture with some skepticism, as it is, to say the least, suspicious.

How can facts A and B both be valid? The problem lies with the word *gene*, which is being used in an entirely different manner in each case.

For fact A, "98 percent of genes" actually refers to 98 percent of the genome, meaning that, should one draw a DNA sample from a human and a chimpanzee, document every base pair of nucleotides in their possession, and match them up, those pairs would be identical 49 times out of 50. This may seem surprising, but it's actually quite logical. For a molecule that divides and replicates so rapaciously, DNA is remarkably stable. Mutations that slip by uncorrected are rare, and when they do happen, it is often in old age, when healthy, uncorrupted versions of the mutated sequence have long since been passed down to the next generation.

Fact B takes the similarities trumpeted by fact A for granted. Using the same logic as fact A, humans are all well over 99.9 percent identical, genetically speaking. That similarity is essential to our continued survival, as it allows humans to breed with humans and not with other animals. Your genome matches 99.9 percent (or 999 base pairs out of 1,000) to your mother and your father.

So what does fact B's 50 percent refer to? Small but critical distinctions between humans called alleles.

Shuffling the Deck

As we have mentioned, a developmentally typical human has 46 chromosomes,[12] of which he inherits 23 from his mother and 23 from his father. Each person receives two copies of chromosomes 1 to 22 (called autosomal chromosomes), plus two sex chromosomes that bear no numeric title. These latter chromosomes are called X and Y, and they determine a person's gender. Women get two copies of the X chromosome, while men get one X and one Y. During meiosis (the creation of gametes, or sperm and eggs), one chromosome of each type is selected at random. The same goes for sperm. During reproduction or fertilization (acts instigated by dopamine, the great motivator!), the two payloads combine, creating a new organism with a full set of chromosomes, a quarter of which (give or take a chromosome or two) came from each of its four grandparents.

Think of your genes as a deck of playing cards. Each deck contains 46 cards divided into two different suits. One suit came from your mother — call it clubs — and the other from your father — let's say spades — meaning you got 23 cards from each of them. When creating reproductive cells, your body sorts through your genetic deck, selecting one card from each of the 23 pairs at random. The result is a half-deck containing one copy of cards 1 to 23, some of them clubs and some of them spades.

Now say you meet a partner of the opposite sex, hit it off, and reproduce.[13] His (or her) half deck combines with yours, contributing its own set of cards 1 to 23, compiled at random from his own maternal and paternal suits (call them diamonds and hearts). The resulting child has a full deck of 46 cards, 23 from you and 23 from your partner. Technically, the 23 cards your child inherited from you are themselves of two different suits — clubs and spades from your mother and father, respectively — but they have become, for all practical purposes, one suit. Genetic inheritance is thus the piecemeal combination of traits from various ancestors. With each subsequent generation, the level of genetic relatedness between elder and younger is roughly halved. After as few as six generations, there is a decent chance that a person doesn't have a single chromosome in common with their ancestor, despite the order of their nucleotides remaining, as with all humans, 99.9 percent identical.

Though we have two copies of each autosomal chromosome, the pairs are by no means identical. If they were, the entire process of chromosomal shuffling would be useless. Every functioning chromosome is largely similar to others of its type, in that it codes for the same genes, is essentially the same length, and for the most part contains the same nucleotide sequences. However, certain genes have mutations that vary from person to person, causing them to function in a different manner. For example, almost everyone has the gene necessary to determine eye colour, but not everyone's eyes are the same shade. Some have genes that code for brown eyes, while others have genes that code for green, or hazel, or blue. Genes with multiple derivatives are called polymorphisms, and they are responsible for the astounding variety of traits between humans. Since human beings have two copies of each chromosome, they have two copies of each polymorphic gene. The precise type (or types) they possess is called an allele.

Sometimes humans have two copies of the same allele, in which case they are homozygous. In other cases, they have two different alleles of the same gene, making them heterozygous. In these cases, the two alleles can interact in a number of ways, the most famous of which was discovered by an Austrian monk named Gregor Mendel. Mendelian genetics divides alleles into dominant and recessive types. When an individual possesses both a dominant and a recessive allele of the same gene, the result is not a compromise between the two. An individual with one brown eye allele and one blue eye allele will not develop murky blue irises, or one brown eye and one blue eye.[14] Rather, the dominant trait supersedes the recessive trait, which lies unexpressed in the gene, awaiting the opportunity to perhaps show itself in a subsequent generation. In the case of eye colour, blue eyes are recessive and brown eyes are dominant.[15] A man with one brown-eye allele (symbolized by a capital B) and one blue-eye allele (symbolized by a lower case b)[16] will have brown eyes. Say that man meets a brown-eyed woman who also has a recessive blue-eye allele, and together they have a child. The child's eye colour genes could look one of four ways. She could be homozygous for the brown-eye allele (BB), heterozygous for the brown and blue-eye alleles (Bb or bB, depending on which allele comes from which parent), or homozygous for the blue-eye allele (bb). In the first three cases, the child, like her parents, will have brown eyes, as the presence of the dominant allele (B) overpowers that of the recessive allele (b). In the latter case, though, the dominant allele is not present, and so the child will have blue eyes.

Very few traits (including the one in our example) truly fit the Mendelian mould of single-gene origin and dominant/recessive binary.[17] Most traits require multiple genes to develop, and some single gene traits vary in their degrees of expressivity, or the extent to which the "dominant" trait dominates. Still others are co-dominant, meaning that neither allele overwhelms the other. Nevertheless, Mendel's insights were remarkable, considering all he had to work with were a few pea plants and his own powers of observation. With these humble tools, Mendel documented the first evidence of genetic inheritance, paving the way for what would become arguably the biggest scientific undertaking of the 20th century: mapping the human genome.

DRD4

As we've already learned, DRD4 (the gene) codes for DRD4 (the receptor), and DRD4 allows the human brain to dole out jolts of positive reinforcement in the form of dopamine. Its connections to drug addiction and depression seem obvious — drugs being a pharmacological shortcut to euphoria, and depression being a chemical imbalance precluding one's ability to experience pleasure — but what links DRD4 to ADHD, heart disease, or any of the other conditions to which it is accused of contributing? Moreover, why DRD4 and not DRD3 or DRD5? The answer lies in the allele.

Within the third exon (or section of codeable, non-"junk" DNA) of DRD4 sits a nucleotide sequence 48 base pairs long. This sequence repeats from 2 to 10 times, depending on the allele, contributing to DRD4's reputation for being one of the most variable genes in the human genome. The 48 base-pair repeat is not the only repeated sequence in DRD4, nor is it the longest, but it is nevertheless the focus of a great deal of scientific scrutiny.

The most common number of repeats found in *DRD4* are 3 and 4, but for susceptibility to depression, addiction, and a host of other maladies, 7 seems to be the magic number. For reasons that continue to elude us, the 7-repeat allele increases a person's predisposition toward risk-seeking behaviour, which includes typical "high-risk" activities, such as drug use, illicit sex, and gambling, but also extends to extreme sports and high-pressure business decisions. This creates an odd schism in public opinion on the 7-repeat allele. While considered an albatross around the necks of junkies and problem gamblers, it can be seen as a positive attribute when possessed by athletes and successful business people, both of whom thrive in high-risk environments.

5-HTTLPR

We've already thanked dopamine for our ability to experience pleasure; it's only fair we now give serotonin its due.

Though a neurotransmitter much like dopamine, serotonin is principally found in the gut, where it regulates intestinal movements. In the brain, it serves a very different function, facilitating feelings of happiness and well-being. The link between digestion and contentment may seem tenuous, but from an evolutionary standpoint, it's actually quite logical. If one considers pleasure outside its cultural trappings, it's ultimately an incentive for continued survival. Pleasure has become far more decadent in modern society, where basic necessities are freely available. But at its humble roots, pleasure is derived from activities necessary for the propagation of our species: sex, warmth, sleep, and, most importantly, food. As a result, we are genetically inclined to feel a sense of contentment when these needs are met, and a drive to meet them when they're not. Serotonin helps us achieve this end.

Studies have linked serotonin levels to food availability, which, in social animals, also relates to one's place in the social hierarchy. When injected with excess serotonin, animals with diminutive statuses in the hierarchy display uncharacteristically aggressive behaviour. In normal circumstances, a crayfish, when faced with a bigger opponent, will perform a supplicating tail-flip gesture that forces it backward, allowing it to flee. However, when injected with serotonin, it becomes more aggressive and attacks its opponent. Curiously, the opposite is true of dominant crayfish. When they receive a boost of serotonin, their behaviour becomes more fearful.

With this in mind, it is interesting to note the number of studies that link *5-HTT* to a host of behavioural disorders in humans and other primates, including both anxiety and excess aggression. There is a wide gulf of evolutionary difference between people and prawns! But the effect of certain chemicals on the neurological system can be remarkably similar across species. The connection is purely speculative, but worth considering.

Unlike *DRD4, 5-HTT* is not itself a gene, but only a section of one. It sits on the promoter region of *SLC6A4*, which codes for a group of serotonin transporters. They affect the efficiency with which the human body can reabsorb and reuse serotonin after it has sent its first chemical message to the receptors. Since *5-HTT* codes for the *SLC6A4* promoter, it decides how much serotonin the body can reclaim. There are only two allelic variations — long (l) and short (s) — but they work in conjunction. Each person has two alleles of any one gene. With two copies of the gene and two possible forms the gene can take — long and short — there are four possible combinations a person can have: long/long, long/short, short/long, and short/short. For the sake of brevity, we will refer to these as l/l, l/s, and s/s (l/s and s/l amount to the same thing, so there is no point in distinguishing between them).

MAO-A

Though less of a key player than either *DRD4* or *5-HTT*, the *MAO-A* gene bears consideration, especially since its function is tied into that of the other two genes. *MAO-A* codes for mono-amine oxidase A, an enzyme that breaks down neurotransmitters like serotonin and dopamine. Its function, or lack thereof, directly affects the amount of dopamine and serotonin in the human body.

Like *DRD4, MAO-A* has multiple allelic variations based on the number of times it repeats a particular sequence of nucleo-tides — in this case, one 30 base-pairs long. Humans can have anywhere from 2 to 5 repeats. Of these, the 4-repeat allele is considered high reactive, meaning it devours serotonin and dopamine more readily than its low-reactive counterparts.

MAO-A has been dubbed "the warrior gene," as recent studies have discovered a correlation between its low-reactive allele and aggressive behaviour in response to provocation. Researchers Rose McDermott and Dustin Tingley devised a study to docu-ment the interaction between a person's *MAO-A* genotype and his response to a perceived wrongdoing. Or, more accurately, a man's *MAO-A* genotype. As *MAO-A* sits on the X chromosome, focusing the study solely on males reduced the list of possible genotypes to either high or low. Girls have two X chromosomes, making their *MAO-A* alleles significantly more complicated (instead of high or low, you have h/h, h/l, and l/l). We do not currently know if one or both of women's *MAO-A* genes func-tion at any one time, or whether a high-reactive allele trumps a low-reactive allele, or vice versa. As a result, our knowledge of *MAO-A*-by-environment interactions pertains only to men.

Ostensibly, men completed vocabulary tests in exchange for financial rewards. However, these tests were only a pretext for a subsequent game, during which an anonymous opponent could steal a certain amount of the man's earnings. In retaliation, men were given the ability to inflict on the thief a somewhat bizarre punishment: making them ingest an unpleasant quantity of hot sauce. If the men chose not to use the hot sauce, it could be redeemed at the end of the game for money. Punishment, therefore, held negative consequences for both the thief and the victim. The thief would be subjected to a dose of hot sauce and the victim would use up a resource that could have otherwise earned back some (but not all) of the money the thief had stolen.

But here's the trick: the thieves didn't exist. Experimenters manipulated the rounds in order to divide men into different test and control groups. Some men had only a small amount of their earnings "stolen" from them, while others faced significantly greater losses. The reactions of each man were recorded and compared to their level of provocation — how much was stolen from them — and their *MAO-A* genotype.

Not surprisingly, men with either genotype who'd had significant portions of their earnings stolen from them acted more aggressively than men who'd lost less. However, among the men who'd lost considerable amounts, those with a low-reactive *MAO-A* were far more likely to pursue vengeance than those with a high-reactive version of the gene. This implies that men with low-reactive *MAO-A* only display greater aggression when provoked by a perceived slight, and not as a result of having an inherently domineering personality.

The warrior gene theory has garnered significant criticism since its inception, particularly because low-reactive versions of the *MAO-A* gene are less prevalent among Caucasians than other races, lending the research an unfortunate air of racial divisiveness. It's not within the stated purpose of this book to weigh in on that particular debate, but whether the "warrior gene" exists or not, it is, at most, only half the story. For behaviours cannot be dictated by genes alone. Genetics may determine how easy it is to push a person's buttons, but the finger that actually pushes them belongs to the early caregiving environment — how a person was parented.

Section 2

The Broken Filter

"*Genes and family may determine the foundation of a house,
but time and place determine its form.*"

—JEROME KAGAN

Chapter 4

Messy Metaphors

Mrs. Munroe has a good group of students this year. Grade eights can be a challenge — precariously balanced as they are between childhood and adolescence, their hormones overcharged and as volatile as nitroglycerin — but for the most part, she can't complain. Only two of her students trouble her, and for very different reasons.

Joey is pure energy. Unfortunately, he rarely puts it to good use. He disrupts classes, swears at teachers, and bullies his classmates mercilessly. Over half a dozen students have complained to Mrs. Munroe about him. One claimed Joey stole his backpack and threw it onto the school roof. Another said Joey shoved her in the janitor's closet and held the door shut until after the second period bell rang. Still another showed Mrs. Munroe her binder, which had been stabbed repeatedly with a pen and defaced with permanent marker. She claimed Joey did it.

Though Joey terrorizes his peers more or less without prejudice, a few students actually look up to him. He flouts rules with an abandon they find hopelessly alluring. He chain-smokes during his lunch hour, standing defiantly just a few feet off of school property, where the teachers are powerless to stop him. He regales anyone who will listen with stories of binge drinking and illicit sex. Mrs. Munroe is pretty sure the sex talk is pure bravado, but the drinking, at least, she believes to be true. Joey has shown up to school flush-faced and giddy on more than one occasion, the smell of stale beer on his breath. None of her punishments seem to have any effect on his behaviour. He careens through life like a transport truck with its brakes cut, flirting with disaster and constantly gaining speed.

Mrs. Munroe's other problem child is Erika, though a less empathetic teacher would hardly consider her a problem at all. She never acts out, or breaks rules, or draws any attention to herself whatsoever. This is not to say she's an ideal student — she doesn't participate in class, and often fails to do her homework. Her test performance is spotty; sometimes she scores very well, but at other times she hands tests in with many questions left unanswered.

For the first few weeks, Mrs. Munroe suspected that Erika had some sort of learning disability, but she has become convinced this is not the case. The work Erika does complete is of exceptional quality. She writes eloquently, and can solve fairly complex math problems without struggle. The trouble is that, more often than not, she simply doesn't bother to do the work. She doesn't seem to have the energy. She smiles wanly when Mrs. Munroe talks to her about her assignments, shrugs off her teacher's concerns, and completes just enough of her schoolwork to get by and stay under the radar.

The other students sometimes tease Erika, but she's not a very satisfying target. Getting a rise out of her is pretty much impossible. A few children give half-hearted attempts now and then, but mostly they just leave her be. She has few friends, and during lunch she sits alone, pushing food around her plate. Her thin arms bear scars from frequent cuts and gashes.

These wounds are not the hallmarks of domestic violence — Mrs. Munroe has never spotted bruises, black eyes, or taped-up fingers. They look self-inflicted.

On the surface, Joey and Erika seem like polar opposites. Joey's personality is aggressive and forceful; Erika's is shy and yielding. Joey does everything he can to draw attention to himself; Erika does everything she can to avoid it. Joey torments others; Erika torments herself. Yet these two seemingly disparate conditions share a common root. Psychologists have found that, beyond the superficial differences in behaviour, aggression and depression are often different symptoms for the same disease: poverty, neglect, emotional distance, and abuse by parents. Spending time with troubled children can often reveal the truth of this seemingly self-contradictory notion. Withdrawn, shy students and bullies alike often share deep-seated and painful insecurities rooted in their family environment. Given this connection, it may not be all that surprising that the same few genes can make a child susceptible to anxiety and aggression, apathy and hyperactivity. The body of research supporting this notion is new and fairly small, but like a well-nourished child, it is growing with astounding speed.

"Internalizing behaviours" are, in a way, the invisible cost of maltreatment. They do not call attention to themselves; if anything, they strive to hide from view. Erika, the self-mutilating student we described earlier, perfectly exemplifies internalizing behaviour. She's shy, withdrawn, constantly fatigued, and prone to depression. Her intelligence and talent are hamstrung by her overwhelming sense of apathy, a black hole sucking away her every ounce of energy and optimism, leaving her feeling hopeless and alone. Nervousness and anxiety are also frequent symptoms of internalizing behaviour, though they can be difficult to see. If Erika experiences them, she hides them well behind a veil of lethargy and indifference.

Children exhibiting internalizing behaviours often feel the same anger as those exhibiting "externalizing behaviour" (think of the rebellious and irascible Joey), but they tend to turn it on themselves, where it manifests in body mutilation, drug use, or eating disorders. They draw their pain inward, but that doesn't mean it can't be felt by those around them. Depression throbs like a wound in a family's flank, one we can spot and bandage with antidepressants, but are all too often unable to actually heal. Though hard to notice at times, internalizing behaviours can be diagnosed, and researchers are growing increasingly confident in their prediction of what causes them. Unfortunately, the answer is complex, subject to variation, and incomplete.

This is not to say it isn't useful. As the following studies will show, even a partial understanding of what causes internalizing behaviours can make treating them significantly easier.

Nothing to Fear but Fear Itself

Mice make ideal test subjects. Though less intelligent than their distant cousins, rats (themselves popular among researchers), mice are smart enough to train, have short birth cycles, and reproduce prodigiously, allowing researchers to observe the effects of an experiment over multiple generations without waiting years for the results to come in. Female mice reach sexual maturity when only 8 weeks old, and can birth 5 to 10 litters per year, each of which contains anywhere from 3 to 14 mice. That's a lot of births, and a lot of mice. It's also an ideal opportunity for selective breeding, and over the years scientists have produced dozens of different strains of mice, each with their own behavioural ticks, temperaments, and characters.

Interestingly, this quest for new and better experimental fodder has itself become grounds for an experiment. What makes these mice different from one another? The obvious answer would be their genes. A series of small mutations occurring over the span of multiple generations have manifested themselves in the mice's tiny brains, changing how each breed looks and behaves. Mice, spanning as many as six generations in a single year, can evolve a lot quicker than humans, who hobble miles behind them with a 20-year generational lag. When assisted by the informed hands of professional breeders, a mouse's evolutionary timeframe can be easily put on fast forward.

But Dr. Michael Meaney and his team questioned this assumption in their 2004 study. To them, a purely genetic explanation for interspecies variation seemed too simplistic. Differences between breeds could be pretty radical, and natural selection is a notoriously slow process, often taking thousands or tens of thousands of years to produce very slight adjustments to the genome. Even when factoring in human intervention, Meaney felt that things were going too fast for genes alone to manage. Something else must be working behind the scenes as well. To prove it, he first selected two very different breeds of mice. The first, called Type A, were skittish, docile, and easily frightened by new places or objects. The second, called Type B, were confident, curious, and almost wholly indifferent to threat.

Mouse Type	Mouse Behaviour
Type A	skittish, docile, and react strongly to stress
Type B	confident, curious, and more or less unfazed by new places or experiences

Meaney took both breeds and performed a cross-fostering study. Six hours after they were born, Type A and Type B mice were taken from their mothers and randomly fostered to mothers of the opposite type. Type A mothers raised Type B infants, and Type B mothers raised Type A infants, hence "cross-fostering." As a control, some infants were taken and fostered to mothers of the same type — Type A infants with Type A mothers and Type B infants with Type B mothers. The mothers raised their adoptive offspring as their own, and Meaney let the infants reach maturity without any further intervention on his part.

When the mice were roughly 70 days old, they participated in a step-down test. Each mouse was placed on a small raised platform in the centre of an open plain. Meaney observed the mouse's behaviour for the next five minutes, noting in particular its willingness to explore its new surroundings — though "explore" is perhaps overselling it. The study broke exploration down into three stages: extending the head over the edge of the platform, stepping two feet off of the platform, and stepping completely off of the platform. Hardly a venture worthy of Magellan or Columbus, but for a laboratory-raised rodent weighing little more than an ounce, step-down testing can be a truly harrowing experience. It evokes a deep-seated fear in a creature whose survival strategies have, for thousands of years, relied principally on its ability to scurry and hide. Aloft on a platform, surrounded by flat, open terrain devoid of grass or rocks or any sort of protective crevice or camouflage, they sense the atavistic dread of their wild ancestors, ears and eyes and nose trained to detect the first sign of an incoming hawk, fox, or bobcat. When confronted with the step-down test, docile mice tend to freeze, overcome by terror, while their more adventurous peers waste little time in exploring the boundaries of their new habitat.

It should come as no surprise, then, that Type A mice tend to take far longer than Type B mice to progress through the stages of exploration. Occasionally, Type A mice don't leave the platform at all, but remain exactly where they're placed, rigid with terror, until the experimenters remove them. Type B mice, on the other hand, barely hesitate before leaping nimbly from the platform and sniffing inquisitively around the perimeter of the cage.

Here was the crux of Meaney's experiment. If Type A mice's skittishness and Type B mice's fearlessness comes hardwired into their genes, then they should exhibit it regardless of who raised them. However, if their dispositions were instead the product of their environment, then adopted mice should behave much like their step brothers and stepsisters, even though they are born from different breeds.

So which was it? Here's the strange thing: it was sort of both.

When raised by Type A mothers, Type A mice acted as skittish as ever. They performed poorly on the step-down test, leaving their platforms with great reluctance or freezing with catatonic fright. But when raised by Type B mothers, Type A mice passed the test with flying colours, exploring their cage with the same gusto as their natural-born Type B brothers and sisters. Though mother mice don't teach their offspring how to react to step-down testing in the conventional sense — few if any of the mothers will have ever even experienced such a thing — something in Type B mice's maternal behaviour imparts in their foster children a bravado they would have otherwise lacked.

It seems that nurture has won the day. Except that Type B mice would beg to differ. Unlike their Type A peers, Type B mice displayed the same inquisitive, devil-may-care attitudes regardless of who raised them. When raised by Type A mothers, they nevertheless acted like their other biological siblings, sniffing eagerly around the testing site.

	Raised by Type A mothers	Raised by Type B mothers
Type A mice	Skittish, fearful, performed poorly on test	Fearless, curious, performed well on test
Type B mice	Fearless, curious, performed well on test	Fearless, curious, performed well on test

You can see why questions like "nature or nurture?" don't have easy answers. They seem to lead us only to more questions. Why do environmental influences only work one way? How can Type B mothers subvert the ingrained timidity of Type A mice while Type A mothers are powerless to uproot the brash gusto of their adopted Type B offspring? What separates these two breeds? Meaney's study can't answer these questions, but it does at least pose them. And in science, new questions can be just as important as answers.

Of Mice and Men

Dr. Meaney's study left us wondering what made Type A mice bend like putty beneath the sculpting hands of their environment, while Type B mice were, behaviourally speaking, rigid as stones. Enquiring scientific minds, spellbound as ever by those vast molecular blueprints, turned once again to genes. Of course, as an answer to Meaney's questions, "genes" is distressingly vague. For the theory to hold any weight, its aim would have to be narrowed considerably. It would have to focus on one gene in particular.

Dr. Joan Kaufman suspected the culprit might be the serotonin transporter gene, known by the tongue-twisting moniker *5-HTTLPR*.[18] As we discussed last chapter, the *5-HTT* gene comes in two different varieties, long (l) and short (s), so named because one of them is built from a larger nucleotide sequence, making it physically longer than the other. In genetic parlance, these varieties are called alleles. Everybody has the same genes, but not everyone has the same alleles, which is why we are not all genetically identical. For instance, imagine two individuals named Tim and Patricia. Tim has brown eyes and Patricia has blue eyes. The gene determining their eye colour is largely similar — it sits on the same chromosome, is more or less the same length, contains an almost identical series of nucleotides, and does the same job in either of them. It is, essentially, the same gene, except that very slight changes have caused it to produce a different outcome in Tim than it does in Patricia. Tim has the brown eye allele of the eye colour gene, while Patricia has the blue eye allele.

Almost every gene in the human body comes in different alleles, which accounts for the tremendous variety of traits between individuals. In the 5-HTT gene's case, the short allele is less efficient than the long allele, meaning it can generate fewer serotonin transporters in a given time. As serotonin is responsible for regulating mood, digestion, and a number of other important biological functions, a less efficient 5-HTT can, under the wrong circumstances, cause a lot of trouble.

5-HTT sits on the 17th chromosome of every human being and non-human primate, and is present in a similar form in most mammals. Since humans have two copies of chromosome 17, they also have two copies of 5-HTT, and they make good use of both of them. This means that a person can have two long alleles (l/l), two short alleles (s/s), or one copy of each (l/s).

Dr. Kaufman knew about 5-HTT's relationship with mood disorders. Many studies have suggested a correlation between 5-HTT and depression. A similar number have implicated it in cases of anxiety and alcoholism. What more likely culprit could there be? Her intuition bolstered by past research, Kaufman hypothesized that the s/s allele of the 5-HTT gene would increase a child's chances of suffering from depression. This is not to say the allele actually made children depressed, only that it provided a foothold for the true causes of depression — in this case, negative environmental influences caused by abusive or neglectful parents — to latch onto.

To prove her hypothesis, Kaufman gathered 101 children ages 5 to 15 for her study, 57 of whom had been removed from their parents' custody by the State of Connecticut Department of Children and Families due to allegations of abuse or neglect. The other 44 participants formed a "community control," meaning they came from similar socioeconomic backgrounds to the test group (their families earned $25,000 a year or less and came from the same geographic region) but had never experienced maltreatment.

Next, Kaufman assessed each child's behaviour to determine if he or she was depressed. Though depression is often considered a somewhat intangible state of being — we've all felt down or depressed at some point in our lives, and for all sorts of reasons — it is also a distinct psychological disorder (known officially by the name Major Depressive Disorder, or MDD) that can be empirically diagnosed. This was the kind of depression Kaufman was looking for, and to find it, she used a diagnostic model called the Short Mood and Feelings Questionnaire, which was originally developed by psychiatrist Adrian Angold. The Short Mood and Feelings Questionnaire is a survey used by psychologists, sociologists, and other researchers to a) determine whether or not a child is depressed, and b) quantify their level of depression on a numeric scale. It is easy to use and highly accurate, making it an ideal tool for experiments dealing with a large number of children, particularly those in which degrees of depression matter — where "is he depressed?" is less important than "how depressed is he?"

With all her data in place, Kaufman ran a series of statistical analyses and measured the findings against her hypothesis. She believed children with the l/l allele of the *5-HTT* gene would be least susceptible to the long-term effects of abuse, and children with the s/s allele would be most susceptible, with l/s children falling somewhere in the middle.

The data proved her right, though "somewhere in the middle" veered a lot closer to the l/l side of things. Among abused and maltreated children, l/l and l/s children were equally likely to suffer from depression. Children with the s/s allele, on the other hand, were nearly *twice as likely* as l/l and l/s children to be depressed. This discrepancy did not exist in the non-maltreated children, who were less likely to be depressed than their maltreated peers regardless of their genotype.

Without exposure to abuse, *5-HTT* doesn't much matter. Or rather, it likely matters in some way we haven't yet discovered, but for the purposes of fending off depression in supportive homes, s/s and l/l both work well enough. When children have stable upbringings, the environment allows their serotonin transporters some leeway, asking only that they function at a certain basic level. Under such lenient conditions, both l/l and s/s alleles have no trouble meeting demand.

Among abused children, however, that benchmark level of functionality doesn't cut it. When burdened by an emotionally fraught environment, children's serotonin transporters need to run at full capacity. If the serotonin transporters aren't up to the task, then things break down and children suffer. We can't yet say for sure what this breakdown entails, but we can make an educated guess. Serotonin helps regulate mood — along with dopamine, it is one of the two chemicals responsible for allowing

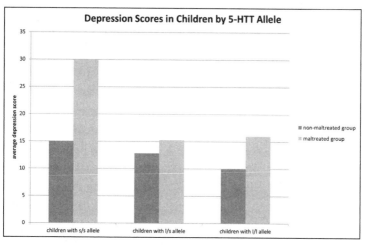

Kaufman, J., Yang, B.Z., Douglas-Palumberi, H., Houshyar, S., Lipschitz, D., Krystal, J.H., and Gelernter, J. (2004). "Social Supports and Serotonin Transporter Gene Moderate Depression in Maltreated Children." *Proceedings of the National Academy of Sciences of the United States of America*, 101(49), 17316–17321.

us to feel pleasure. Transporters are a protein product vital to the processing of serotonin in the human brain, and *5-HTT* is responsible for building them. The better it does its job, the more serotonin transporters there are doing theirs and the smoother the whole system runs. Switch the l/l allele for the less efficient s/s model and production dips. That's fine if serotonin is in low demand, but if the body needs more to cope with the stress it is continually bombarded with at home, and if demand can't match supply.... You see the problem.

Though different in a lot of ways, Meaney's cross-fostering experiment and Kaufman's maltreatment studies suggest a similar relationship between genes and environment. In Meaney's experiment, Type A mice had the equivalent of the s/s allele, while Type B mice had the l/l. When reared in adverse conditions (remaining with "scaredy-mouse" Type A mothers), the Type A mice succumbed to environmental pressure, adopting the timid disposition that is the hallmark of their breed. However, when brought to a more stable, supportive environment (being cross-fostered to "tougher" Type B mothers) their timidity failed to develop. Conversely, Type B mice — the resilient l/l children of the rodent world — were unaffected by the troubled Type A environment, maintaining their extroverted personalities regardless of who raised them.

Building the Human Brain

In 2006, Kaufman performed a follow-up study in order to confirm and expand upon her initial findings. Her new experiment was identical in structure to her old one, except that it included an extra variable: a gene on the eleventh chromosome called *BDNF*. *BDNF* codes for brain-derived neurotrophic factor, a protein responsible for developing and maintaining brain cells. Studies have linked the gene to child-onset depression, and Kaufman hypothesized that it might worsen symptoms of depression in children already made vulnerable by the l/s or s/s *5-HTT* allele. To confirm this, she genotyped (or genetically tested) children in search of a specific polymorphism (or variety) of the *BDNF* gene.

Like *5-HTT*, *BDNF* has two alleles of interest to researchers: "val" and "met."[19] They work on exactly the same principle as *5-HTT*'s long (l) and short (s) alleles. Val is the more common and stable allele, the equivalent of *l*, and met is the rarer, more troublesome allele, the equivalent of *s*. As with *5-HTT*, *BDNF* is active on both chromosomes. Individuals can be val/val, val/met, or met/met (the equivalent of l/l, l/s, and s/s, respectively).

The val/met and met/met alleles are associated with a number of neurological conditions, including Alzheimer's disease, Parkinson's disease, eating disorders, depression, and bipolar disorder. People with val/met or met/met alleles also perform relatively poorly on tests measuring their ability to remember places or events. This may come as a result of the val/met and met/met alleles' effect on the hippocampus, a region of the brain responsible for transitioning memories from short-term to long-term storage. On average, people with the val/met or met/met allele have a smaller hippocampus by volume than those with the more common val/val allele.

Considering *BDNF*'s role as a developer of neural tissue, it's not hard to imagine how even a small mutation in the gene could greatly impair functionality in an organ as intricate as the brain. If one's hippocampus somehow shrank, its ability to consolidate short-term memories into long-term ones would be reduced, which would explain why individuals with the val/met or met/met allele perform poorly on memory recollection tests while doing as well as their val/val peers on tasks that scarcely involve the hippocampus, such as learning new words and planning ahead — their hippocampi have been built with a suboptimal protein material. The hippocampus still works, of course, or anyone with a met allele would be functionally brain-dead. But it works, broadly speaking, a little *less well* than it could. Memories come a bit slower, slip away quicker, and make easier prey for Alzheimer's, which regularly chooses the hippocampus as its first target.

Of course, this is only half the story. The environment always has its say as well, which is why Kaufman included *BDNF* in her gene-by-environment study. She wondered if rather than directly causing these ailments, the val/met and met/met alleles might, like the s/s *5-HTT* allele, simply make the individual more susceptible to them.

Kaufman's new experiment mirrored its predecessor. As in her previous study, participants were 5 to 15 years old and recruited in the same manner — maltreated and non-maltreated children were drawn from the same community and lived in similar socioeconomic environments. The only difference between them was that maltreated children, unlike the control children, had at some point been taken from their parents for a minimum of 96 hours due to allegations of abuse.

Kaufman divided the children into two groups based on their *BDNF* genotype, creating a val/val group and a val/met group.[20] She treated each group as a separate study and recompiled her data. In both groups, maltreated children with s/s *5-HTT* alleles were the most likely to exhibit symptoms of depression. But among this statistically disadvantaged group, those who also had the val/met *BDNF* allele were more susceptible still.

Among the val/val group, maltreated children with the s/s *5-HTT* genotype scored an average of 5 points higher on the depression scale (meaning they were more depressed) than maltreated children with the protective l/l alleles; in the val/met group, this discrepancy more than doubles. The val/met genotype acts as a kind of susceptibility multiplier, expanding the gap between s/s and l/l children, *but only when those children were maltreated.* Among children who were not maltreated, neither the *BDNF* nor the 5-HTT allele they possessed had a more than marginal impact on their odds of suffering from depression.

Kaufman's findings paint a bleak picture for val/met, s/s children living in abusive conditions. Is there any hope for these kids at all? Are the odds so thoroughly stacked against them that they are, in effect, born into lives of poverty, addiction, and crime? The statistics may seem damning, but we prefer to reject such fatalism. And lucky for us, Kaufman's study offers a tangible cause for optimism.

During her study, Kaufman asked participating children to list people in their lives whom they confide in, count on financially, tell good or bad news to, have fun with, and approach when they have a problem. Children described their relationships with each person they mentioned, and told researchers how often they were able to see him or her. Kaufman used this information to measure each child's level of social support. The more people children named as supportive presences, and the more often they were able to see these people, the higher their rating on Kaufman's social support index.

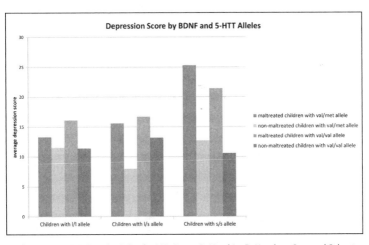

Kaufman, J., Yang, B.Z., Douglas-Palumberi, H., Grasso, D., Lipschitz, D., Houshyar, S., ... and Gelernter, J. (2006). "Brain-derived Neurotrophic Factor–5-HTTLPR Gene Interactions and Environmental Modifiers of Depression in Children." *Biological Psychiatry*, 59(8), 673–680.

Focusing solely on the maltreated cohort, Kaufman once again measured the effects of genes and environment on children's depression scores. Except this time, instead of separating children into maltreated and non-maltreated groups, Kaufman divided the children into high support and low support groups, based on their answers to her social support questions. High support children knew a number of adults outside of their parents whom they regularly went to for advice, comfort, and support. These adults included grandparents, family friends, other relatives, favourite teachers, friends' parents, and community members to whom the children had a strong connection. They were a frequent presence in the child's life, providing the emotional and intellectual nourishment he or she might not necessarily have gotten at home. Low support children did not have this same advantage. They had few close relationships with adults outside of their parents (or perhaps none at all), and those whom they did trust were not always available to them.

Having constructed a new framework, Kaufman reassessed the data. Keep in mind, every child participating in this leg of the study experienced maltreatment at home. Living in houses fraught with anxiety, anger, and pain, it's difficult to imagine that a kind word from a grandparent or uncle or extra attention from a particularly dedicated teacher could make much difference to how they behaved. Yet it did.

The results of Kaufman's high support/low support study and her maltreated/non-maltreated study possess an eerie symmetry. In each experiment, the effects of *5-HTT* and *BDNF* genotype are identical, with high support children filling in for the non-maltreated group. High support children were as impervious to genetic influence as non-maltreated children *in spite of the fact that they had been abused.* Their depression scores were on the whole higher, but they displayed none of the genetic volatility characteristic of abused children. Those with the s/s *5-HTT* and val/met *BDNF* alleles — the devastating one-two punch of genetic oversensitivity — were no more depressed than children with the protective l/l and val/val alleles. The presence of stable, supportive adults in their lives mitigated the effects of an abusive home life, particularly among those who, because of an accident of genetics, would have been most affected.

Kaufman's research can teach us two things. The first is that human intervention can trump genetics. When the odds are stacked against you, when your home life taxes your emotional and intellectual development, when not one but *two* genes undermine your brain's ability to cope with the strain, even then you can find solace in a friendly face or a guiding hand or a shoulder to cry on. As fragile and beholden to the whims of their parents as children seem at times, they nevertheless have a stunning tenacity about them, an ability to derive comfort and support from wherever they may find it. This ability speaks volumes about the plasticity of child development. It also leads us to Kaufman's second point: development is complex. Research has pushed aside the notion of predominance in either nature or nurture, ushering in a more nuanced paradigm of gene-by-environment interactions. In this new theory, the quality of a child's environment influences how he or she behaves, but the extent of that influence is determined by the presence of certain genes. The environment sets the station but genes control the volume. And there isn't just one volume knob, either. The *5-HTT* gene can dial up depression a good 10 decibels, say, but then the *BDNF* gene can keep it capped there, or crank it up another 10. Suddenly our simple transistor radio has become a home stereo system. But then consider the moderating influences enjoyed by high support children. When the family environment is stable and supportive, does that dial down the depression? Does it dial up anything else? Where does that fit in our analogy? A separate bass or treble knob on the speakers themselves? The metaphor has grown ungainly. It falls apart.

Child development doesn't take well to pithy metaphors. The human body is an immensely, perhaps even infinitely complex organism, a sprawling network of molecules responding to commands issued from both inside (our genes) and out (our environment). Genetic and environmental influences clash, converge, and collude with one another, holding court over a seething mass of cells that somehow function in perfect (or perhaps only near-perfect) harmony. Sometimes it seems the more we learn, the less we know. Fortunately, this isn't the case. We don't know everything, but we know quite a bit. A lot more now than we did 10 years ago, surely, and in another 10 years we'll know a lot more still.

And, most important of all, we have learned how to harness this knowledge. Scientists and policy makers have already begun advocating for change in the way our communities support their most vulnerable children. But their research does not apply solely to cases of dire poverty or criminal abuse. It affects all children, even those from loving, supportive homes.

Chapter 5

Knowledge Is Power

Unlike depression, anxiety, and other internalizing behaviours, externalizing behaviours are highly visible. We see them in graffiti-covered storefronts and kicked-over newspaper vending boxes; in bars or on buses, where a furtive glance or an arm brushed accidentally against a shoulder turns in an instant into a shouting match; and on the news, in stories of robbery, domestic violence, and murder. Think of Joey from our last chapter. A classic example of externalizing behaviour, he drew attention to himself at every opportunity, openly flaunting rules, disrupting class, and bullying anyone who dared to meet his eye. Unlike Erika, who could be easily overlooked by a teacher less empathetic than Mrs. Munroe, Joey saw to it that he was noticed. To Erika, attention was a vile tincture, a medicine she hated taking and that didn't seem to do her any good; to Joey, it was a drug.

The negative effects of externalizing behaviour ripple outward from the individual, affecting his family, his peers, his co-workers, and ultimately his community — and we use "his" here deliberately. Boys are far more likely than girls to exhibit externalizing behaviour in response to a stressful environment. Girls, by contrast, are more likely to suffer from depression or anxiety, though internalizing behaviours are significantly less gendered than externalizing behaviours.

Hundreds of studies have shown that stress caused by verbal and physical violence, mental illness, and substance abuse greatly increases children's chances of suffering from excessive aggression, alcoholism, and ADHD. Though this correlation is well-documented, it is not incontrovertible. Plenty of children come from stressful homes yet grow up to be well-adjusted adults. What benevolent force saves them from the downward spiral of anger and violence that claims so many of their peers? Is it blind luck? Is it social support? Or do they possess some innate genetic filter that keeps environmental pollutants out of their systems?

A Canary in the Coal Mine

A 2005 study led by Sara Jaffee compared the effects of a stressful home environment on identical and fraternal twins. Fraternal twins are conceived when two eggs are fertilized by two different sperm, while identical twins occur when a fertilized egg — called a zygote — splits into two separate organisms during its first few replications. Identical twins have identical genomes, which explain their great physical similarities. Fraternal twins, on the other hand, are simply two siblings who shared a womb. Genetically speaking, they are no more alike than a typical brother and sister.

In technical terms, identical and fraternal twins are distinguished by their zygosity, or the number of fertilized eggs from which they were born. Identical twins, born from a single zygote, are called monozygotic, while fraternal twins are called dizygotic.[21]

Zygosity	Twin type	DNA in common
Dizygotic	Fraternal (non-identical) twins	50 percent
Monozygotic	Identical twins	100 percent

The goal of Jaffee's study was to show that a person's genes were correlated to his or her sensitivity to the long-term effects of maltreatment. She developed a framework that stratified children's risk of exhibiting externalizing behaviour based on their zygosity and the presence or absence of externalizing symptoms in their twins. This premise may seem confusing, but it is actually fairly simple. If a trait has a genetic link, then one of your relatives possessing that trait increases your chances of possessing it as well. The closer that relative is to you genetically, the more alleles you share, and the greater the odds that you both display the same version of a given trait. Dizygotic twins have roughly 50 percent of their polymorphisms in common, so the odds of them sharing a genetic trait are approximately one in two. Monozygotic (identical) twins, on the other hand, have 100 percent of their polymorphisms in common, so the odds of them *not* sharing a genetic trait are slim to none (although it is possible for a gene to mutate shortly after the zygote separates, and certain genetic traits can be switched on or off by the environment, a phenomenon we will address in more detail later in this book). Therefore, if you observe a genetic trait in one dizygotic twin, there is a decent chance it will be visible in the other twin as well; observe the same trait in a monozygotic twin, and its presence in the other twin is basically guaranteed.

Bearing this in mind, Jaffee developed a 4-point scale of genetic risk, its underlying principle being that a symptom in one twin predicts the presence of that same symptom in the other twin. Your sibling becomes a sort of canary in the coalmine of your genes, their behaviours a genetic portent of what you may one day face.

The lowest-risk children were those whose monozygotic (identical) twins showed no signs of externalizing behaviour. Considering these twins share all of their DNA, the absence of a genetic trait in one twin can safely predict its absence in the other. Next were children whose dizygotic twins showed no signs of externalizing behaviour. Though the trait could arise from the 50 percent of alleles the children don't share, we can at least guarantee that one half of their DNA is safe. Riskier still were children whose dizygotic twins showed signs of externalizing behaviour. At this level of the scale, we have confirmed that the trait exists within the subject's immediate family. Perhaps they inherited it or perhaps they did not, but it is a confirmed possibility. Lastly, children whose monozygotic (identical) twins showed signs of externalizing behaviour were the highest risk of all. If one twin has the trait, and the trait comes from a polymorphic variation, then the other twin almost certainly has the offending variation, too.

Which is not to say that he or she has the trait.

Anyone who has met a set of identical twins could tell you that the term "identical" is not, in the most technical sense, accurate. Spend enough time with them and you will be able to distinguish one from the other just by looking at them. The telltale sign may be a mole or a freckle, or a slight difference in height or weight, or a result of their varying mannerisms and inflections. Though casual acquaintances may not be capable of discerning one from the other by appearance alone, a brief conversation should suffice. The "identical" aspects of monozygotic twins rarely extend to their personalities. In fact, identicals often exaggerate the differences between each other, perhaps in order to more firmly establish unique identities. A twin girl who is slightly more extroverted than her identical sibling will make a point of acting as outgoing as possible, while her more reserved twin will draw further inward. These behaviours change the way each twin is treated by her teachers, her peers, and even her own family, which in turn reinforces the differences between them.

Living things are more than the sum of their parts. Genes are not our overlords, especially when it comes to complex behavioural traits. One's environment is equally important, and we would expect the home life of these children to play an important role in their development (or lack thereof) of externalizing behaviours. Jaffee is, of course, aware of this, which is why her study grouped children based on environmental factors as well as genetic ones. More specifically, she considered whether or not they had been physically maltreated.

Interviewers asked the twins' mothers a series of "probe questions" designed to elicit conversation about their children's past maltreatment without coming across as accusatory or hostile. Questions included "Do you remember any time when your child was disciplined severely enough that he may have been hurt?" and "Did you worry that you or someone else may have harmed or hurt your child?" The interviewers chose their words carefully, avoiding any implications that the mother may have been at fault. If the mother reported any maltreatment, the interviewer probed for details, keeping careful notes on what happened, when, how often, and if the police or child services were involved. They also kept an eye out for subtler clues, observing how the mother and child acted during their conversation. A nervous glance, downcast eyes, fidgeting, and increased tension in the presence of the father, or any hint at a darker truth was noted, analyzed, and used to determine whether the child was potentially being maltreated. The evidence didn't need to be ironclad; for inclusion in the study's test group, children could be classified either probable or definite cases of maltreatment.

Jaffee took the maltreated and non-maltreated cohorts (containing 307 and 809 children, respectively), subdivided each of them into groups based on her 4-point risk scale, and tallied the frequency of conduct problems in each group, as reported by the children's mothers and teachers. Conduct problems included fighting, bullying, lying, stealing, cruelty to people or animals, vandalism, and breaking rules. As expected, each degree up the maltreatment risk scale correlated to an increase in conduct disorder in both cohorts. Lowest risk children, regardless of whether or not they were maltreated, were less likely to act out than children of the same cohort in the next bracket up. However, within each risk group, the maltreated children were more likely to exhibit conduct disorders than the non-maltreated children. Moreover, the gap between risk levels was wider in maltreated than non-maltreated children. As the risk level rose, the amount of maltreated children displaying conduct disorders increased considerably more than it did in the non-maltreated cohort. In the lowest genetic risk group, maltreatment caused conduct disorders to rise 2 percent compared to non-maltreated children of the same risk level; in the highest genetic risk group, the increase was 24 percent.

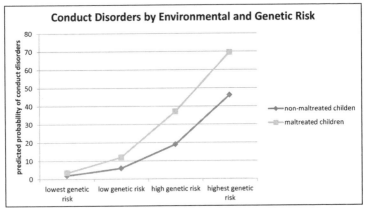

Jaffee, S.R., Caspi, A., Moffitt, T.E., Dodge, K.A., Rutter, M., Taylor, A., and Tully, L.A. (2005). "Nature × Nurture: Genetic Vulnerabilities Interact with Physical Maltreatment to Promote Conduct Problems." *Development and Psychopathology*, 17(1), 67–84.

Jaffee's study is a helpful example of how genes and environment interact. Maltreatment affected children negatively regardless of their genetic risk; maltreated children were more likely to misbehave than non-maltreated children in every risk group. Predicting how much more likely is where genes came into play. Though an excellent model, the weakness of Jaffee's study lies in its generality. Much like Meaney's experiments with Type A and Type B mice, Jaffee showed that genes influence our susceptibility to abuse without targeting any one gene. In order to understand the relationship between genes and environment, we need to narrow our focus to a precise genetic target.

Pleasure, Anger, and Dopamine

Dopamine is, arguably, the most powerful motivator in the human brain's arsenal. Without it our entire species would collapse into despondency, indifference, and extinction. But dopamine is no good on its own. In order to reap its benefits, our brains need a way to process it. For this, we have a protein product called a dopamine receptor, a tiny neurological trigger fired by contact with a dopamine molecule. The human brain has many different types of these receptors, but perhaps none has come under more scientific scrutiny than the DRD4 family, a class of dopamine receptors implicated in a host of adverse conditions, including schizophrenia, Parkinson's disease, bipolar disorder, anorexia nervosa, bulimia nervosa, and drug addiction. A protein product, DRD4 is coded for by the *DRD4* gene, and much of its reputation as a hotbed of neurological strife comes from a single allelic variation called the 7-repeat allele. As its name suggests, 7-repeat is a variation of the *DRD4* gene where a brief sequence of 48 nucleotides (the microscopic molecules from which genes are constructed) repeats seven times.

Repetition is not what makes the 7-repeat unusual; different varieties of *DRD4* have the same sequence repeated anywhere from two to eleven times. What makes the 7-repeat allele unique is its weaker-than-average reaction to dopamine, compared with other versions of *DRD4*. To put it crudely, the 7-repeat allele is not all that good at its job. While its compatriots handle influxes of dopamine with ease, 7-repeat struggles to stay on target. This idiosyncrasy has made 7-repeat a subject of great interest to scientists across multiple disciplines, as a person's neurological response to dopamine influences, on a very fundamental level, how that person behaves. It seems inevitable that such an infamous allele — particularly one so intimately involved in regulating human behaviour — would catch the eye of perceptive scholars studying child development.

Among those paying attention were Dutch researchers Marian Bakermans-Kranenburg and Marinus Van IJzendoorn. Together, the two professors from Leiden University in the Netherlands have spearheaded multiple studies investigating the effects of 7-repeat on children's behaviour. They are, arguably, among the world's foremost experts on the subject. And they have found a link between the troublesome gene, early rearing environments, and children's behaviour that you, having read the results of Joan Kaufman's studies earlier this chapter, may find awfully familiar.

First, Bakermans-Kranenburg and Van IJzendoorn recruited 47 mothers when their children were 10 months old and followed them until the children were three. They visited each mother at home and filmed her performing normal, unstructured activities — cleaning, cooking, feeding, or changing or playing with her child, etc. Mothers weren't told what the two researchers were looking for, or even whether they or their children were the focus of the study. They were instructed to act as normally as possible and, after a brief period of self-consciousness, settled quickly into their typical routine.

Bakermans-Kranenburg and Van IJzendoorn studied the tapes, documenting the behaviour of each mother-child pair.

In the children's case, they were interested in signs of externalizing behaviour — talking back, hitting, throwing food and toys, fits of anger, hyperactivity, any outward display of excessive aggression or unchecked energy. For mothers, the focus was a bit different. Less attention was paid to actions, and more to interactions. Bakermans-Kranenburg and Van IJzendoorn wanted to gauge something called maternal sensitivity, a variable that measures how adept mothers are at anticipating, interpreting, and responding to their children's needs.

Mothers' actions were rated on the Maternal Sensitivity Scale, a sociological measure comprised of four categories: a mother's awareness of her child's signals of needs or wants, her accurate interpretation of those signals, the appropriateness of her response, and how promptly she responded. Mothers who scored on the upper half of the scale — meaning they responded quickly and appropriately to their children's needs — were placed in the high-sensitivity group, and mothers on the lower half — those who responded slowly or infrequently to their children, or who misinterpreted their needs — were classified low sensitivity.

To acquire the study's final variable, researchers took DNA samples from each child participating in the study and determined which polymorphism (or variation) of the *DRD4* gene they possessed. More specifically, they wanted to know whether or not the children had the infamous 7-repeat allele. Bakermans-Kranenburg, Van IJzendoorn, and their observation team were kept clear of the results of these tests until after they had reviewed the tapes and submitted their appraisals of mother and child behaviour. Sequestering data is critical in these types of studies, where objectivity is a goal that is exceedingly difficult to reach, and the slightest potential for bias in the researcher can poison the entire experiment. If the researchers charged with scoring mother-infant behaviour knew which children had the volatile 7-repeat allele, they could — either consciously or unconsciously — rank them higher on the externalizing behaviour scale in order to prove their hypothesis correct. This problem — called confirmation bias — is a constant hazard to experiments in the social sciences, and researchers must guard against it vigilantly.

When all the data was in place, Bakermans-Kranenburg and Van IJzendoorn put it through rigorous analyses. The results were significant. For children with the 7-repeat allele, mothers' behaviour greatly influenced their odds of acting out. The 7-repeat children with low-sensitivity mothers (mothers who misinterpreted their children's needs, or who responded indifferently to them) exhibited a great deal of externalizing behaviour, while 7-repeat children with high-sensitivity mothers (mothers who understood their needs and met them promptly) barely showed any externalizing behaviour at all. They were *less than half* as likely as 7-repeat children with low-sensitivity mothers to talk back, act out, or show signs of ADHD. Children without the 7-repeat allele fell somewhere in the middle, though they were closer to the

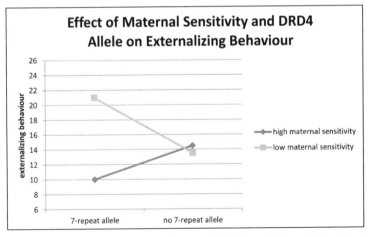

Bakermans-Kranenburg, M.J., and Van IJzendoorn, M.H. (2006). "Gene–Environment Interaction of the Dopamine D4 Receptor (DRD4) and Observed Maternal Insensitivity Predicting Externalizing Behavior in Preschoolers." *Developmental Psychobiology*, 48(5), 406–409.

well-behaved 7-repeat high-sensitivity children than the defiant 7-repeat low-sensitivity children. Their mothers' level of sensitivity didn't make much difference to their odds of displaying external-izing behaviour.

Keep in mind that the women in the low-sensitivity group were not necessarily bad mothers. The study did not recruit parents accused of child abuse or neglect, nor did it focus on families from groups generally considered to be high-risk (impoverished, uneducated, suffering from alcoholism or drug addiction, prone to violence, etc.). Low-sensitivity mothers didn't leave their children home alone for hours on end to go party, or drink themselves sick, or bully their children with taunts or smacks or insults. Some of them were absent-minded. Many of them were overworked and exhausted and didn't have the energy or patience required to meet their children's every immediate need, but loved their children all the same and wanted nothing but the best for them. The vast majority were probably doing their best, and would be horrified at the thought that their actions might be hurting their children. And yet, their children were over twice as likely to display aggressive or violent behaviour as those of high-sensitivity mothers — assuming, of course, the children in question had the 7-repeat allele of the *DRD4* gene. That is not a small discrepancy, and it shows that in parenting, the little things matter just as much as the big ones.

Fixing the Problem

Having established a link between genes, maternal sensitivity, and children's behaviour, Bakermans-Kranenburg and Van IJzendoorn strove to use this knowledge to help those children who were most at risk. Their study showed that children with the 7-repeat allele and low-sensitivity mothers were by far the most likely to display signs of externalizing behaviour. Having just one of the two traits — 7-repeat but a high-sensitivity mother, or a low-sensitivity mother but no 7-repeat — was pretty much as good as having neither. Therefore, it stood to reason that changing one of those two variables in vulnerable children would lower their risk considerably. Genes can't change. Maternal behaviour can.

The two researchers recruited 157 families with children who exhibited signs of externalizing behaviour, such as aggression, hyperactivity, and hostilely defiant behaviour toward authority figures. The families were randomly assigned to either a test or control group. Families in the test group underwent an intervention program Bakermans-Kranenburg and Van IJzendoorn had developed.

Each family in the program received six home visits from female consultants called interveners. During these visits, the interveners observed how the family interacted, appraised their parenting strategies, and offered tips and suggestions for improved communication between parents and children. Each visit was themed, focusing on different skill sets, such as responding promptly to children's signals, sharing emotions, and using positive reinforcement. The last two sessions were review, where interveners helped bolster previously learned skills. At the end of the program, parents received brochures filled with tips and exercises on the key issues of the intervention.

Meanwhile, the control group participated in a largely insubstantial program called a dummy intervention. Researchers contacted parents by phone and discussed parenting issues with them. Parents were encouraged to talk about their children's development, but the "interveners" did no intervening whatsoever; they did not observe the participants' parenting strategies, nor did they offer any tips on how to more effectively parent children with externalizing behaviour disorders. The entire point of the control was to make parents think they were participating in an intervention program without actually providing one. Bakermans-Kranenburg and Van IJzendoorn met with both groups a year after the program's completion and noted the change, if any, in children's externalizing behaviours.

The results were, at first glance, lukewarm. As expected, 7-repeat children benefited from the real intervention, but the effect was marginal; 7-repeats who underwent the intervention program scored an average of 2.5 points lower on the externalizing behaviour scale than 7-repeats in the control group, who received the deliberately ineffective "dummy" intervention. Non-7-repeat children varied even less. Although 2.5 points is enough to be statistically significant, given the respectable sample size of the study, it is hardly earth-shattering. The intervention program seemed like a dud.

Bakermans-Kranenburg and Van IJzendoorn were not to be dissuaded. Pushing the control group aside, they considered their data from a new angle. Perhaps, they thought, merely participating in the program wasn't enough. A far more influential factor would be whether or not the parents who received this information actually *did anything with it*, or whether they promptly fell back into old habits after the intervention program concluded.

The two researchers set out to ascertain exactly that. They took parents who had participated in the real intervention, re-observed them interacting with their children, and broke them into two groups based on whether or not they had continued to follow the techniques prescribed by the program.

Suddenly, the intervention seemed far more promising. Among children with the *DRD4* 7-repeat allele, those whose parents took the program's lessons to heart scored 6 points lower on the externalizing behaviour scale (meaning they were calmer, happier, and less prone to anger) than children whose parents chose not to follow the plan, a difference *more than twice that between the intervention and control groups*. Even among families in the dummy intervention group, those who had adopted a more engaged and interactive parenting style — be it through advice gleaned from a parenting book or the suggestion of a grandparent or simply by learning from their own experiences as parents — saw a precipitous drop in their children's externalizing behaviour, with children scoring 4 points lower on the externalizing behaviour scale than those of less adaptive parents. The drops were less substantial in children without the *DRD4* 7-repeat allele, though even they showed a marked improvement.

Bakermans-Kranenburg and Van IJzendoorn's intervention was a rousing success, but not because it was a brilliant or life-altering program. Its power didn't come from comprehensive lesson plans or advanced technology or extensive funding — in fact, it possessed none of these traits, just half a dozen chats with an informed third party and several pages of accessible parenting literature. Nurses or social workers or perhaps even trained parents could provide programs like this in our communities.

The true success of the program rested on the parents' desire to better understand and relate to their children. Without that spark, the program meant nothing.[22]

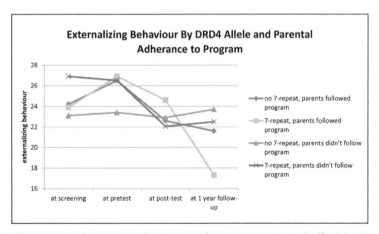

Bakermans-Kranenburg, M.J., IJzendoorn, M.H.V., Pijlman, F.T., Mesman, J., and Juffer, F. (2008). "Experimental Evidence for Differential Susceptibility: Dopamine D4 Receptor Polymorphism (DRD4 VNTR) Moderates Intervention Effects on Toddlers' Externalizing Behavior in a Randomized Controlled Trial." *Developmental Psychology*, 44(1), 293.

In the insular, almost solipsistic world of infant development, small actions have big consequences. Young brains grow at a feverish rate, and their constant, relentless expansion makes them ravenous for stimuli. Everything they see, hear, taste, touch, and smell is gobbled up, pored over, processed, and neatly filed away for future consideration. Much of it will ultimately be discarded, but a surprising amount of it will be absorbed and incorporated into the child's beliefs, attitudes, and behaviour. Minds, as mysterious and intangible as they may seem, are rooted in the physical world. They are built experience by experience and neuron by neuron, materials as real — and as crucial — as the bricks and mortar of a house's foundation. Mislay the bricks or skimp on the mortar and the house stands crooked or crumbles to the ground.

Sounds scary, doesn't it? And you know what, it *is* scary. Parenting is a hard job. It requires creativity, discipline, intuition, compassion, tenacity, and wisdom. It comes with long hours, tremendous responsibility, and no pay. It forces you to become the parent your child needs you to be, to adapt your responses, emotions, and behaviours to the benefit of your child. It demands the best of you at all times. It is tough. But it is far from impossible. Your parents did it, after all, as did your grandparents before them, and your great-grandparents before them. Trailing behind you to the distant horizon of human history is a chain of parents thousands of generations long. Some of them did a better job than others. Yet every single one of them, in their own way, succeeded at humanity's most important endeavour. They kept the ball rolling for another generation. If they could do it, surely you can too. Think of all the advantages you have over your ancestors 10 generations back. You have clean water and family doctors and hand sanitizer. You have penicillin and daycare and the polio vaccine. You have freedom from famine and pestilence and war. You have *knowledge*, more than any generation that came before you.

We also have civilizations and governments that can afford to attend more to the needs of families, encouraging and helping parents to be the sensitive, attentive people their children need them to be. Parenting needs to be recognized as the cornerstone of greater public health and supported in as many constructive ways as possible. But we are getting ahead of ourselves. There is much more evidence still to come that will reveal the true scope of parenting's influence on individuals, families, and the societies in which they dwell.

Scientific studies, with their complex behavioural scales and near-inscrutable graphs, can seem abstract and sterile. But beneath the tables and jargon and rhetoric lies a rich and ever-deepening pool of knowledge. We are the beneficiaries of a grand and storied tradition of scientific inquiry, but also of practical experience. It is at the crossroads of these two variables that our understanding of early child development is at its most lucid. And perhaps no field of study gets it better than attachment theory.

Chapter 6
The Eyes of a Child

In the wake of the Second World War, thousands upon thousands of children were left without parents. Six years of warfare on an unprecedented scale had caused a dramatic influx of orphans. Most were homeless, friendless, and hopelessly alone, their entire families slaughtered and their villages bombed to rubble. Their shell-shocked faces neatly encapsulated the horrors that had plagued Europe for over half a decade, and the World Health Organization (WHO) was desperate to help them in any way it could. But building and staffing orphanages wasn't enough. The WHO strove to correct not just the physical and financial hardships faced by orphans, but the psychological ones as well. They wanted to understand the effects of such profound loss on the human mind in order to better help those who suffered through it. For this they turned to the renowned psychiatrist John Bowlby.

Bowlby was the perfect candidate. An award-winning and well-educated scholar, he had experience working with maladapted and delinquent children and an avowed passion for helping disadvantaged young people. The WHO asked him to write a pamphlet on the psychology of orphans, how the loss of both parents affects children's mental and emotional development. Bowlby accepted, and the task so captivated him that he made studying children the basis of the rest of career. Attachment theory was an extension of his original work, drawing inspiration from psychology, biology, and ethology in an attempt to explain how and why children bond with their early caregivers. Though received with some reluctance by the academic community of the day, attachment theory ultimately became the go-to model for exploring early child development.

Dr. Mary Ainsworth, Bowlby's star pupil, reinforced his theory, amending to it various tools and strategies designed to measure and categorize the children it sought to study. Ainsworth's research begat two intelligent and ambitious disciples: Patricia Crittenden and Mary Main. Crittenden and Main both believed strongly in the basic tenets of attachment theory, and both used the new science as a diving bell with which they plumbed the murky and shifting depths of infant psychology. It is what they found down there — or rather, how they chose to interpret it — that caused a rift to form between them.

Severed Bonds

Do you remember Sophie from the beginning of this book? She wasn't an only child. She had a sister named Sandra and a brother named Darren, both younger than her. Though their traumatic upbringing forged a certain bond between them, the three siblings were never close. They got along fairly well, all things considered, but were all very different people.

For one thing, Sophie and Sandra reacted very differently to their parents' fighting. Sophie, we know, cowered in her room, drowning out the noise as best she could and doing everything in her power to avoid the situation. Sandra took the opposite approach. She was a heavier sleeper than Sophie, but on nights where the fighting got heated enough to wake her she would scream and cry and beat her fists against the headboard until her parents came running, drawing their attention to her and away from each other. When things calmed down she seemed more or less content, oblivious to the subtler domestic tensions that buzzed discordantly in Sophie's ears more or less constantly.

Sophie made self-sufficiency and people-pleasing her mantra. Sandra, on the other hand, relied on her parents for everything. She constantly mooched money, demanded attention, and whined whenever she didn't get her way. Though she demanded constant affection, she herself was not particularly affectionate, treating her parents with a confused jumble of sycophancy, indifference, and disdain.

Unlike Sophie, Sandra didn't take well to school. She struggled to pay attention in class and spent most of her time daydreaming and doodling. Though not one to act out, Sandra scarcely made an effort and squeaked by with poor grades. By the time she finished high school she was already married to a man four years older than her, and the only job she could find was at Burger King.

Now an adult, Sandra has three children and barely enough money to feed and clothe them. Her husband works at a warehouse loading boxes of frozen food onto trucks. He spends most of his time playing video games, ignoring Sandra pretty much completely. Sandra takes her aggression out on the children. She constantly calls on Sophie for help, but Sophie has her own problems and there's only so much she can do.

As for Darren, he was still in the womb when Sophie and Sandra's home life started to crumble. His mother took care of him as best she could, but some days the weight of her life grew much too heavy and she stayed in bed, ignoring his cries and flicking through channels on a small, grainy television. His father convinced himself that Darren wasn't really his child and he offered the boy nothing but insults and barbed criticism.

At school, Darren was habitually sent to the principal's office. He picked fights, talked back to teachers, and disrupted classes. Not a month went by where he didn't face suspension. Twice he was held back a year for failure to complete any of the course material. In seventh grade, he was expelled for stabbing a classmate in the arm with a compass and had to enroll in another school across town. By grade 10 he was expelled again, this time for selling pot. When he was 18, he was squatting in a friend's downtown apartment.

Darren worked briefly as a stock boy at a grocery store, but mostly he sells drugs — soft stuff like pot and pills. He doesn't have the connections or the muscle necessary to move crack or heroin, but he doesn't really mind. That stuff is far more dangerous to work with, and he doesn't need to earn that much. He crashes on couches, eats fast food, and spends the rest of his cash on booze and cigarettes. He has a child he never sees with a woman who nearly had him arrested for domestic abuse.

A Tale of Two Theories

Attachment theory, as defined by Dr. Mary Ainsworth, divides 12- to 24-month-old babies into three groups based on how they act in relation to their parents — when and how they seek comfort, the affection (or lack thereof) they display when their parents hold or play with them, and the degree to which they are comfortable exploring their environment. To distinguish between groups, Ainsworth represented each one by a letter, giving us attachment types A, B, and C. Each group of babies has developed a different and distinctly recognizable strategy to ensure that their attachment figure (parent) provides them with protection, comfort, and the necessities of life. Without a successful strategy for attachment to a caregiver, babies would be hopelessly alone and vulnerable to all manner of threats — disease, starvation, predators, and exposure to the elements.

Attachment is therefore an evolutionary adaptation to ensure survival.

Groups A, B, and C represent three distinct attachment strategies, each comprised of specific behaviours that children adopt in order to cope with and function in the world around them. The strategies derive from infancy but persist over the lifespan and affect behaviour and mental health into adulthood.

Type B children are securely attached. They are comfortable being left alone for short periods but happy to see their parents return. Type A children, called "avoidant," tend to avoid contact with caregivers. They have come to expect neglect or disinterest on the part of their guardians, often because their early cries for attention have gone unheeded. As a result, they aren't bothered by spending short periods of time on their own, nor do they seem at all excited to see their parents when they return. This is in direct contrast to Type C or "reactive/ambivalent" children, who fuss and cry upon being left alone for even a moment, but are not consoled by, and often show resentment toward, their parents' presence. Type C behaviour is often a response to inconsistent or partial neglect — when a parent comes running at the first sound of their child in one instance, but leaves them unattended for hours in another. Type A behaviours, on the other hand, come from consistent neglect. Children whose parents never answer their cries or react indifferently to their presence learn to seek comfort from themselves, developing a fierce inward yearning for self-reliance and emotional numbness to outside caregivers. There is, we believe, another cause of Type A attachment: "Tiger" parenting. The Tiger Mother, a term popularized by Amy Chua's 2011 book *Battle Hymn of the Tiger Mother*, emphasizes control, harsh discipline, and a relentless drive for scholastic pursuits in child-rearing. Proponents of Tiger Mothering argue that children lack the capacity for self-motivation needed to achieve their best, and a firm, strict, and unwavering pressure, applied by the parent, is necessary to make children reach their full potential. The parent becomes a kind of crucible, facilitating the high temperatures necessary to smelt a child's raw components into a strong, successful adult. However, predicating affection purely on scholastic or musical success can create in a child an overwhelming need to please others. Using affection as a reward for good behaviour is essentially a sort of Pavlovian conditioning and leaves children with a fairly tenuous grasp on their self-esteem. Children reared in this way often find their sense of self-worth hinges on the approval of others, creating a person not unlike Sophie: outwardly successful, but inwardly pained.

Type B children are well-adjusted for today's world, while Type A and Type C children adopt alternate strategies to assure attention from their parents. These strategies are initially adaptive, meaning they improve a child's ability to form attachment relationships with their caregivers. But as children grow, those once-advantageous behaviours of infancy become trap doors of childhood. These trap doors swing open perilously beneath their feet as they attempt to navigate their widening social and emotional landscape.

For Type A children, this means that indifferent behaviour in infancy can lead to excessive people-pleasing in childhood, promiscuity in the teenage years, and an externally assembled adult self, in which the individual's entire personality is derived from his or her interactions with others. Externally assembled individuals equate praise with self-worth and criticism with self-hatred. Their self-esteem is as capricious as a flag in the wind, held aloft by the breeze and changing direction with each passing gust or zephyr. For Type C, the path embraces contrasting yet ultimately connected aspects of internalizing and externalizing behaviour, ranging from aggression and passivity in milder forms to sadism and seduction, and finally, in extreme forms, rabid paranoia.

We can see these trends in Sophie, a classic Type A child, and Sandra, a typical Type C. Both are haunted by their past, but each woman's burden takes a distinct shape. Sandra suffers more overtly, her fractious behaviour making relationships difficult and sabotaging her education, leaving her unequipped to function in society. Ostensibly, Sophie did much better. Type A individuals are often outwardly successful people, as their need to please others and thirst for self-sufficiency and approval find natural outlets in career-building. But their drive comes at a price. Type A people find it extremely difficult to trust others, yet at the same time desperately seek their positive regard. We saw as much in Sophie, whose successful teaching career masked the many psychological issues festering beneath the surface: her obsessive people-pleasing, her postpartum depression, and her recurring bouts of crippling anxiety. A harsh word from a student or colleague would slice her to the bone.

Mind you, not every Type A or Type C child will stray to the corrosive fringes of this continuum. Neither Sophie nor Sandra is doomed to a life of rabid paranoia; with professional help and family support, they may even grow more secure over time. Patricia Crittenden's Dynamic Maturation Model of Attachment eschews rigid boundaries of "normal" and "abnormal." A person can veer a little to either side their whole lives and still be okay. Nor will their attachment strategy necessarily remain in any one place on the continuum. No developmental authority stamps "Type A" or "Type B" onto one's baby-self psyche, neatly categorizing the individual for life. Crittenden's model emphasizes fluidity and movement, as seen in its popular depiction as a wheel. Type B balanced comfortably at the top, a buffer on either side. Proceeding clockwise brings you farther into reactive/ambivalent Type C territory, while moving counter clockwise elicits more and more avoidant Type A behaviour. Go too far in either direction and you wind up at the bottom of the wheel, in the dark and vicious mires of psychopathy.

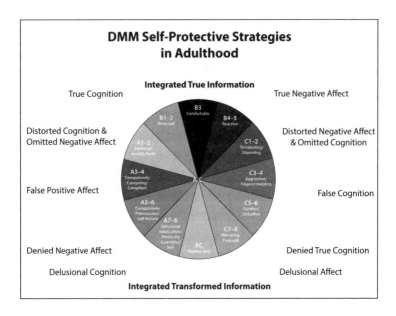

Mary Main, on the other hand, takes a more rigidly defined, categorical approach to attachment theory. In place of Crittenden's fluid extremes, she created a separate attachment category altogether, called disorganized, or Type D. Disorganized attachment is, somewhat paradoxically, the strategy of having no strategy at all. According to Main, it occurs when children perceive their parents as aggressive or frightening figures, but also as their only source of comfort and security. The schism produced by these conflicting perceptions breeds confusion, anxiety, and, ultimately, what appears to be disorganized attachment.

Crittenden and Main would probably diagnose Sophie and Sandra the same way, but would butt heads over how to classify Darren. Main would consider him an obvious Type D, while Crittenden would place him somewhere far along the Type C end of the behavioural spectrum.

This might seem like a fairly small point of contention, but it has placed a divide not just between the two theories, but between their major proponents. Crittenden's Dynamic

Maturation Model has been castigated as an unfounded corruption of Ainsworth's original theory, while Main's disorganized attachment has been described as a lazy catch-all for behaviours that, ultimately, adhere to either Type A or Type C strategies. And that, really, is the crux of the matter. According to the Dynamic Maturational Model, all attachment behaviour is "organized," in that children invariably interact with their caregivers in a manner they deem most conducive to their survival. These strategies, though damaging in the long run, are not mere aberrations. They exist for a reason. Even in infancy, children know to look out for number one.

Now any parent whose young child has managed to lay their hands on a pair of scissors, or toddled gleefully toward a busy road, or reached idly for the handle of a pot of boiling water will regard this claim with understandable incredulity. Children, especially young ones, are walking maelstroms of calamity. However, this behaviour stems not from a deliberately foolhardy or self-destructive impulse, but from incomplete neural development. Their little brains simply haven't matured enough to properly assess risk. Yet even infants know enough to know they're helpless, and that their survival depends wholly on their ability to charm the enormous, benevolent, and deeply strange creatures that have thus far deigned to feed and clothe and shelter them. Human babies can't rely on their wits or speed or protective poisons or appendages; they lack any conventional means of self-defence. Their only chance of surviving those tumultuous early years is to forge a bond with their caregivers strong enough to keep them out of harm's way.

Children will adopt whatever behaviour will best serve them in those first few years where they have only the tiniest modicum of control over their lives, even if it causes innumerable problems for them down the road. This idea is the underpinning principle of the Dynamic Maturational Model. In Patricia Crittenden's view, all attachment behaviour is adaptive — while an infant may be classified as insecure in the DMM, that child has adapted perfectly to its environment. Mary Main, on the other hand, believes that children do sometimes get it wrong, and in situations of extreme and unrelenting stress, they may behave in a reckless, irrational, and detrimental way.

Which side do we take in this particular feud? As our stance on nature versus nurture should indicate, we aren't much for "sides." Our opinion is that, as is often the case when two theories are presented and neither can be easily discredited through observation or analysis, the truth lies somewhere in the middle. Which does not mean both Crittenden and Main are half wrong — both of their views may be correct. They would simply, in that case, be incomplete. Like two artists standing on either side of an object, each puts metaphorical brush to canvas and reproduces with skilled strokes the object's dimensions, colour, texture, and features as they see them. Both artists paint a stunning picture, reproducing the object perfectly while completely ignoring any aspect of its opposite side. Their paintings may look entirely different, but the object displayed on either canvas is one and the same.

So, in short, we take neither side. We see no practical reason why we should have to. Despite their disagreements, Crittenden's and Main's theories are not all that different from one another. Both emphasize the influence of early child behaviour on adult development; by extension, both focus almost exclusively on nurture. Their reasons for doing so are not unfounded — both theories are backed by extensive research showing strong correlations between parenting style and child attachment behaviour. Among the general population, roughly 15 percent of children display some characteristics of disorganized attachment (or what Crittenden would refer to as extreme Type A or C attachment); among maltreated children, that number is 80 percent. Clearly parents have an enormous influence over how their children learn to deal with other human beings — after all, they are the ones on whom children first hone their social skills. However, a small but growing body of research suggests that, though they may sometimes have to shout to be heard, genes still manage to get their say.

The Return of the 7-Repeat

Van IJzendoorn and Bakermans-Kranenburg turned their attention once again to the DRD4 7-repeat allele, although this time they were interested in different child outcomes. Knowing 7-repeat's influence on externalizing behaviour, the two researchers believed the troublesome allele may hold similar sway over disorganized attachment. But 7-repeat can only increase a child's susceptibility to behavioural disorders; it can't actually cause them. An environmental factor must also be at play, and it needn't be anything as extreme or deplorable as physical or mental abuse. Bakermans-Kranenburg and Van IJzendoorn thought a shift in parents' mood brought on by recent emotional trauma would suffice.

What sort of emotional trauma? Feelings can be hard to measure, as subjective and messy as they are, which is why Van IJzendoorn and Bakermans-Kranenburg set far more specific guidelines for inclusion in their study. They recruited 85 mothers who had recently lost a friend or relative, someone who they either a) lived with or b) visited at least once a week, prior to the loved one's passing. Van IJzendoorn and Bakermans-Kranenburg videotaped the mothers as they went about their day, much as the two researchers had done in their externalizing behaviour study. They also conducted extensive interviews with mothers, asking them about the nature of their recent loss, their memories from childhood, and the state of their current relationships with friends and loved ones.

The videotapes were scrutinized, their contents parsed for three distinct classes of actions, deemed "frightening behaviours": threatening behaviour, frightened behaviour, and dissociative behaviour. These three categories compose a scale designed by attachment theory proponent Mary Main, and together they quantify the degree to which a mother's behaviour can potentially disturb her child, creating the conditions that cause disorganized attachment. In order to use the scale, researchers observe tapes of the participants and pick out every incident, however minor, that can be classified as threatening, frightened, or dissociative in nature.

Despite their ominous names, frightening behaviours are not necessarily abusive. Threatening behaviour includes scolding, shouting, and spanking. Frightened behaviour is exactly what it sounds like: a mother responding in an emotional or dramatic way to a threat their child doesn't comprehend, such as a snarling dog, a high ledge, or a busy road. Dissociative behaviour is perhaps the most abstract, and includes any behaviour that separates a mother from her children mentally but not physically, be it a daydream, a trance, or simply a few minutes spent ignoring them in favour of watching television or reading a news article. None of these actions fit our romanticized image of what a perfect mother — that flawless, mythic, Stepfordesque creature — would do, but if a woman invited us up to her apartment and we saw her scold her child for scribbling on the walls, or let out a shriek when she noticed him poking experimentally at an electrical outlet, or tune out his crying while she finished making a cup of tea, we probably wouldn't feel obligated to call Child Services.

Next, Van IJzendoorn and Bakermans-Kranenburg tested the children when they were between 14 and 15 months old. Each child underwent the Strange Situation Procedure, a test developed by Dr. Ainsworth — Mary Main and Patricia Crittenden's mentor — to gauge infants' attachment strategy. The test itself is fairly simple. Researchers subject children to a series of mildly stressful events and record their reactions. Before you recoil at the thought of infants as unwilling participants in some traumatic experiment, we should stress the *mild* aspect of "mildly stressful events," which include having an adult the child doesn't know walk into the room, allowing the child to explore the room on his own, and separating the child from his parents for a five-minute period.[23] Trained observers interpreted the children's responses to the test and placed them in one of the four attachment categories we discussed previously: secure (Type B), avoidant (Type A), reactive/ambivalent (Type C), or disorganized (Type D). Type B children enjoyed exploring the room. They sometimes became unsure of themselves or frightened, but when they did they found comfort in the arms of their parents, were easily consoled, and happily resumed explored shortly after. Type A children enjoyed exploring, but did not seek comfort from their parents, even when frightened; mostly, they acted as if their parents weren't there. Type C children hated exploring. They clung to their parents, terrified and inconsolable.

Type D children were harder to classify, as disorganized attachment takes many shapes. Children suffering from it run to their parents for comfort, only to fall silent and turn their heads away. They cringe at their mother's touch, smile, and claw violently at her face, all in the span of a single thought. They wander the room like shiftless ghosts, ignoring cherished toys and seeking comfort from the walls or furniture. They freeze, fuss, fidget, twist their limbs about in a ceaseless, obsessive-compulsive rhythm, or move as if underwater, stepping and flailing in slow motion. Their behaviour is varied and unpredictable, but bespeaks confusion, anxiety, and profound inner turmoil.

Observers watched for such behaviour, and ranked the children who exhibited it based on the severity of their symptoms.

Though the Strange Situation Procedure is designed to allocate children to one of the four attachment groups — Types A through D — Van IJzendoorn and Bakermans-Kranenburg were only interested in whether or not children were disorganized. Type D (disorganized) children were thus assigned to one group, and Type A, B, and C children were lumped together in another.

After sorting through the data, Van IJzendoorn and Bakermans-Kranenburg didn't seem to have found much of interest, except that older mothers were more likely than younger mothers to raise Type D children. Beyond that, there appeared to be no meaningful correlations between the variables at all. In spite of previous evidence linking maternal frightening behaviour to infant disorganized attachment, the study found no such connection. Disorganized attachment seemed almost random in distribution, as if abiding by rules lying outside the purview of both genes and environment.

The answer lay in the maternal interviews. Unlike the videotapes, which documented specific observable behaviours in mothers (the "frightening behaviours"), the interviews rooted beneath the surface. Through meticulous questioning, Van IJzendoorn and Bakermans-Kranenburg psychologically assessed each mother to determine whether or not she had successfully come to terms with her loved one's passing. This was not to say mothers no longer missed the departed or felt sad at the thought of them, but that they had passed through the five stages of grief and were able to move forward with their lives. These mothers were classified as having a "resolved loss." Mothers with unresolved losses, on the other hand, had not yet moved forward. Grief held them in thrall, keeping them from discussing the event rationally or without jarring emotional outbursts. Unresolved mothers provided bizarre or contradictory details about their lost loved ones, muddled their tenses (speaking of the deceased in the present tense; i.e., "Mary likes flowers"), or suffered significant lapses in memory. Van IJzendoorn and Bakermans-Kranenburg placed resolved mothers in one group and unresolved mothers in another, and compared the prevalence of infant disorganized attachment in each.

The discrepancy was stark, and it hinged, as always, on the *DRD4* 7-repeat allele. Without the 7-repeat, children showed signs of disorganized attachment at roughly the same rate, regardless of whether or not their mothers' losses were resolved. Among children with the 7-repeat it was a whole different story. In their case, having a mother with an unresolved loss made them almost *three times as likely* to exhibit signs of disorganized attachment as 7-repeat children whose mothers' losses were resolved.

Van IJzendoorn and Bakermans-Kranenburg's findings are surprising. Both logic and past evidence suggested that mothers' frightening behaviour should be far more influential to their children than their private, inner pain. If anything, frightening behaviours were thought to be how that pain manifested itself — even if unresolved loss was the disease infecting children with disorganized attachment, frightening behaviours were supposed to be the syringe that injected it. But Van IJzendoorn and Bakermans-Kranenburg's study suggests that children see beyond simple cause and effect — Mom shouts, Mom is upset; Mom spanks me, Mom is angry — and pick up on behavioural quirks so subtle that Van IJzendoorn and Bakermans-Kranenburg needed to implement psychiatric assessments to unearth them. Perhaps children are more perceptive than we give them credit for. Or perhaps our measurement of parenting behavious and attachment strategies is too imprecise.

These are, of course, only the findings of a single study. But Van IJzendoorn and Bakermans-Kranenburg's experiment underscores the limitations of our understanding. They question the parameters of our knowledge of genetics, psychology, and child development. They prove that the lens through which we watch children grow, as refined as it might be, is not yet fine enough. Above all, they teach us to question our assumptions and look deeper into the ways that our children's genes and environment interact.

The Broken Filter

For years, the prevailing metaphor for genes was "the blueprints of development," a master plan on which every facet of an individual is meticulously drafted. The image fit nicely with the predominant theory of genes at the time, called the genetic dogma, which stipulated that the flow of information from DNA to RNA to polypeptide chains to protein is unidirectional and irreversible. According to the genetic dogma, DNA is strictly read-only; RNA cannot rewrite it, nor can a protein be translated back into RNA. However, the latest research shows top-down, dictatorial genetic dominance to be an incorrect, or at least incomplete, characterization of how genes work.

As important as genes are, they are not the only plan from which a person is built. *DRD4*, *5-HTTLPR*, and *BDNF* are not genes "for" anything more than the products after which they are named (dopamine receptors, serotonin transporters, and brain-derived neurotrophic factor, respectively). These products can, in turn, regulate physiological and mental development, but there's a lot of give and take between genetic and environmental factors. The environment works in conjunction with genes, and through changes to the epigenome (a process we will discuss in greater detail later), it can actually influence when and how these genes are expressed. Nor are these influences always obvious or simple. Think of the cumulative effects of the *5-HTT* and *BDNF* genes, or the protective properties of a friendly adult outside of the family, or the ability of children to ignore their parents' dramatic behaviour while latching onto their inner turmoil. Through the course of this chapter, we've learned how ineffably complex and muddled and messy child development can be. Beneath the surface, where nature and nurture spiral, clash, and converge, the concept of anything as neat and orderly as a "genetic blueprint" seems trite, or even absurd.

As scientists became aware of this discrepancy, they adopted a new image: the genetic recipe book. As a metaphor, it is more accurate than the genetic blueprint, as it suggests a set of guidelines that rely on the availability of select ingredients and remain open to a certain degree of flexibility. More importantly, following a recipe creates a product greater than — and distinct from — the sum of its parts. After baking a cake, one cannot pick it apart and prescribe one line or word of the recipe to each individual crumb. The recipe metaphor also concedes some influence to environmental factors, rather than supposing that genes alone dictate the end result. The ingredients may combine correctly, but set the oven to the wrong temperature and the cake will be burnt or underdone.

But even the genetic recipe seems somehow insufficient. It implies a clear and straightforward relationship between genes and environment, one that can be easily replicated by following a few basic instructions. Mix thoroughly to combine ingredients. Apply leavening agent to make baked goods rise. Cook at 400 degrees for 35 minutes, or until golden. It's too neat, too easy, too *comprehensible*.

Perhaps genes are too sprawling and complex an idea to be housed in a single metaphor. In that case, we propose a more modest analogy, one that focuses specifically on the gene-by-environment interactions we've explored in this chapter. When considering the interplay between genes and the environment, think of a gene as a filter, and the environment as a stream of water passing through it. Should the stream contain some debris — anxiety, obesity, behavioural difficulties, and so on — a functional filter will strain out the impurities. Similarly, a broken filter can cause no harm, should the stream itself be pristine. However, when the water is murky and the filter malfunctioning, environmental pollutants will pass through unrestricted, causing a great deal of trouble for the unlucky individual swimming downstream.

We're fairly fond of this image, we must admit. But it does place a value judgement on various filters, and that can lead to problems. Remember Joey and Erika from chapter 4? If the broken filter theory is correct, it would suggest that their brains were built from inferior genetic material. Joey's defiant anger and Erika's depression may be the result of troubled home lives, but with better supplies of serotonin or dopamine, their symptoms never would have appeared in the first place.

Therein lies the theory's main problem. If one filter is functional and the other is broken, then one gene is clearly better than another. And if that is the case, why has evolution not selected against the "broken filter" genes? They are not recent mutations — we can find examples of them in almost every animal on earth. Surely such a glaring genetic defect couldn't survive a billion years of natural selection if it didn't also carry an equal or greater advantage.

Perhaps our metaphor needs work. What if, instead of a broken filter, we simply had one with looser, more permissive netting? Such a filter wouldn't do as good a job of catching debris as would a more stringent model, but it may also permit the passage of beneficial materials — nutrients, for instance — that the more functional filter would block. In this case, one filter would not be invariably better than the other. Instead, each would be useful in one environment and detrimental in another. Perhaps, if raised in more supportive environments, Joey and Erika would not only recover, but excel. Their permissive filters, completely unsuited to troubled environs, would suddenly become a tremendous asset. Such a concept would radically recontextualize the findings we've discussed so far, necessitating a lot of research, several well-designed studies, and a revolution-ary new theory of gene-by-environment interactions.

For this, we turn to a man named Thomas Boyce.

Chapter 7
The Orchid and the Dandelion

———————————●————————————————————●————————————

Maria looked at the pregnancy test with disbelief. It couldn't possibly be right. She was 17, barely three weeks into grade 11, and according to the small plastic rectangle in her hand, her life was about to change dramatically.

She went to her boyfriend's apartment, resolving to break the news to him over dinner. She made pasta, overcooking the noodles and clumsily dropping a skillet of sauce onto the floor. Her hands trembled and her mind felt shrouded in thick, roiling mist. After 30 minutes of awkwardly puttering around the kitchen, she told him. Her declaration was terse: "I'm pregnant," she said, the last syllable disintegrating into a long, terrified sob.

Tom, her boyfriend, was stunned but supportive. He'd moved away from home at 16 after a brief and bloody fistfight with his father, and lived on his own in a one-bedroom apartment above a pizzeria. Two years Maria's senior, he'd finished high school with poor marks and, after a protracted stretch of unemployment, landed a job as a deliveryman for UPS. He told Maria he would stick by her and the baby, and though he wasn't truly sure of it at the time, he meant it.

Maria gave birth to a baby boy midway through her second semester of grade 11. She named the child David. He was a happy baby. Maria fully intended on returning to school after weaning him, but somehow never got around to it. Instead, she got a job working nights as a waitress, and another as a cashier at 7–Eleven. She and Tom tried to arrange their schedules in such a way that one parent was always home. When this wasn't possible, an elderly neighbour babysat for them. In exchange, Tom helped her out with a few simple chores. She became a surrogate grandparent to David, whose biological grandparents either didn't know of his existence or wanted nothing to do with him.

Even with external support, David was often alone. He became self-sufficient at a young age, pouring his own cereal and dressing himself for kindergarten. His parents were kind and loving, but they maintained their social lives and enjoyed smoking pot, which they studiously avoided doing in front of him. As a result David was often left to his own devices, which suited him fine. He was happy entertaining himself and playing with the other children living in his apartment complex. The parents of these children, aware of David's somewhat peculiar family situation, treated him warmly, feeding him and letting him sleep over and generally looking out for him.

When David was five years old, Maria got pregnant again. The ultrasound confirmed she was carrying twins. Maria panicked. She'd been excited about the idea of having another baby, but even one was sure to stretch her meagre budget to the breaking point. Two seemed utterly unfeasible. After talking things over with Tom, she decided to give one of the children up for adoption.

Maria named the girl she kept Melissa. She was a tiny baby, born about a month premature, and fussy. She cried often, especially at night. Maria and Tom's sleep schedule became increasingly fragmented, Melissa's incessant wailing denying them any more than an hour's uninterrupted slumber. This, combined with the financial strain of raising another child, took its toll on Maria's mood. She grew sulky and withdrawn, increasing her pot-smoking habit and occasionally yelling at her children, which she'd never done before. She still loved her kids, and cared for them to the best of her ability, but her efforts became increasingly threadbare as the conflicting demands of work and child-rearing wore away at her.

David took his role as big brother very seriously. He cared for Melissa as she grew, dressing her for school, making her meals, helping her with her homework, and doing his best to cheer her up. As a little girl, Melissa could be sweet and charming, and David could always make her smile. However, as she grew, she became more moody and distant. Her teacher reprimanded her frequently for her disruptive behaviour in class, and sent her home on two separate occasions: once for maliciously pouring a jar of paint over the carpet, and again for biting another student. At home, Melissa oscillated wildly between temper tantrums, pleading forgiveness, and silent, brooding withdrawal.

As David grew, he began to indulge in the rebellious acts typical of adolescence. He stayed out late, talked back to his parents, took up smoking for a brief period, and drank at the odd party where alcohol was available. But his grades remained fairly high, and his behaviour calmed down near the end of high school, when he became more focused on getting a proper postsecondary education. School didn't excite him, but he understood its importance. Attending university seemed like an obligation he needed to fulfill; the consequences of not doing so far outweighed the benefits. He studied economics for two years, dropped out, and went to college instead, where he majored in computer science. He got a job shortly after receiving his diploma, and made a modest but happy life for himself.

While David mellowed, Melissa grew increasingly volatile. She partied incessantly, spent days on end away from home, and dated seedy men several years — and in one case an entire decade — older than her. Not content with the more common narcotic offerings of adolescence, she snorted cocaine and took dangerous amounts of ketamine. Sometimes she stayed up for days, or awoke in strange places without any idea of how she got there. On the surface, it seemed she delighted in making her parents worry, and appeared vindicated when she managed to make her mother cry. Her parents scolded her, grounded her, and pleaded with her, but nothing worked. When they told her their concerns, Melissa would scoff.

"Like you even give a shit," she'd say. To Melissa, her parents' neglect during her early years was unpardonable. They didn't care about her then, she thought, so why should they all of a sudden care about her now? David she listened to, to a point, but when he would suggest she straighten up she would accuse him of being a shill for their mom and dad and storm off. He couldn't reason with her and eventually stopped trying. Their relationship grew cold.

Overreacting

It's hardly a surprise that siblings in the same family can have very different temperaments; anyone with a brother or sister could tell you that. Yet doesn't it seem odd that two children raised by the same set of parents in the same household with roughly the same means can come to such radically different ends? It happens all the time, of course, but what exactly causes two children to react so differently to the same caregiving environment?

The answer has, in part, revealed itself through the studies we discussed in our previous chapter. Certain genes (*DRD4*, *5-HTT*, *MAO-A*, etc.) can, depending on the allele (or version) one possesses, make a person more susceptible to adverse rearing conditions. In our scenario, David would be a low-reactive child, while Melissa would be high-reactive. Perhaps Melissa's DNA contains the 7-repeat *DRD4* allele, or one of the other problematic polymorphisms we've explored, making her more likely to act out in the face of her parents' benign but persistent inattentiveness.

The question, then, is why do high-reactive traits exist at all? From an evolutionary standpoint, it seems unlikely that an increased disposition toward self-destructive behaviour would be selected for in the long run. Over generations, one would expect 7-repeat, s/s *5-HTT* and their hypersensitive ilk to be outstripped by their more stalwart allelic brethren. Are these mutations simply too recent to have been selected out, or is our species too buttressed by its advanced technology and social structure for natural selection to take effect? Not likely. Many of the "problem" alleles we've discussed so far have counterparts throughout the animal kingdom, from primates all the way down to crustaceans, implying they've been around for a very, very long time. But what benefit could high-sensitivity provide?

To provide a possible answer, let's check in on Melissa's sister.

Separated shortly after birth, neither twin was aware of the other's existence. As far as Marcy knew, she was the only child of Roger and Evelyn Davenport, a wealthy couple in their late thirties. Roger worked as an engineer and Evelyn as a travel agent. The Davenports were attentive and loving parents. They had tried for years to have biological children, but they couldn't conceive on their own, and their repeated attempts at in vitro fertilization all failed. Though adopting was not exactly how they'd expected to have children, their love for Marcy knew no bounds, and they dedicated their lives — and their considerable means — to providing only the best for her.

Marcy went to a private school, took swimming lessons in the family pool, and had a playroom full of educational toys. Her parents hired skilled tutors to give her lessons in French, the piano, and gymnastics. Evelyn read to her from infancy, and Roger took her to every museum within five hours of their house. The family travelled often, and always took pains to experience and learn about the local culture of whatever country they visited. By the age of 10, Marcy was fluently bilingual, was proficient on three instruments, and had visited four continents.

Marcy loved school. She excelled in science, consistently handled mathematics at a grade level above her own, and devoured every book put in front of her. Every teacher she had considered her a natural student. Her grades were always the highest in class, and by the time she finished elementary school she'd amassed an impressive collection of scholastic awards.

In high school, she became an active member of student council, running in every student body election and winning almost every time. No one was surprised when she was elected valedictorian. Though affording school was not going to be a problem for her regardless — Roger and Evelyn had it covered — she was awarded generous scholarships that, supplemented by her savings from her part-time job, allowed her to pay her own way.

Marcy rocketed through university, got accepted to med school, and landed a residency less than two months after earning her degree. She seemed to thrive under pressure, a quality that, coupled with her fierce intelligence and love of challenging work, led her to specialize in neurosurgery. By 30, she was on track to becoming one of the most respected surgeons in her province.

She'd known she was adopted since she was old enough to start asking questions about it — and for a girl as smart as Marcy, this wasn't very old at all — but it wasn't until adulthood that she began pursuing her biological parents. It was during this process that she learned she had a twin sister. The news was exhilarating, though a little hurtful — part of her couldn't help but wonder why her parents had given her up for adoption while her sister got to stay. In spite of these feelings, she sought out her sister, and was surprised at what she found.

Marcy had been told she was an identical twin, and though she knew their differing tastes and circumstances meant that they probably wouldn't look as similar to one another as she might have imagined, she was nevertheless startled by Melissa's appearance. She was 20 pounds thinner than Marcy, and dressed in leggings and a tacky jacket made of fake leather. Marcy's silk blouse, though far from opulent, likely cost more than Melissa's entire wardrobe.

Melissa clasped a cigarette between two fingers topped with artificial fingernails. Her face resembled Marcy's but was prematurely lined. A child tugged at her leg and she patted his head distractedly as Marcy introduced herself. The conversation was polite but the two found they had little to talk about. Secretly, they both nursed doubts as to whether they were actually related. It just seemed so improbable that twins could turn out so differently.

Such stories take some of the wind out of genetic determinists' sails. Marcy and Melissa are, genetically speaking, identical to one another. And though they were reared apart, they did spend the first eight and a half months of their existences (they were premature, remember) in an identical environment. During that time, they coexisted within a single uterus, absorbing the same nutrients and chemicals, reacting to the same stimuli, breathing in the same amniotic fluid. Sure, from that point on their paths diverged dramatically — Marcy was ushered into a life of privilege and intense intellectual nourishment, while Melissa remained in a home that was financially struggling and structurally laissez-faire — but neither were subjected to heinous abuse or dire poverty. Melissa had fewer advantages, but she never wanted for food, clothing, or shelter, and though she would probably scoff at the suggestion, she was loved.

Is it that simple, then? Do well-meaning but inattentive parents doom their children to a life of alcoholism and drug abuse? Hardly. Even within our brief example, we have David, who turned out well despite growing up in suboptimal early rearing conditions. We've already put forth one hypothesis for this discrepancy: David is a low-reactive child, while Melissa is high-reactive. Does this mean that Marcy, somehow, inherited a low-reactive gene not imbued to her sister?

Not necessarily. In fact, according to the theory of Biological Sensitivity to Context, it is probable that Marcy, like her sister, possesses high-reactive genes.

Biological Sensitivity to Context

When differences in reactivity among children first came to the attention of the scientific community, the predominant assumption was that high reactivity was a maladaptive trait — a genetic mutation that made those carrying it less likely to survive into adulthood than their unaffected peers. On first blush, high-reactive genes do appear to be something of a burden to those who possess them, a ball and chain shackled to their chromosomes, leaving their unfortunate heirs prey to whatever trauma the surrounding environment may decide to throw at them. We've presented this viewpoint once already, and explained its overarching flaw: these traits are *old*. In the face of hundreds of millions of years of evolutionary scrutiny, the 7-repeat *DRD4* allele and its histrionic brethren should have been selected out eons ago, replaced by their staunch, stable, and unwavering counterparts. The fact that they haven't suffered such an ignoble fate strongly suggests that they may provide some benefit to offset their potential costs, and a researcher named W. Thomas Boyce has compiled substantial evidence as to what that benefit might be.

Boyce is a professor of pediatrics at the University of British Columbia. In 2005, he released a paper explaining his theory of Biological Sensitivity to Context. Boyce was understandably skeptical of the notion that some genes were "worse" than others yet had somehow remained floating in the global gene pool all this time. He posited that high reactivity may be a double-edged sword, but can nevertheless be wielded effectively in the right circumstances. Increased sensitivity to one's environment is not the same as increased sensitivity to pathogens, or exceptionally brittle bones, or haemophilia, or any other conditions that leave one in a vulnerable state without providing any tangible benefit. Rather, it is a difference in malleability. The behaviours of more reactive children — who, in Boyce's theory, would be considered to have high Biological Sensitivity to Context (BSC) — are more easily sculpted by the surrounding environment than those of low-reactive children — those with low BSC. For Melissa, this meant succumbing to the more unfortunate aspects of her upbringing, and acting out against them in a short-sighted, self-destructive way. David, a low BSC child if ever there was one, took his home life in stride. Between the two of them, David seems to have the evolutionary edge.

But then there's Marcy. Raised by exhaustingly attentive parents, ensconced in wealth and privilege, provided with every learning resource imaginable, she excelled at everything she put her mind to. For her, high BSC was a tremendous advantage, as it allowed her to make the most of the resources her privileged upbringing afforded her.

Boyce divides children into two poetically named categories: orchids and dandelions. Drawn from an old Swedish aphorism, the term "dandelion children" refers to hardy, rugged individuals with low BSC. Like the plants they are named for, they seem to thrive equally well in manicured lawns and cracks in the sidewalk. Orchid children, on the other hand, have high BSC. Like orchids, they flounder in substandard environments. But if the soil is pH balanced and nutrient rich, and the sun is shining just right, and the rain falls gentle but often, they grow into flowers of exceptional beauty.

Think back to some of the studies discussed in the previous chapter, namely those dealing with the DRD4 7-repeat allele.

As you may recall, those with the 7-repeat allele — the "high-reactive" version of the gene — responded much more poorly to hardship than children with different, less reactive alleles. The precise nature of the response (depression, aggression, ADHD, etc.) and hardship (poverty, etc.) varied between studies, but the results were markedly similar.

The severity of these results swept aside a second finding. High-reactive children struggled in adverse living conditions while low-reactive children soldiered on; but in supportive conditions, where low-reactive children achieved about the same as their peers in "high risk" environments, high-reactive children *thrived*.

Monkey Business

Thirty miles from Washington, D.C., away from the crowds and the noise and the politics, the National Institute of Health's Laboratory of Comparative Ethnology nestles into the bucolic Maryland countryside. Its location is well-chosen, for the LCE is not the stereotypical lab bedecked with stainless steel counters and finicky instruments awash in harsh fluorescent light. Most of the lab is outdoors, comprised of a swath of Appalachia demarcated by twin bands of electrified chain-link fence. Inside the fence live a colony of rhesus macaques, a primate not quite as closely related to us as chimpanzees or bonobos but that nevertheless shares about 95 percent of our DNA. The LCE is run by Dr. Stephen Suomi, a distinguished psychologist with a long history of working with macaques. Compared to some of his earlier studies, his present work is largely hands off. Much (but not all) of the research done at LCE is observational; aside from having food provided for them — in the form of a delightfully named substance called "monkey chow" — and living within borders defined by a two-tiered cyclone fence, the macaques at Suomi's lab exist very much as they would in the wild. They feast and fight and fornicate, form alliances, and make power plays, all the while observing a strict and complex social hierarchy.

Macaque troops are matrilineal, stabilizing around a dominant and typically elderly female in groups of between 30 and 300 macaques, called troops. Females born into a troop stay there for life, their position rising and falling within the confines of that matrilineal line, until they themselves are, potentially, among the elder alpha females. Males, by contrast, exist on the fringes of macaque society. At adolescence (which, in macaques, occurs when the male is roughly four years old) they leave the clan of their birth — be it voluntarily or by force — and join roving gangs of similarly disenfranchised males. Life in a gang is a turbulent time for macaques, a Darwinian trial by fire where only the strongest, swiftest, and smartest escape the flames. Mortality rates in these gangs are exponentially higher than in any other facet of macaque society, and males are understandably eager to leave their shiftless existence and rejoin a troop in order to engage in the far more enjoyable pursuit of siring offspring.

Life among the macaques is relentlessly social. Size and strength undeniably help determine a macaque's place in the hierarchy, but the truest predictor of success is a macaque's ability to understand and interact with other macaques. In humans, we might call this emotional intelligence. A successful macaque knows exactly where she stands in the hierarchy. She knows which matriarch is the quickest to anger, and which is showing signs of weakness. She can recall without hesitation which macaques have her back in a fight, and which would just as soon bash her brains in with a rock. Macaque society thrums with political intrigue; to thrive, social graces are essential.

Sadly, when it comes to social graces, not all macaques are born equal. Over years of careful observation, Suomi noticed two recurring deviations in macaque behaviour. Macaques of the first deviation have what Suomi deemed to be neurotic personalities, and comprise roughly 20 percent of the total population. These macaques are reluctant to leave their mothers' sides, and remain anxious and withdrawn well into adulthood. Anxious macaques socialize far less often than other macaques do, form fewer alliances, and swing dejectedly from the lower rungs of macaque society.

Macaques of the second deviation face similar yet opposing challenges. Suomi calls them bullies, and they comprise a smaller portion of the macaque population than do neurotic macaques: between 5 and 10 percent. This is a very good thing for macaque society at large, because, unlike the anxious subgroup, who meekly sidestep conflict and cause no harm, bully macaques are a nuisance to everyone and a danger to themselves. They get between high-ranking mothers and their children — a folly on par with stepping blindly onto a freeway at rush hour. They leap madly from treetop to treetop, taking risks at which more sensible macaques, despite being dextrous and acrobatically gifted, would balk. They challenge macaques twice their size to combat, and when they are inevitably beaten and shamed, they don't learn their lesson; they attack again and again. Play fighting is a normal and healthy part of macaque development, but bullies have trouble grasping the "play" part — they bite and scratch and hit for real, alienating potential playmates and earning the ire of their mothers.

Anxious macaques and bullies have a lot in common. Both have trouble relating with other macaques in their troop. Both show signs of behavioural disorder, a fact neatly ascertained by the reaction of anxious and bully macaques to a "happy hour" test. For a one-hour period, macaques are given unrestricted access to a fruity beverage containing 9 percent alcohol. Well-adjusted macaques know their limits. They have between three and four drinks and call it quits. Anxious and bully macaques show no such moderation. They drink to excess, though each group goes about it in a different way. Anxious macaques drink more than they should, but they do so in a manner that suggests self-medication. They drink until they're good and drunk. Bullies take it one step further. They are the frat boys of the animal kingdom, hitting the bottle as if it were an endurance contest. They drink until they are practically unconscious, their drunken bodies reeling and their blood alcohol content skyrocketing to dangerous levels.

But perhaps the most important connection between anxious and bully macaques is their origins. Both have genetic susceptibility to problematic behaviour, but genetic cause ends precisely there. In order to activate these behaviours, young macaques must experience them during childhood. Anxious macaques came from anxious mothers, and bully macaques from bully mothers. When these macaques grow, they adopt the same parenting flaws they themselves experienced as infants and impart them on a number of their children, lending the cycle of neuroses and violence an air of inevitability. But take the neurotic or aggressive macaque away from his troublesome upbringing and foster him to a nurturing, affectionate mother, *and these adverse behaviours disappear.*

The culprit, therefore, is poor parenting, though it is aided and abetted by certain high-reactive polymorphisms. If you've read this far, it shouldn't surprise you that one of them goes by the name *rh-5HTTLPR*, the macaque equivalent of our notorious friend *5-HTT*. As with *5-HTT*, *rh-5HTT* has a long (l) and a short (s) allele; when you genotype bully macaques, guess which one you find? Consistently, the s allele makes an appearance, either paired with an l allele (l/s) or doubled up with another s allele (s/s).

Genetically susceptible individuals, when raised in nurturing environments, are no more likely than genetically resistant individuals to succumb to their grim, ostensibly gene-predicted fates. Genes may be the trigger, but the environment is the finger that pulls it. And different environments choose very different targets, and so trigger very different outcomes. Suomi's genetically vulnerable macaques may become bullies when raised by bullies, or suffer chronic anxiety when raised by anxious mothers, but when they are raised in supportive environments, they don't just do okay, they flourish.

In a number of ways, high-reactive macaques fostered with love and affection actually exceed their low-reactive, similarly coddled peers. They consume less alcohol in happy hour tests. They become exceptionally caring mothers, their nervous energy channeled into a productive pursuit. They rise high in the social hierarchy, often becoming prize mates or matriarchs of top-ranking troops. And, on a molecular level, they process serotonin (the neurotransmitter responsible for modulating mood) roughly 10 percent *more* efficiently than l/l macaques, despite having the supposedly less efficient serotonin transporter gene.

Not all primates have an exact equivalent of the *5-HTT* serotonin transporter gene. In fact, only two species do: macaques and humans. Macaques may not be our closest relatives, but we and they share another trait that every other primate lacks: versatility. Apes, chimps, and bonobos are fine-tuned to their environments; attempt to relocate them even in the most tightly controlled conditions and the results will be, at best, lukewarm. Macaques are a different story. Pluck a troop of macaques from their native home and drop them just about anywhere on Earth,[24] and they will not only survive, but prosper. Given adequate resources and sufficient means to avoid predators, their numbers will steadily increase until they reach the upper limits of sustainability.

On the Indian subcontinent, where indigenous macaques can be found, they dwell in jungles, hardwood forests, savannahs, the fringes of deserts, and the rocky outcrops of the Himalayan foothills. They have made their homes happily in rural Maryland, islands off the coast of Puerto Rico, the swamps of Louisiana, the high arid plains of Texas, and the San Fernando Valley. And while

many of these macaque colonies are bolstered by human intervention, they are more than capable of surviving without us.

In the 1930s, a tour boat operator known as Colonel Tooey
released a troop of rhesus macaques into the forests of Silver
River State Park, Florida, in order to provide his river cruise
business with a bit of exotic colour. Eighty years later, the
descendants of these monkeys have become a significant part
of the local ecosystem despite the repeated attempts of local
farmers to wipe them out. These are not Great Apes in cap-
tivity, their environment meticulously regulated, their intergenerational survival hinging on the constant efforts of trained
zoologists. These are monkeys that we're actively *trying to kill*,
but can't. That's truly impressive, because if there's one thing
human beings are good at, it's killing our competition.

There exists a correlation between high-reactive serotonin
transporter genes and primate adaptability. Does the former
cause the latter? We cannot yet definitively say. Causation is a
far harder relationship to prove than correlation. Yet it remains
a tantalizing hypothesis. After all, our ability to adapt to new
environments has been paramount to our success as a species;
without it we would all remain nestled in the cradle of civiliza-
tion, our numbers culled by severely limited resources and our
ingenuity stunted by an absence of necessity. And studies have
shown that high reactivity is only a liability when it and the surrounding environment clash. When they harmonize, it can prove
to be a tremendous advantage. Could this two-tiered reactivity
be the key to the success of us and our rhesus macaque cousins?
Bold, high-reactive wagers hedged with a larger population of
low-risk, moderate-yield alleles? We may never know for sure,
but any new parents left wringing their hands as they await the
results of their child's genotype testing can relax. An s/s *5-HTT*
allele is not a death sentence. In fact, under the right environmental conditions, its presence could very well be an advantage.

The Two Faces of *DRD4*

Remember our Dutch friends, Bakermans-Kranenburg and Van IJzendoorn? They designed a study examining the effects of maternal sensitivity on externalizing behaviour. Researchers videotaped mothers as they interacted with their infants, noting both how much attention the mother paid to her baby and how the baby responded to that attention. A distracted, inattentive, or easily frustrated mother received a low maternal sensitivity score, and a crying, inconsolable, aggressive child ranked higher on the scale of externalizing behaviour. Bakermans-Kranenburg and Van IJzendoorn's theory was that the presence of the 7-repeat *DRD4* allele in children would make them more likely than average to act out when raised by low-sensitivity mothers.

The numbers agreed with them. Among children from low-sensitivity homes, those with the 7-repeat allele scored an average of 7 points higher on the Child Behavior Checklist externalizing behaviour scale than those without the 7-repeat. This is not surprising, as these children learned from an early age that, to ensure a response from their parents, they had to act out vigorously.

The results were more dramatic still when comparing 7-repeat children from low- and high-sensitivity homes. Those with low-sensitivity mothers scored over *twice as high* on the externalizing behaviour scale as those whose mothers were more cognizant of and attentive to their needs. That is a big jump. However, one comparison the researchers glossed over was between 7-repeat and non-7-repeat children in high-sensitivity homes. Among these two groups, the children with the 7-repeat allele (the high-sensitive version of the gene) scored over 4 points *lower* than their peers without the offending allele. In other words, the children with the risky, "problem" allele were actually better behaved than those with the stable, less reactive allele. Four points is a less significant discrepancy than 7 points, and not even close to the 10-point, 100 percent markup seen between 7-repeat children in low- and high-sensitivity homes. But it's not peanuts, either.

The Dutch duo were not the only researchers to document this trend. Half a dozen different studies have reached similar conclusions. Dr. Kim-Cohen, a psychology professor from Yale University, found children with the less efficient "low reactive"[25] allele of the *MAO-A* gene — a polymorphism responsible for doubling incidents of externalizing behaviour when found in unsupportive households — accounted for below-average externalizing behaviour when possessed by children in supportive, nurturing homes. Again, the kids with the "trouble alleles" were the ones causing less trouble.

One of the more surprising findings came from Hungarian psychologist Dr. Judit Gervai. In many ways, Gervai's study mirrored that of Van IJzendoorn and Bakermans-Kranenburg. Both looked at the prevalence of disorganized attachment as mediated by the *DRD4* 7-repeat allele. Both divided mothers into groups of low and high risk — for Van IJzendoorn and Bakermans-Kranenburg, this meant separating grieving mothers based on whether or not they were still struggling to resolve their loss. Gervai, meanwhile, grouped mothers based on whether or not they engaged in "disrupted maternal communication," meaning they appeared disoriented, excessively needy, withdrawn, or childish in their behaviour toward their children. And both found that children's genotypes dictated whether they would be susceptible or immune to their environments.

The only difference was which gene did which.

In Van IJzendoorn and Bakermans-Kranenburg's study, as in every other experiment we've reviewed that incorporated the *DRD4* gene, the 7-repeat allele increased children's reactivity (or, as Boyce would put it, their Biological Sensitivity to Context). The 7-repeat children did as well or better than non-7-repeats in stable conditions, but when put under strain by poverty, neglect, parental depression, or any other hardship, they fared particularly poorly. Gervai reached the opposite conclusion. In her study, comprising 96 middle-class Hungarian families and 42 low-income American families, the 7-repeat allele acted as a moderating variable. Those who possessed it exhibited disorganized behaviour with roughly equal frequency regardless of whether or not their mothers engaged in disrupted maternal communication. Conversely, children without the 7-repeat allele were four times more likely to exhibit signs of disorganized attachment if raised by disruptive mothers than if raised by mothers who showed no signs of disruptive behaviour. When compared to a 7-repeat child, a non-7-repeat child was twice as likely to be disorganized if each were raised by a disruptive mother, but only half as likely if raised by a non-disruptive mother. The pattern is familiar; only the variables have been reversed.

Does this mean that either Gervai or Van IJzendoorn is wrong? Not necessarily. Their studies were similar, but they weren't identical. By focusing on slightly different environmental causes — disrupted behaviour and communication in Gervai's study versus more subtle responses to unresolved loss in Van IJzendoorn and Bakermans-Kranenburg's — the two studies point to different gene-by-environment interactions. For children with the 7-repeat allele, mothers' disrupted communication and childish behaviour did not seem to matter in predicting whether or not children were disorganized in their attachment. However, more subtle psychological responses to unresolved loss did make a difference. You could conclude, then, that parenting (particularly with high-reactive children) involves more than a specific set of behaviours, but rather a certain amount of psychological preparedness that likely could benefit from external sources of support like fathers, friends, and, if necessary, counsellors. Clearly, context matters more in some cases than in others.

Boyce's Studies

Data from dozens of papers supported Boyce's theory, but in order for Biological Sensitivity to Context to gain real traction, he needed to do some studies of his own. One of these measured the effects of biological sensitivity and environmental stressors on children's susceptibility to respiratory illness.

Many human studies — including almost all of those we've discussed so far — measure children's environmental stressors based on the disposition, behaviour, and socioeconomic situation of their parents. As parental bonds are the closest that children experience until at least adolescence, and as parents are the people with whom children spend most of their time, the quality of a child's home life is a logical way to gauge his or her degree of exposure to environmental stressors. But it is not the only way. With more families finding it necessary to have both parents join the work force full-time, children are spending more of their early years in childcare facilities. Though parental influence remains important, Boyce thought a daycare centre could produce an environmental impact significant enough to affect a high-sensitive child.

Boyce measured the level of environmental stress in two ways. First, he disseminated questionnaires to four childcare facilities. The questionnaires contained descriptions of 20 minor stresses a child could experience during daycare: rejection by peers, change in drop-off or pick-up routine, toilet problems, etc. The events described were not deeply traumatic, but could conceivably embarrass or upset a child. Preschool teachers completed the forms every two weeks, noting the stresses, if any, experienced by each child in her care.

Boyce's second measure was broader. Observing each of the four participating childcare centres, Boyce's researchers noted the teacher-to-child ratio, staff turnover rate, proportion of full- and part-time teachers, teachers' average education level, and overall quality as measured by the venerable Clifford Early Childhood Environment Rating Scale. These five criteria were tabulated and used to place each childcare facility on a continuum of environmental stress, with two centres in the low-stress field and two considered high-stress.

Next, Boyce needed to measure each child's Biological Sensitivity to Context. As we've already mentioned, this is not as simple as genotyping each child and grouping them based on which allele of a given gene they have. Without any sort of genetic calibration, Boyce needed to assess each child's sensitivity the old-fashioned way: through experimentation and empirical evidence.

The test was carefully designed. Boyce needed a series of activities enjoyable enough to engage 3- to 5-year-old children, but challenging enough to stimulate physiological stress responses, namely an increased heart rate and heightened blood pressure. He would then measure these stress responses and, based on his findings, declare a child to be high- or low-reactive.

The trouble with performing stress tests on children is keeping results consistent. Strange environments, the presence of a person the child finds frightening or unpleasant, or a tantrum on the ride over can act as emotional and biological white noise, weakening the signal the test picks up and garbling its results. Distortion is inevitable, but a good study keeps it to a minimum. Bearing this in mind, Boyce allowed the children to see, touch, and even operate the testing equipment a week before testing, in order to make them more familiar — and hence more comfortable — with the experiment while it was being performed. He held the tests in a quiet, secluded room within the childcare facility to keep the children focused but comfortable. The examiner was a woman the children had not met before; a familiar face may have been more comforting, but also would have come with its own collection of biases, both positive and negative.

Children are usually more comfortable with women than men, and the examiner had experience working with young children.

The experiment's content was as meticulously crafted as its setting. Participants completed seven activities that provided a physical, intellectual, and emotional challenge at a level that young children would find difficult but not daunting. The tasks were as follows: an interview, using building blocks to replicate a structure built by the examiner, remembering and reciting a series of numbers, a gestalt closure task,[26] solving a dispute between hypothetical classmates, identifying an object while blindfolded, and describing an emotional event. Throughout the procedure, children wore a blood-pressure cuff on their non-dominant arms that measured their heart rate and blood pressure.

Lastly, pediatric nurses and doctors checked the children each week for respiratory illnesses. Neither the doctors nor the nurses knew anything of the children's sensitivity or the child-care centre's level of environmental stressors. Each section of the experiment was performed in isolation from the others, and the three variables were only brought together after the data was tabulated and ready for analysis.

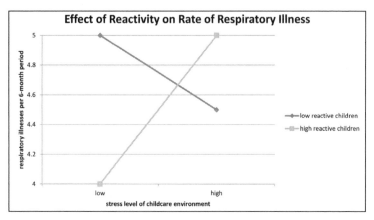

Boyce, W.T., Chesney, M., Alkon, A., Tschann, J.M., Adams, S., Chesterman, B., ... and Wara, D. (1995). "Psychobiologic Reactivity to Stress and Childhood Respiratory Illnesses: Results of Two Prospective Studies." *Psychosomatic Medicine*, 57(5), 411–422.

The findings confirmed Boyce's suspicions. High-reactive children were 20 percent more likely to develop a respiratory illness if they attended one of the high-stress childcare facilities than if they attended a low-stress facility. Conversely, low-reactive children were 10 percent *less* likely to catch a respiratory illness if they attended a high-stress facility. Of the four groups, high-reactive children in low-stress daycare actually showed the lowest rate of respiratory illness, with an average of only four incidents per six-month period.

Boyce conducted several similar studies and scoured peer-reviewed journals for dozens more, amassing an impressive body of evidence to support his theory and fitting it eloquently within a broader evolutionary framework. Diversity has been the key to an organism's survival almost since life began. Without it, even the most fearsome apex predator will inevitably be exterminated when some industrious microbe or parasite devises an effective way to attack them, or the environment becomes hostile, or a valued food supply dwindles. It's the reason that sexual reproduction has been such a rousing success among just about every creature more complex than bacteria. If you don't shuffle the deck, you may draw nothing but kings and queens at first, but eventually you'll face a run of threes and twos that will almost certainly be your undoing.

Biological Sensitivity to Context is an extension of that premise. Varying degrees of sensitivity assure that the human species will be able to cope with a wide and ever-shifting range of environments. High-reactive children are humanity's high-stakes bet. If the cards don't fall their way, they lose big, but if they hit a hot streak, the payout is enormous. Low-reactive children, by contrast, are the human gene pool's conservative investment, a kind of genetic GIC. The returns may not dazzle us, but the pool is, at least, safe. This diversified take on genetic investing works for the rhesus macaques, and it seems to be working for us, too.

But Boyce takes it farther. Prior to his theory, gene-by-environment interactions were considered to be much as we've described them thus far: a method of diversifying the gene pool to better assure our species' survival. Boyce agrees with this concept, but does not consider it to be a purely passive phenomenon. Instead, he argues that Biological Sensitivity to Context is determined in part by the surrounding environment.

Tuning Our Reactivity

Think of environmental stress as a spectrum with a safe, well-adjusted, and financially stable upbringing at one end and an insecure, impoverished, and violent upbringing at the other. According to Boyce, children at either end of this spectrum are disproportionally likely to be high-reactive, while children in the middle are more likely to be low-reactive. Boyce believes that the environment does not simply predict a child's chances of success, considering his or her genotype. Rather, it actually helps dictate the strategy that a child will adopt in order to cope with his or her surroundings, not just psychologically, but biologically.

But if Boyce is right, and BSC is determined by environmental factors early in life, why do children faced with severely adverse conditions become high-reactive? Every study we've reviewed shows that, under stressful conditions, high-reactive children perform worse physically, intellectually, and emotionally than their low-reactive peers. Shouldn't an environmentally determined BSC account for this poor standing by making every child low-reactive unless they are born into a stable, nurturing family?

Consider Patricia Crittenden's interpretation of attachment theory, the Dynamic Maturational Model. As you may recall, the crux of Crittenden's theory is that children adopt seemingly self-destructive attachment behaviours because, during the first few years of their lives, they are the best strategies children have at their disposal. When a parent is consistently neglectful, a child cannot afford to waste energy by crying every time he or she is hungry or cold, since that behaviour has proven ineffective. Instead, the child becomes withdrawn, seeking comfort in his or her own self-sufficiency. When crying sometimes summons a caregiver and sometimes doesn't, the child learns that the affection of his or her capricious protectors is fleeting, and as a result, he or she becomes clingy but not trusting. These behaviours often cause trouble for people down the road, straining their relationships with their family and peers, and hindering their ability to function effectively in a market society, where co-operation is paramount. But if in the child's eyes the alternative is death, then such behaviours are, in the short term, advantageous. It doesn't matter if the child isn't actually likely to die (few parents are deliberately negligent enough to kill their children, and in many cases where they are Social Services will step in before they get the chance); the child is acting on basic evolutionary instincts, not rational thought, and so can only make decisions (though even calling them decisions is somewhat misleading) based on the lesson imparted to him or her.

Biological Sensitivity to Context operates in much the same way. When a given trait first rose to prominence, an adverse environment meant something very different than it does today. In modern times, few denizens of the first world face famine or drought on par with that experienced by our ancestors. We are at little risk of attack from vicious animals or rival tribes, and have developed our own protection from many of the diseases that once threatened to wipe our entire species from the face of the Earth. These dangers have shrunk or disappeared, but new ones have risen to take their place. Modern threats are complex and intuitional, and require a new set of defences that, from an evolutionary standpoint, we have not yet developed.

Here is the key difference. When we consider a trait mal-adaptive, we do so through the lens of an affluent and highly structured 21st-century society where the goal is to survive not just physically, but economically. People continue to die young, and probably always will, but making it to a procreationally viable age is no longer the feat of prowess and ingenuity it once was. Ten thousand years ago, it was all that mattered. Responding to a violent upbringing by becoming exceptionally aggressive, or mistrustful, or self-sufficient was, at the time, a fairly effective way to go about things. If times were hard, predators plentiful, and food scarce, then being the biggest and baddest primate on the block was the best way to assure that you survived long enough to pass on your genes. But now, when our body responds to similar cues of hardship, these ingrained survival traits become liabilities. Children grow up too aggressive to get along with others, too hyperactive to hold down a job, too anxious to make the social connections necessary to succeed in a service-based market economy. Our instincts have turned against us. Or, perhaps more accurately, the world has turned against our instincts.

Stressing Out

If BSC is environmentally determined, then why have so many studies linked reactivity to the presence of certain alleles? Boyce doesn't discount the role genes play in determining BSC. Indeed, his studies have been among those that indicate their importance. He merely argues that the environment exerts an additional influence on our BSC on top of the effects of genes like *DRD4* or *5-HTTLPR*. It does so, says Boyce, by influencing the way our body responds to stress.

In both highly stressful and highly supportive environments, children become exceptionally attuned to stressful stimuli. Their heart rate rises, adrenaline floods their veins, and their minds become instantly alert, ready to respond to danger (or opportunity) in a fraction of a second. In a high-stress environment, it's easy to see how this could have been an advantage. When danger continually looms in the form of a bear or a lion or an enemy tribe, quick reflexes and increased vigilance can be the difference between life and death. But for low-stress environments, the benefits of a heightened stress response system are less clear. Why would a child raised in a secure, nurturing, and supportive environment require a stress response system on par with a child for whom danger is a constant companion? The short answer is he wouldn't, but Boyce offers a compelling theory as to why he got one anyway.

Do you remember the crash course in genetics we gave you back in chapter 3? If so, you'll recall that genes aren't the neatly ordered units of code they have often been described as in mainstream science articles. Rather, they are a conglomeration of nucleotide sequences interspersed with introns — commonly (and somewhat erroneously) called "junk DNA" — and spread across tens or hundreds of thousands of base pairs, and sometimes even multiple chromosomes. They overlap with other genes sharing the same nucleotide sequences, and can be reassembled in different ways at different times.

It should come as no surprise, then, that an organism built from such ostensibly chaotic instructions should possess some traits with unusual or unexpected connections. High BSC is one such trait. A number of studies have found a positive correlation between heightened stress response and a number of indicators of intelligence. On the surface, this seems strange. Stress, at sufficiently high levels, is supposed to elicit our most primitive instincts, forcing us into simple, atavistic responses like fight, flight, or freeze. We are more likely to associate intelligence with calm, rational, nuanced thinking, hardly the sort of thing one should engage in when being chased by a tiger or shot at by an advancing army. Yet deeper down, the link between the two traits becomes more apparent.

Researchers have found high-reactive children to be more reflective and more conscious of themselves and their environment. They are more capable of delaying gratification in pursuit of long-term goals, and have better self-control, than low-reactive children. One could see how these traits — particularly an awareness of oneself and one's environment — could be useful at both ends of the environmental stress spectrum. To children in high-stress environments, it means an above-average ability to assess risk, spot danger, and remain vigilant in the face of a longstanding threat. To children without such dire concerns, the same trait can be put toward exploration, introspection, and invention, all hallmarks of high intelligence. Coming from the other direction, a 2006 study found that more intelligent, introspective individuals have trouble coping with stress. This is true not just of humans, either. Going back to Dr. Stephen Suomi's Maryland compound, you may recall how members of the two major socially aberrant groups — the neurotics and the bullies — developed previously unseen advantages when raised by supportive mothers. The neurotics, genetically destined to fretful, low-status lives, became model parents, their anxiety honed into perception and forethought. The bullies, meanwhile, channeled their killer instincts into the political arena, allowing them the edge necessary to rise in the macaque ranks, while their more stable upbringings taught them the importance of the soft touch as well. In humans, as in macaques, intelligence and high-reactivity may be two sides of the same coin.

The Orchid-Fringed Garden

To turn speculation into data, Boyce conducted a pair of studies. The studies were similar in nature, both to each other and to experiments we've discussed in previous chapters. Boyce determined environmental stress through surveys and questionnaires, taking into account both demographic data (family income, mother's level of education, etc.) and personal responses (whether there is much fighting at home, if mothers felt overwhelmed by the responsibilities of child-rearing, had the children been excluded by their peers or experienced a change in their routine, etc.). The studies each used slightly different measures, but the general category of questioning was the same.

To determine children's Biological Sensitivity to Context, Boyce used the same stress test featured in his respiratory illness study reviewed earlier this chapter. Children performed a series of seven activities designed to stimulate their spatial and emotional reasoning while machines monitored their heart rate and blood pressure.

So why two tests? Given the similarities, it may seem redundant not to bundle them into a single experiment. Except Boyce differentiated between the two of them in one key way: focus. Boyce's theory regarding BSC's distribution can be graphically represented as a large U shape, with environmental stress represented by the x axis (left to right) and child reactivity by the y axis (up and down).

High-reactive children are largely distributed to the low- and high-stress ends of the environmental stress axis, represented by the two prongs of the U, while low-reactive children congregate in the middle of the axis, represented by the U's round bottom. A number of studies we've reviewed have reflected this general trend: only the left, low-stress half of the U has been, in most cases, decidedly atrophied, failing to reach the same heights as the U's right, high-stress half. Boyce argues that this discrepancy does not prove his theory wrong, but rather speaks to the imbalance of significantly low-stress and significantly high-stress environments in a normal population sample. To put it crudely, sore thumbs stick out. While high-stress environments are fairly common, exceptionally low-stress households are, unfortunately, fairly rare. Much more common are households in which there is a moderate — and completely normal — level of stress, as parents fret about bills, bemoan juice spilled on carpets or crayon scribbles on walls, or struggle to cram yet another doctor's appointment or visit to the mechanic into their already hectic lives.

To counter this trend, Boyce ran his two studies with different scopes. The more broadly focused of the pair looked at three levels of environmental stress —low, medium, and high — and found the same lopsided U shape implied in the data from Bakermans-Kranenburg and Van IJzendoorn's studies, and several others we've reviewed. Child reactivity was higher in low-stress environments than in middle-stress environments, but highest by far in high-stress environs. The other study, however, put aside high-stress environments entirely. It divided environmental stress into three more narrowly defined groups: very low stress, low stress, and moderate stress. Essentially, Boyce cut his original graph in half and focused solely on the left side of the U. He thought the shift in focus would invert the typical trend of higher-stress environments producing more high-reactive kids. And it did.

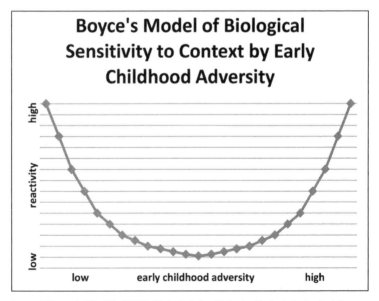

Boyce, W.T., and Ellis, B.J. (2005). "Biological Sensitivity to Context: I. An Evolutionary-Developmental Theory of the Origins and Functions of Stress Reactivity." *Development and Psychopathology*, 17(2), 271–301.

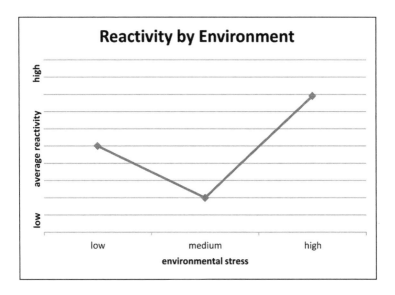

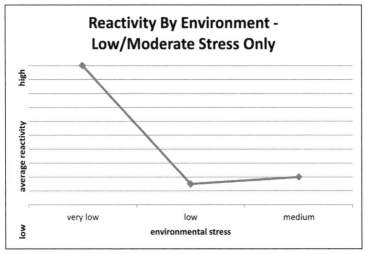

Ellis, B.J., Essex, M.J., and Boyce, W.T. (2005). "Biological Sensitivity to Context: II. Empirical Explorations of an Evolutionary–Developmental Theory." *Development and Psychopathology*, 17(02), 303–328.

Moving from very low-stress to low-stress environments, the drop-off in child reactivity is stark; from low-stress to moderate-stress, the difference is non-existent. Compare this to the almost linear increase in environmental stress from very-low to moderate groups, and the reason for all those lopsided U's seems pretty clear. Highly supportive environments produce a disproportionate amount of high-reactive children, but only when those environments pass fairly rigorous standards of quality. In households like Marcy's — the gifted child we talked about at the start of this chapter — high-reactivity is the BSC de jour. In less affluent homes, or households where parents don't have the luxury of devoting every second of their lives to nurturing their children, low-reactivity becomes far more common. This trend continues until we reach a place where stress becomes intense and commonplace and child reactivity promptly rises to levels equalling those at the opposite, low-stress end of the spectrum.

Migration

Of course, there is another possible explanation for the prevalence of high BSC children in highly supportive and abusive homes, one that allows genes like *DRD4* and *5-HTT* a more prominent role. The increased number of high-reactive children in adverse environments may have come, in large part, from a gradual migration of genetically susceptible individuals to the fringes of the environmental adversity scale. For instance, think back to David and Melissa, the brother and sister introduced at the start of this chapter. Though raised in the same household, the two went on to live very different lives. David became a programmer for a fairly large company, earning a decent middle-class salary. His wife, whom he met in university and married shortly after graduation, worked in data processing, and the two of them made enough to provide a decent life for their children.

Sometimes money was tight, but there was always food on the table, a roof over their heads, and enough left over to pay for field trips and piano lessons, and to take the odd vacation. Melissa, meanwhile, descended into a dark and gloomy cavern of adolescent debauchery from which she never fully emerged. She drank too much, partied too hard, tripped too intensely, and had her first child before she was emotionally or financially capable of shouldering that kind of responsibility.

David was a classic dandelion child, living comfortably and happily despite his less than idyllic home life. Melissa, on the other hand, was an orchid, and the care and climate of her childhood failed to meet her high standards. Their respective dispositions had an enormous impact on the outcome of their lives, and beyond that, the lives of their children. Not only are Melissa's children at a socioeconomic disadvantage, living in near poverty and raised by an emotionally immature mother with a drug problem, they also have a 50 percent chance of inheriting the genes responsible for causing high biological sensitivity to context. Among her several children, those who inherit low BSC genes may overcome their adverse circumstances, while those with high BSC have the odds stacked much higher against them. Exposed and susceptible to poor rearing environments, high BSC children will often continue the cycle of poverty and addiction, passing it down to their own children, and so on.

Melissa and David aren't the only people in this situation. Millions of families like theirs will show similar patterns, where dandelion children soldier on despite emotional and financial setbacks, and orchid children flounder. And since people typically meet, befriend, and marry people in their own socioeconomic level, the genes for low and high BSC may begin, over many generations, to separate. And the same is true on the opposite end of the spectrum. Marcy — Melissa's prosperous twin sister, who was adopted by a wealthy family — is able to offer her children a life of privilege, opportunity, and unwavering support. Though all of them have a great shot at doing well and succeeding in any career they choose, the ones with high BSC will be able to truly maximize their potential, much as Marcy herself did.

Thus, just because a majority of high BSC children live in adverse circumstances doesn't mean the environment directly *caused* high BSC; generations of genetic susceptibility may have simply attracted the more high-reactive individuals to the far ends of the environmental spectrum.

However, our reluctance to endorse every aspect of Boyce's model doesn't mean we reject his theory outright. Quite the opposite. His claim that biological sensitivity to context is an adaptive trait, as opposed to a maladaptive one, is well-documented. Nor do we entirely reject the notion that BSC is environmentally determined. We simply think that these influences might have a slightly different origin than Boyce describes.

We've known for some time that nature and nurture aren't diametrically opposed, and that the enmity between genetic determinists and behaviourists was little more than political posturing and a case of tunnel vision. Not only are the two factors entwined through the gene by environment interactions we've discussed so far, they are actually linked by an intricate network of molecules capable of brokering exchanges between them. How they do so forms the crux of an important and exciting new science called epigenetics.

Section 3

Let's Talk About Stress, Baby

─────────●───────────────────────────────●─────────

*"We are running 21st century software, our knowledge,
on hardware that hasn't been upgraded for 50,000 years,
and this lies at the core of many of our problems."*

— RONALD WRIGHT

Chapter 8

The Genetic Fuse Box

Autumn 1944: The memory of D-Day burns like a righteous fire in the furnace of the American military, driving the troops on with renewed vigour. Allied forces have made comfortable advances into Western Europe, carving out swaths of mainland and gunning for the heart of the Third Reich. On the Eastern Front, the Soviet war machine trundles inexorably westward, fueled by an endless stream of soldiers and a slow-burning anger at Germany's betrayal. Things look bad for the Axis. Their westernmost holding, the Netherlands, seems next in line to fall. The Dutch are mutinous and the Allies are closing in. In a fit of desperation and petulance, the Germans cut off the food supply to the western half of the Netherlands and flood the fields, ruining the remains of what was already a subpar crop. American attempts to ship in supplies by barge fail, as winter has set in early and the canals have frozen solid. The Dutch, sealed off on all fronts and left with dwindling food supplies, face the harshest famine in their recent history.

Wait. This sounds familiar, doesn't it? We described the Dutch Hunger Winter in chapter 3. As you may recall, the effects of the famine did not dissipate in the spring, when the embargo was lifted and the canals unfroze. They reverberated throughout the generations, affecting the children and even the grandchildren of those who had experienced the famine firsthand. Women pregnant during the famine gave birth to children predisposed to heart disease, breast cancer, and obesity. And these conditions didn't just appear randomly in the affected cohort. Each one correlated to a set of distinct variables, particularly the gender of the child and how far along they were in their gestation when food supplies hit their nadir.

When we first mentioned the Dutch Hunger Winter, it was to illustrate how the environment influences child development in a manner once considered the sole dominion of genes. But we didn't tell you *how* the environment went about exerting this influence. We touched on some relatively crude mechanisms, such as how our surroundings provide the basic materials genes need to build their protein products — you may recall the example of hair colour being determined in part by the body's supply of copper — and attachment theory covers the development of less tangible traits, such as personality or behaviours. But obesity and heart disease aren't behavioural conditions accounted for by neural plasticity. Nor can the environment's influence over them be explained away by simple molecular supply and demand. Something more complicated is at play here, something that accounted for environmental conditions (food scarcity) and instructed the fetus to adjust accordingly (store energy in fat cells at an above-average rate). This kind of complex physiological action is generally the purview of genes, but genes aren't that proactive. They can't deliberately adapt to abrupt changes in the environmental landscape — at least, not on their own. Perhaps the gene for nutritional thriftiness exists in all of us, but remains to varying degrees inactive, waiting for some outside influence to crank up production. That outside influence is what epigenetics is all about.

Spool and Thread

Picture a strand of DNA in your mind's eye. Chances are you conjured up, without much effort, an image of two thin ribbons spiralling around one another in the famous double helix pattern, the twin strands connected at regular intervals by nucleotide bonds like rungs on a twisted ladder. This picture is not fundamentally wrong, but it lacks some key details. When not being transcribed, DNA wraps itself around proteins called histones, which cluster tightly together in groups of eight called nucleosomes. Nucleosomes congregate in a squat, highly dense material called chromatin, which, as its name suggests, forms chromosomes.

Think of histones as spools and DNA as the string wound around them. Without these genetic spools, DNA would drift through our cells like giant hairballs, bulgy and tangled and constantly snagging on every protruding protein edge, leaving our genes tattered and ripe for mutation. Histones keep our DNA organized and protected. They also help control the frequency at which our genes code.[27]

When a gene is ready to be transcribed, its portion of DNA unravels itself from the histone, allowing access to the double helix strand. At all other times, our DNA remains neatly wrapped around its histone spools. By adjusting their grip, so to speak, on the DNA spooled around them, histones control how often the genes it protects are available for transcription. And the tightness of their grip is determined by a loose array of proteins and molecules called epigenetic tags.[28]

Nor are histones the only part of our chromosomes controlled by epigenetics. Various molecular hangers-on festoon the outer edge of our DNA, manipulating our genes' behaviour. Among the most common of these interlopers are a series of alkane molecules called methyl tags. Comprised of carbon and hydrogen, methyl tags latch onto our DNA, annexing the associated gene and discouraging it from coding. The more methyl molecules present, the less inclined the affected gene is to be transcribed. In this sense, methyl molecules act as a dimmer switch, their presence lowering a gene's activity and, if attached in sufficient numbers, shutting it down entirely.

Methylation, unlike genetic mutation, is completely reversible. A methylated gene will, if unmethylated, resume operating as if it had never stopped working in the first place. However, just because methylation is not necessarily permanent doesn't mean that its influence on genes is fleeting. Methyl tags can stick with us for years, stowing away during cell replication and remaining in place for thousands of cell generations. Many of the methyl tags in your body right now have been there since you were born, and will stay there until you die. Your children will inherit some of them along with the 23 chromosomes with which you provided them (or will provide them, if said children are currently hypothetical).

The idea of methyl molecules latching onto your DNA seems vaguely sinister, like tiny parasites hijacking your genome, but epigenetic marks are not only common, they're downright essential to life. They can be found in every cell in the human body; are, in fact, the reason we have different cells in the first place.

Each one of us begins life — in the loosest sense of the term — as a single cell called a zygote, which itself came from the fusion of two gametes (or sex cells): one sperm and one egg. Gametes are, in a sense, half cells, in that they possess only 23 of the typical 46 chromosomes present in every other cell in the human body.

Upon formation, the zygote is almost entirely unmethylated, meaning that every gene present in its cells is unfettered and ready to code. This is a very good thing, because the zygote's cellular offspring will go on to form every part of the human being it is destined to become, and every one of those genes will have its own part to play in the process.

As the zygote divides, it begins to take the shape of a hollow sphere called a blastula. Blastula cells, like the original zygote cells, are unmethylated.[29] Every gene they possess is capable of transcribing its corresponding protein product.[30] Beyond this stage of development, that begins to change. The blastula cells continue to replicate, and eventually form multiple layers, each with a unique cellular destiny. The outermost layer, called the ectoderm, will become skin and nerves; the middle layer, or mesoderm, will become muscle and bone; the inner layer, or endoderm, will become internal organs.

Development continues. The blastula becomes an embryo, which becomes a fetus, which grows and changes until it becomes a being capable of living outside the womb, at which point the mother goes into labour and gives birth to her baby, who in nine short months managed to transform from a single-celled organism into a complex, breathing, crying, nursing bundle of joy. Along the way, junior's cells didn't just divide; they specialized. Ectoderm became skin cells and nerve cells and brain cells. Mesoderm became muscle cells and bone cells and blood cells. Endoderm became stomach cells and liver cells and large intestine cells. And that specialization, though vital, comes at a price of flexibility.[31] Once an ectoderm cell becomes a skin cell, that's it. Every cell it produces, and every cell those cells produce, and so on all down the line, will be a skin cell. It can't double back and become a blood cell or a brain cell or a muscle cell. Its career path is set for life.

Why do cells submit to such fatalism? Skin cells aren't missing the requisite genes for becoming blood cells, or brain cells, or any cell you care to name. With a few exceptions — sex cells being the most obvious — every cell you possess contains all the genetic instructions needed to perform any job in the human body. What stops a blood cell from having a mid-life crisis of sorts and switching fields, becoming a skin cell or a liver cell or a neuron? In a word: methylation. By selectively methylating genes, cells can dedicate their finite resources to performing their assigned duties to the best of their ability. Having cells switch careers would not be beneficial to the organism in its entirety, which benefits from a rigid and highly codified division of labour.

Think of each cell in your body as a tiny nanocomputer, and your DNA as the computer's organic circuit board. The circuit board dictates the myriad processes responsible for keeping you alive, sending commands from the CPU, or nucleus, to the cell's many components, regulating enzymes and releasing hormones and synthesizing data from your sensory inputs. Attached to this circuitry is a fuse box called the epigenome, a vast array of tiny methyl fuses, each linked to a distinct gene. Trip the switch and the gene falls silent, its current interrupted by a methyl tag. Remove the tag by reinstating the fuse and the gene comes back into play, its semiconductors alight with a fresh thrumming of energy. It doesn't matter if the fuse was turned off for five minutes or five years; a flick of the switch is all it takes to get things running again. By contrast, rewiring genetic circuitry is cumbersome, dangerous, and permanent, the result of rogue molecules haphazardly soldering wires and scraping down bits of silicon — in short, mutations. Occasionally, by pure serendipity, these changes allow the machine to function more efficiently at its particular task. Far more often they are disruptive and damaging, and tiny molecular technicians must be called in to fix them.

Unlike genetic mutations, which are accidental and unpredictable, epigenetic tags are easy for the body to regulate. They assure that the most useful circuits get sufficient energy and any processes working contrary to the cell's goal are silenced, streamlining efforts and increasing efficiency.

Tabula Rasa

Epigenetic effects are not always as predictable as those that determine which cells get which job. Some are downright bizarre. Consider the agouti mouse, an animal intent on proving the misnomer inherent in the term "genetically identical." For though the genotypes of two agouti mice can be indistinguishable down to the last nucleotide, their phenotypes[32] often appear to be anything but. In adulthood, some have grey-brown coats and svelte physiques, while others have yellow coats and great, rotund bellies. The fat and yellow mice not only suffer from decreased mobility, but also from an increased risk of developing diabetes and cancer. The difference between them and their slim counterparts is the agouti gene, identical in both but only active in the fat mice. In the slim mice the agouti gene is highly methylated, keeping it from producing its affiliated protein; in the fat mice the gene is unmethylated and codes freely, accounting for both the affected mouse's yellow coat and its corpulent frame.

Having discovered this distinction, the obvious question is what causes it? There is no one culprit, though exposing pregnant mice to bisphenol A — a chemical compound found in a number of plastic products, including, alarmingly, baby bottles — has been found to increase the frequency at which their infants are born with their agouti genes unmethylated. The unmethylated agouti mice are more likely to sire offspring whose agouti genes are also unmethylated, compounding the disorder. Happily, this problem has a remarkably easy fix: feeding mothers pellets laced with methyl molecules greatly reduces their offspring's chance of having an unmethylated agouti gene. What's more, when mice who have had their agouti gene "fixed" sire children of their own, the next generation retains the correction despite never having been fed the methyl pellets themselves.

Bearing this research in mind, the effects of the Dutch Hunger Winter no longer seem quite so mysterious. As with agouti mice, pregnant women experiencing the famine gave birth to children with an epigenetic predisposition to a number of adverse conditions, including — again, as with agouti mice — obesity, heart disease, and diabetes. And the famine's effects didn't stop at that generation. The Hunger Winter study continues to this day, and researchers still find traces of the famine's impact on the descendants of those who suffered through it.

Unfortunately, one detail the agouti mice and Dutch Hunger Winter studies do *not* share is a tidy and easily remedied epigenetic cause. There is no agouti-like gene in humans solely responsible for the intergenerational ramifications of famine, no simple solution obtainable through a judicious addition or removal of a few methyl molecules. There are likely a number of genes at play,[33] some which should be methylated but aren't, and others that shouldn't be methylated but are. And even if we developed technology capable of tracking down and altering each offending gene and methyl tag, we couldn't say for sure that "correcting" the problem wouldn't cause another more serious ailment to appear in a different system or organ. After all, who could've guessed that the same gene responsible for producing yellow pigment in mouse hair also leads to chronic obesity?

Ultimately, the findings of the agouti mice and Hunger Winter studies are less about developing a solution and more about reinventing the way we look at the problem. Epigenetics is a new science, but it has undergone a substantial shift within its short lifetime, and studies like the agouti mouse experiment have been at the helm of this change.

According to conventional genetic theory, inheritance consists of 46 chromosomes passed from parents to their child, 23 from mom and 23 from dad. That's it. Geneticists acknowledge that nurture is important as well, but its work begins after genes have already spent a full nine months doing their thing. Sure, environmental influences are in a broad sense inherited (since mothers teach children who become mothers who then teach their own children, etc.), but such inheritance is subject to a number of conditional clauses and assumptions (children aren't adopted, parents raise their children in a manner analogous to how they themselves were raised, etc.) that make them inconsistent and unreliable. Genes, say geneticists, are stalwart messengers, grimly striding through the harshest conditions in unwavering pursuit of their goal: passing their vital chromosomal missives on to the next generation. The environment shifts and slides and changes like the weather. Genes are sturdy as stone.

Except that we are garnering more and more evidence that implies this might not be the case. Environmental influences may not be as capricious as once assumed; indeed, they may stick to our genes for generations. And epigenetics provides the glue that holds them in place.

In its earliest incarnation, epigenetics was not expected to adopt that sort of role. Its methyl tags, though vitally important to proper gene expression, were thought to remain only on the genes of the individual, and not be passed along with the rest of their genetic legacy. The zygote, with its absolute cellular potential, was supposed to be a kind of blank state, the dry-erase epigenetic scribblings of previous generations wiped clean, leaving 46 unadulterated chromosomes ready to be methylated again from scratch. Yet somehow epigenetic information is being inherited. To understand how this happens, we need to think of inheritance as more than a molecular transaction.

Umbilical Telegraphs

Unlike with genes, we haven't yet developed a satisfactory theory as to why and how epigenetic inheritance occurs. We do know, however, that certain epigenetic traits have critical periods where an action or chemical or experience is especially likely to trigger a long-term change in a gene's methyl pattern. Often, these critical periods can be found early in a person's life, particularly when they're still in the womb. During the Hunger Winter, for instance, the gender and gestational period of affected fetuses determined what condition they would be predisposed to as they grew. Women whose mothers experienced famine during the first trimester of their pregnancy were twice as likely as the normal population to develop schizophrenia. For men, having a mother who experienced famine during the first two trimesters of their pregnancy greatly increased their odds of becoming obese; if the famine extended well into the third trimester, they faced the opposite problem, becoming chronically underweight. These conditions were highly gender specific; women showed no spike in obesity, nor did men show an increase in their odds of developing schizophrenia as a result of early exposure to famine.

Things get stranger still. Consider two genetic disorders, Angelman syndrome and Prader-Willi syndrome. On the surface, they don't seem to have a lot in common. People with Angelman syndrome have severely reduced cognitive function, lacking the ability to say more than a few simple words. Their movement is clumsy and irregular, marked by jerks and tremors. Yet for all the adversity they face, people with Angelman syndrome — informally called "angels" — are almost universally happy. Their faces alight with beatific smiles. Giggles cascade constantly from their lips, often accompanied by a joyous and endearing flapping of their hands. Indeed, it was the grouping of these characteristics — the smiling, angelic features and erratic, jerky movements — that inspired Dr. Harry Angelman's original name for the disorder: happy puppet syndrome (the name was eventually changed, as it seemed patronizing).

Compared to "angels," individuals with Prader-Willi syndrome are far less mentally impaired. Their biggest challenge is in the physical realm. Prader-Willi sufferers have insatiable appetites. They also store fat at unusually high rates. By their teenage years, individuals with Prader-Willi syndrome often become morbidly obese, and those who don't remain highly susceptible to substantial weight gain for their entire lives.

The Angelman and Prader-Willi syndromes could scarcely be more different. Yet both of these conditions are caused by a partial deletion of chromosome 15, meaning a section of the chromosome was either badly damaged prior to conception or was never present in the sperm or egg in the first place. What's more, the deletion in both cases is not simply on the same chromosome, or overlapping. It is *identical.* The exact same genetic defect, down to the last missing nucleotide, causes two completely unrelated syndromes. And the allocation of each syndrome is in no way random; it depends solely on which parent supplied the offending chromosome. If inherited from the father, the deletion causes Prader-Willi syndrome; if inherited from the mother, it causes Angelman syndrome.

It's difficult to articulate to anyone who is not a biologist how big an upset this is to the understanding of genetic inheritance. Imagine learning that water sometimes flows uphill or gravity takes the odd holiday. A chromosome's lineage wasn't supposed to matter. Genes were just genes, and they did their job regardless of where they came from. Yet the Angelman and Prader-Willi syndromes, the Dutch Hunger Winter study, and the agouti mouse experiments all suggest that we don't have nearly as full a grasp on how inheritance works as we once believed. And there's no reason to believe these examples are isolated phenomena and not part of a larger trend. Hedonistic pursuits once thought to harm only those who participated in them — smoking, drinking alcohol, eschewing sleep for another night out with friends, eating burgers with unsettlingly honest names like "the Artery Clogger" — might actually be worming their way into subsequent generations. The dangers of fetal alcohol syndrome and smoking during pregnancy have thankfully become well-known, but epigenetic inheritance, it seems, can draw from experiences occurring outside that critical nine-month window.

Our intention is not to send you screaming to the nearest monastery for a life of unyielding austerity. Nor are we suggesting that every cheeseburger you eat is going to haunt your children and your children's children to the seventh generation like some trans-fat-sodden biblical curse. We simply want to emphasize that the science of inheritance is undergoing a sea change. Parents' actions can hide in their genes, molecular stowaways riding along unbeknownst to the chromosomes carrying them. We don't yet understand every motive epigenetic influences have for climbing aboard, but we are aware of one particularly prominent cause: stress.

Chapter 9
The Neural Garden

Sophie lies awake in bed. Tonight sleep has been slow in coming. She mulls over the day's events in her mind, wincing at each commitment she willfully piled onto her already overburdened schedule. At every request, absurd promises rise to her lips: offers to tutor Timmy McManus two nights a week until his math grade improves, to take over coaching the girls' volleyball team, to meet with Mr. and Mrs. Deluca again about their spoiled son. Dwelling on it now is pointless and painful and will only delay her getting the sleep she desperately needs; but Sophie can't help herself. Her brain returns to it again and again like a tongue to a sore tooth, poking and prodding despite the pain.

For a moment the pressure becomes a physical thing, its weight on her chest malicious and unbearable. Sophie's heart beats faster, her hands clench, her breath freezes into a cold, hard clump in the back of her throat. She takes slow, measured breaths, counting each one off as her therapist taught her until she gets to 10. Her heart rate slows. Her hands loosen, revealing angry half-moon marks where her fingernails bit into her palms. She heaves a heavy sigh of mingled exhaustion and relief.

We tend to think of panic as a primarily psychological response to stress or fear. The physical symptoms we associate with it — sweaty palms, trembling fingers, shortness of breath — seem like superficial manifestations of a much deeper mental anguish. Stress response, we feel, is all about mindset. But much like the outmoded concept of nature versus nurture, assuming that stress must be either a wholly physical or a wholly mental condition creates a false dichotomy between the two. Your mind and body are not separate parties ruling over you through coalition; they are very much linked. Those seemingly superficial cues — the sweating, the trembling, the rattling breath — betray a deeper and far more complex physiological response, one that engages an elaborate series of glands, nerves, and neurons called the hypothalamic-pituitary-adrenal (HPA) axis.

The HPA axis consists of three segments: the hypothalamus, the pituitary gland, and the adrenal glands. The hypothalamus is a tiny part of the brain — in humans, the entire thing is roughly the size of an almond — located just above the brain stem. Despite its small size, the hypothalamus's duties are manifold, though its most vital function is facilitating communication between the nervous system and the endocrine system. The nervous system links the brain to the rest of the body, allowing it to move muscles and receive sensory input through the transmission of electrochemical signals. The endocrine system comprises a series of glands that secrete hormones responsible for regulating a number of important bodily functions, including internal temperature, hunger, thirst, circadian rhythm (or sleep cycle), and, most germane to our current discussion, response to stress.

The HPA axis is itself an endocrine system, which is why its first junction is the hypothalamus. When our body acquires sensory data (captured by our eyes, ears, nose, tongue, and sense of touch) indicating a potential threat, the hypothalamus takes that information — brought to it by the nervous system in the form of electrochemical impulses — and translates it into a chemical-based language that the HPA axis can understand. It does this by secreting a hormone called "corticotropin-releasing hormone," or CRH, which travels from the hypothalamus to the nearby pituitary gland, where it stimulates the release of — you guessed it — corticotropin. However, this was apparently too self-evident for anatomists, who reissued corticotropin a clunkier and less intuitive name: adrenocorticotropic hormone, or ACTH.

The pituitary gland is even smaller than the hypothalamus: about the size of a pea in humans and weighing less than a gram. Like the hypothalamus, its duties are manifold. Though most renowned for its role in human sexual development, the pituitary gland is also a vital part of our stress response system. As we've mentioned, it secretes the hormone ACTH, which travels through the bloodstream to a pair of glands perched atop the kidneys. Here, at the adrenal cortex, we have reached the final stop along the HPA axis. This is where we truly get down to business.

Upon receiving a dose of ACTH, the adrenal cortex instructs its glands to secrete a pair of hormones responsible for implementing our physiological stress response. The first of the two is adrenaline, a name you've probably heard before. We attribute to adrenaline the "rush" we feel in the face of danger, the jackhammering heart and sweaty palms and manic burst of wide-eyed energy. Yet adrenaline is only one half of an integral stress response partnership. It's other half is a far less celebrated hormone, but one that is no less important: cortisol.

Cortisol's main role in responding to stress is redistributing energy (in the form of glucose, or sugar) to the parts of the body that need it most in a time of crisis — the brain for making snap decisions, the major muscle groups to carry those decisions out, and the heart to provide the muscles with the surplus oxygen they need to work at full capacity. Cortisol acts as a kind of override switch, drawing power from other areas of the body (such as digestion, immune system response, and gamete production) and allowing us to make full use of our adrenaline. Adrenaline rushes headlong into battle, ramping up our heart rate and boosting our muscle tone and readying our fight-or-flight response, which is why it tends to get all the glory. But cortisol is no less vital. It provides a critical support role in the stress response system, overseeing our glucose supplies and keeping the troops well-nourished for the duration of the battle.

It's easy to see how a stress response system can come in handy. When fleeing from a sabre-tooth tiger or defending your village from a warring tribe, the ability to dip into the reserves and muster up that extra bit of energy could make the difference between life and death. But eventually the threat passes, at which point our energy is no longer well-spent on muscle tone and a hammering heart. The surplus glucose needs to be returned to the systems from which it was initially drawn, or else we'll have escaped from whatever triggered our stress response system in the first place only to die from malnutrition or disease, as our digestive and immune systems failed to shift back into gear. Fortunately, our HPA axis has a nifty way of returning to business as usual. Once cortisol reaches a certain concentration in the bloodstream, it makes its way up to the hypothalamus and pituitary gland, where it dampens the production of CRH and ACTH, respectively. As our stress hormone levels drop, the amount of cortisol in the bloodstream gradually decreases until the body returns to its original, pre-stress state. This is called a feedback loop, and it's an incredibly valuable trait. In essence, it's like having your bathwater reach up and shut off the tap before the tub gets too full and floods the washroom.

Thanks to the feedback loop, there's nothing unhealthy about experiencing occasional bouts of stress. This is a good thing, as it's a very fortunate few who can live their entire lives

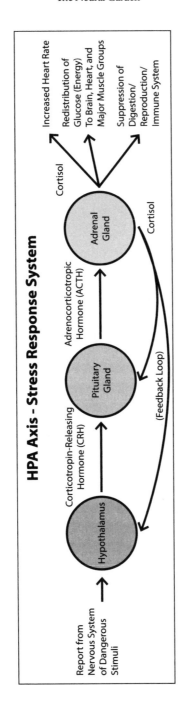

HPA Axis - Stress Response System

without succumbing to feelings of anxiety, frustration, or fear. When we do experience these unpleasant sensations, our body provides us with the extra energy needed to respond to them, then dials us back down to a state of hormonal equilibrium called homeostasis. Homeostasis is our body's natural resting point, where internal temperature, pH, and hormone levels coexist in perfect harmony. An organism in homeostasis is functioning optimally — in utilitarian terms, it is expending the least possible amount of energy to perform the most work. Less waste means a more efficient conversion of food into energy, greater production of gametes (or sex cells), a more disciplined and well-staffed immune system, and a smarter, sleeker, swifter brain. An organism in homeostasis is, in short, better equipped to survive, which is why our bodies have a number of mechanisms in place designed to make homeo-static harmony sturdy and, in the event of a shakeup, easy to re-obtain. The HPA cortisol feedback loop is one of them.

Think of cortisol as a kind of hormonal ballast, keeping our bodies on an even keel in calm or choppy waters. Only sometimes the waters are more than just choppy. Sometimes life steers us into the arms of a raging hurricane. If the waves of stress and fear batter us too intensely, allowing no chance for us to rest and recalibrate, our ballast may shift. At this point, our body is no longer able to manage itself effectively. With our homeo-static equilibrium compromised, our beleaguered ship begins to sail at an uneven keel. Stress sloshes onto our decks, and our poor vessel is suddenly at risk of sinking. The captain calls all hands on deck in a desperate attempt to keep our ship afloat. The cook stops cooking. The navigator abandons his charts. The ship doctor closes his clinic. Our body's many systems, sup-pressed by cortisol in a desperate attempt to weather the storm, stop working. Our immune system shuts down, increasing our risk of contracting diseases and reducing our ability to fight them.

Our digestion and sleep schedules become interrupted, weakening us further still.

This is bad enough in adulthood. During early childhood, when the bulk of our energy should be directed toward our physical and mental growth, excessive stress can have disastrous lifelong consequences. Chronic exposure to high levels of stressful stimuli — called toxic stress — among children corrodes the very foundation of human development. And when the groundwork is poorly set, everything built atop it risks collapse. Problems we associate with adulthood or even old age — heart disease, diabetes, alcoholism, etc. — all have their roots in early childhood.

We should clarify that toxic stress is very different from the mild anxieties, injuries, and upsets that comprise a normal and healthy childhood. Your child stubbing their toe or being scolded for colouring on the walls or throwing a tantrum in the supermarket are not signs of toxic stress sinking its poisonous fangs into their defenceless minds. A little stress isn't a bad thing; in fact, it can actually be good from a developmental standpoint.

Stress, as defined by experts in child trauma, comes in three levels. The first, called positive stress, is a normal part of growing up. Every child gets stressed out at some point, and moments of mild frustration, anger, or anxiety serve to calibrate their stress response system, giving their HPA axis a sort of trial run in order to get the kinks worked out and prepare it for more serious crises later in life. A child is dropped off at daycare, or gets a booster shot, or pinches his finger in a cupboard. He cries, his heart rate rises, cortisol circulates through his bloodstream. A few moments later his mother comforts him, and after a bit of coddling and gentle reassurance, the child is tottering happily through the house again, his discomfort forgotten and his cortisol levels back to baseline.

The second level, called tolerable stress, occurs when a child undergoes a significant traumatic event. She breaks her leg, survives a major earthquake, or loses her grandmother to cancer. These experiences are not part of an ideal childhood, but they aren't prescriptions for lifelong hardship, either. If they occur infrequently, and if the child has in her life a supportive and nurturing adult presence to help her through it, she'll almost certainly recover with no negative long-term effects.

However, when stress is severe and ongoing *and the necessary parental support is not present,* the stress becomes toxic. Aside from extreme circumstances like war and famine, the parental support, or lack thereof, is really the key distinction between tolerable and toxic stress. For the first six months of a child's life, the HPA axis isn't very reliable. It needs to learn to do its job, and it can't do so if it's constantly bludgeoned with stressful stimuli at levels that would challenge even a grown adult. Mastering hormonal self-regulation under conditions of toxic stress would be like trying to teach a child the rules of touch football by pitting him against an NFL linebacker. It's not a fair fight. Children need shelter from the storm of stress, and parents are the ones to provide it. For the first six months of your child's life, *you are the HPA axis.* Any stress they experience filters through you first, and the better equipped your own stress response system is for metabolizing adverse stimuli, the more effectively you'll be able to shield your child from the emotional fallout of life's many traumas.

When a parent isn't up to the task, due either to their own malfunctioning HPA axis or an overpowering flood of adverse stimuli (no parent, no matter how well-adjusted, could protect their child from the abominable brunt of the Holocaust if its nefarious agents kicked down their door), toxic stress bleeds through. And as its name suggests, toxic stress is dangerous stuff. It poisons children, weakening their immune systems and adversely affecting their emotional, physical, and intellectual development. Children raised in environments rife with toxic stress suffer disproportionately from a vast and deeply troubling array of conditions. Worst of all, a hyperactive stress response system undermines the body's attempts to build a strong neural framework. Cortisol is neurotoxic, meaning it kills brain cells. If excess cortisol is present in infancy, the time when brain cells are rapidly growing and connecting, the brain doesn't develop as it should. It becomes weaker, its neurons less densely packed, its operational capacity compromised.

The Neural Garden

Infancy and early childhood encompass a period of unparalleled brain growth. Neurons are rapidly generated by neuronal stem cells, and the connections between them multiply frantically. Each neuron releases a mad tangle of tiny filaments called dendrites, microscopic cables connecting one neuron to the next. The brain grows thick with them, a jungle canopy teeming with electrochemical impulses. And as in the jungle, Darwinian selection looms ever-present. When neural connections are used often they flourish, their wispy dendrites growing into sturdy trunks. Meanwhile, dendrites that go unused atrophy — a process called pruning — until the jungle of neural connections becomes sparser and more cultivated, a garden of the mind.

This in itself is not cause for concern; dendritic pruning is an integral part of neurological development. It might seem somewhat inefficient — why waste precious energy growing dendrites when you're just going to till them under? — but an initial surplus of synapses (or neural connections) gives our brains a certain amount of wiggle room during our early years. We call this feature of our brains "neural plasticity," and it is vital to our ability to adapt to diverse and changing environments.

By providing a dense network of synapses, our brains allow for every contingency. Once in place, the connections go on a kind of probation. If a dendrite is used often, the brain assumes it must be valuable and reinforces it. If a connection is used rarely or not at all, the brain assumes our circumstances don't require that particular informational pathway and lets it wither. By the time we are adolescents, our brains have turned from lumps of unformed clay into highly individualized sculptures, shaped by the deft and meticulous hands of our early rearing environment. It is for this reason that children pick up new skills — especially languages — with an ease that leaves most adults flummoxed. Their brains are more pliant than ours and new abilities can be incorporated easily into the folds of their neocortex, while our synapses are far more set in their ways.

Dendritic pruning is a highly effective early learning system, but it has one major drawback. Growing all those dendrites takes a lot of energy. Under normal conditions this isn't a problem, but if some other part of the body starts demanding the bulk of the resources — an overactive stress response system, say — then the dendrites aren't able to grow at an ideal rate. And if the stress response system continues to tap the body's energy reserves at an unsustainable rate, many useful dendrites will wither alongside their unused peers. Those that do manage to survive will languish in impoverished neural soil, their stalks sickly and weak. To make matters worse, an environment rife with toxic stress isn't likely to provide children with a lot of intellectual stimulation; not only is the child starved for physical resources, but the environment is simultaneously failing to stimulate his brain in a meaningful way. With both biological and sociological factors stacked against them, these children are effectively fighting a war on two fronts. Nurture bombards them with adverse stimuli while nature besieges them, cutting them off from the resources they need to feed their growing brains.

Rodent Rules

In 1957, a young researcher named Seymour Levine observed a strange phenomenon among the rats in his laboratory. He took newborn rat pups and, at regular daily intervals for the first several weeks of their lives, separated them from their mothers for 15-minute periods. The separated mice spent their brief diasporas exploring the confines of a small, unadorned cage. When the 15 minutes were up they were returned unharmed to their mothers. This procedure is called handling, and though it may not seem like much of an occurrence, it has a significant impact on a rat's stress response system. Handled pups, when compared to their non-handled peers, react to stressful stimuli in a far more relaxed manner. The effect is both behavioural and physiological. When presented with a novel environment, handled rats are much calmer than non-handled rats, and their cortisol levels don't surge nearly as high.

The opposite effect can also be achieved. Should you for some reason — be it scientific or sadistic — want to produce rats with highly sensitive stress response systems, simply separate them from their mothers for more prolonged periods. An hour or two will do it. Repeat the process — called, appropriately enough, "maternal separation" — a dozen or so times, and the rats in question will grow into neurotic, fretful creatures rife with cortisol, their HPA axes pumping loads of the stuff into their bloodstreams long after their handled brethren have already returned to homeostasis.

A number of established scientists repeated Levine's results. As the studies piled up, not only was the efficacy of handling and maternal separation confirmed, but the reason *why* it worked became clear. Handling and maternal separation weren't changing anything about the rats directly. Rather, these practices changed the way their mothers treated them. The real cause was a series of affectionate and nurturing actions collectively called licking, grooming, and arched-back nursing[34] behaviour, or LG-ABN. Rat dams (mothers) who engaged in high LG-ABN — those who licked, groomed, and nursed their offspring more often than usual — produced rat pups with tempered, easy-going stress response systems. Meanwhile, low LG-ABN mothers — those who spent little time licking and grooming their young, and made little effort to nurse them — produced jittery, easily agitated offspring with hyperactive stress response systems. Handling, it turns out, increases LG-ABN behaviour, while maternal separation decreases it. Levine's findings remained accurate, but the context surrounding them suddenly changed. Handling and maternal separation were catalysts, not causes.

LG-ABN behaviour is highly heritable. When the pups became mothers themselves, those raised by low LG-ABN mothers acted cold and distant to their offspring while those raised by high LG-ABN mothers became warm and affection-ate parents. This led scientists to question whether LG-ABN behaviour really altered rats' stress response systems at all. Perhaps, they thought, LG-ABN was just an extension of rats' genetically preprogrammed HPA behaviour, and handling and maternal separation were, at most, enhancing behaviours that would have appeared regardless.

To counter this claim, researchers Michael Meaney and Moshe Szyf of McGill University in Montreal performed a cross-fostering study. Pups of high LG-ABN dams were given to low LG-ABN mothers, who raised them as their own. In turn, pups of low LG-ABN mothers were given to high LG-ABN mothers. Additionally, some pups were cross-fostered to mothers of the same type — low LG-ABN pups to low LG-ABN mothers and high LG-ABN pups to high LG-ABN mothers — to confirm that the act of cross-fostering pups wasn't itself causing a change in stress behaviour.

Meaney and Szyf have performed dozens, if not hundreds, of these studies. The results have been consistent and profound. Again and again, rat pups adopted the stress response system of the mothers who raised them, both on a behavioural level, in their nervousness or lack thereof, and a physiological level, in the degree of stress hormones found in their bloodstream. Regardless of the disposition of their birth mothers, rat pups raised by high LG-ABN mothers were calm and self-assured, and displayed a measured and stable hormonal stress response, while those raised by low LG-ABN mothers were invariably timid, edgy, and rife with cortisol. And these effects didn't go away after a single generation. Pups cross-fostered to low or high LG-ABN mothers raised their "children" in the same manner as their adoptive parents, perpetuating the cycle of low or high stress response.

So what is causing this physiological change? The answer appears to be epigenetics. To demonstrate, let's follow the development of two rats, one born of a low LG-ABN mother and one of a high LG-ABN mother. From fertilization to birth — spanning a period of about 22 days — our two subjects are essentially identical. Most germane to our interests, their stress response genes[35] are free of any methyl molecule tags that might impede their function. In rats of both high and low LG-ABN mothers, these genes are switched on and ready to make proteins. However, shortly after birth, the region becomes methylated (or turned off) in both rats and remains so until the pups are six days old, at which point our two subjects' genomes diverge. In pups raised by high LG-ABN mothers, the sequence switches back on, shedding the shackles of its methyl molecules and resuming the ability to produce proteins. In pups of low LG-ABN mothers, the methyl tags remain in place, locking down the gene and restricting its ability to operate. Importantly, this divergence always occurs at *precisely the same time* when mothers start really licking and grooming their young and the differences between high and low LG-ABN mothers become readily apparent.

We are beginning to see evidence of these same effects in humans. Unfortunately, the highly invasive nature of cross-fostering studies makes them impractical (not to mention unethical) to perform on human beings — it is a rare mother indeed who would willfully allow her newborn daughter to be taken from her arms and replaced with a squalling infant born of strangers. Understandably, human studies have been less invasive and more roundabout. Yet they do occur.

In 2011, Dr. Marilyn Essex approached participants in the long-running Wisconsin Study of Families and Work, which began following an initial 570 pregnant women and their partners beginning in 1990 and continues to the present day, albeit with reduced numbers. Of the original 570, many were ineligible for Essex's study, and still others declined the offer to participate. All told, 109 mothers and their children partic-ipated in Essex's study. Not a huge number, but big enough for her purposes.

Poring through stacks of medical data, Essex traced the rise and fall of stressful life events occurring in each participant's household during their children's early years, noting every death, car accident, divorce, nervous breakdown, and any other unfortunate occurrence that could have conceivably raised the stress levels of the affected family. She then genotyped those children — now in their teens — and noted the patterns of methylation present on a number of key genes, particularly those pertaining to the stress response system. Her hypothesis was that traumatic events in parents' lives, if they occurred at a certain critical period of development, would alter the patterns of methylation found on their children's genomes. As it turned out, they did. Adult stress and child methylation synced up in complex, surprising, and remarkably consistent ways.

Essex found that if stressful events occurred during certain trigger periods in a child's life, they would leave an epigenetic imprint on that child's genes. These trigger periods, though consistent, were not cut and dried across the entire population of the study. Rather, they were highly dependent on the gender of both the affected child and his or her parent. The parent's gender determined the time at which their stressful experience had the most bearing on the methylation patterns present in their children. For mothers, the period was during their child's infancy. Mothers who reported experiencing a great deal of stress when their children were just babies — be it from losing a job, relationship trouble, or grieving the loss of a loved one — had children who displayed a distinct and unconventional pattern of methylation in certain target genes. Fathers produced a different but no less distinct methylation pattern, but only when stressed during their children's preschool years, and only in their daughters. Sons showed no abnormal patterns of methylation regardless of their father's stress patterns. Mothers, on the other hand, impacted the methyl patterns of their sons and daughters equally.

What does all this mean? From a short-term standpoint, admittedly not all that much. If you were hoping for a silver bullet solution, a lone methyl tag placed at a critical moment in childhood responsible for all of our problems, then we're about to disappoint you. None of the genes Essex monitored in her study have a direct link to heart disease, cancer, depression, or any other genetically modified malady. A panacea bearing Essex's moniker is, sadly, not forthcoming. However, to the more far-seeing among us, Essex's findings are truly groundbreaking. A profound truth about the power of motherhood, proven again and again in Meaney and Szyf's rodents, has now been officially seen in humans. And where one epigenetic influence goes, others will surely follow. There is no telling what shocking and far-reaching discoveries the next decade of epigenetic research will bring.

Conduits

Bruce Perry could be called a Hobbesian, though that would perhaps be uncharitable. Like the dour 17th-century philosopher Thomas Hobbes, Perry believes that humankind, despite great leaps forward in social structure, quality of life, and technological innovation, has not ventured far from the jungle from whence it came. Yet Perry does not believe bloodshed to be an innate part of human behaviour, which is where he and Hobbes differ. Hobbes could not have known about genes, having died almost 200 years before Gregor Mendel had so much as planted his garden, but had he the ability to learn of DNA, he would almost certainly believe violence to be tangled up in there somewhere. Perry, however, rejects this fatalist notion. To him, violence is a learned behaviour, a tragic legacy passed down through a thousand generations. It may be our birthright, however much we may begrudge those who gave it to us, but it is not innate.

Earlier this chapter, we discussed how the infant brain develops: a fecund flourishing of dendritic foliage thick as a jungle canopy, pruned and harvested and organized by our earliest experiences into something more orderly and productive, a kind of intellectual agriculture. We select the dendrites we use most and tend to them closely, watering them and weeding them and fertilizing their soil. The dendrites we don't use we yank free in order to provide greater resources to our more desirable neurological crops. But managing such an immense and complex garden takes work, and work takes energy. The body accounts for this under normal conditions — infants don't have much to do with their energy besides learn and grow. But when we are besieged by ever-present toxic levels of stress, our stores are gradually depleted. Tending to our intellectual nourishment is put on hold in favour of our more immediate survival, and gradually our garden begins to wither. The soil becomes parched, its dendrites weak and wilted. Weeds choke the life from our desired neurons, filling our heads with bitter, spiny synapses from which we in no way benefit. Dr. Perry is fascinated with this unfortunate process, though intellectual stimulation is not his chief concern. He is far more interested in the effects of *emotional* stimulation on a child's life, studying how a supportive adult presence filters the toxins from otherwise toxic stress, and how that same parent's absence allows those toxins to flow unimpeded.

Perry is no stranger to trauma. A senior fellow of the Child Trauma Academy, he has served as an expert witness on many high-profile cases in which children and adolescents were traumatized, including the siege of the Branch Davidian compound in Texas, the Columbine High School massacre, and the Oklahoma City bombing. He stood on the front lines of mental health support during Hurricane Katrina and 9/11, assisting children and adults who suffered from post-traumatic stress disorder, depression, and other emotional fallout. His research has informed our modern understanding of how young minds respond to violence, and the profound effect parents have on moderating, or exacerbating, this response.

Certainly, neglectful parenting has an adverse effect on children's development. Our neural gardens need more than fresh soil to truly flourish. They need pruning and weeding and watering. An untended garden may grow thick and green if the sun is shining and rain comes often enough, but it will be a wild, chaotic patch of earth, fruitful perhaps, but also cluttered and choked with weeds. The same goes with young minds. Infants need more than food and warmth and safety; they need stimulation and interaction and play, and the more of it they get, the better they'll be at thinking and reasoning and, above all, feeling. Emotional intelligence and intellectual intelligence (what we generally mean when we just say "intelligence") are closely connected attributes, but they are not identical. Perry gives a chilling example of this point in his 1997 paper on the cycle of violence.

Six o'clock in the evening in inner-city Baltimore. A 15-year-old boy named William sees a classmate shooting hoops on the neighbourhood basketball court. It's twilight and the city feels deserted. There are no pedestrians on the sidewalks, no cars on the streets, no conversations drifting though open windows. The classmate dribbles his way up the court, the thwack of his ball on the pavement echoing off the nearby tenements. William's eyes drift from the basketball to his classmate's shoes. Air Jordans, their vamps and laces an immaculate white, the fresh rubber of their soles squeaking against the tarmac with each step. William approaches his classmate, who eyes him nervously.

"Hey," the classmate says.

"Gimme your shoes," says William.

"What? No way."

William lifts up his jersey and pulls a handgun from the waistband of his pants. He'd been wearing the gun for no particular reason except that it felt good against his stomach. It feels even better in his hand, he notes. The classmate's eyes go wide. He raises his hands, backing up slowly.

"The shoes," says William.

"Y-yeah, okay, sure," the classmate stammers. Very slowly, he bends down and unties his laces. He takes off the shoes and hands them to William, who takes them with an approving smile. He holds them up to his face and looks them over, the gun still trained on his classmate.

"Cool. Thanks," he says, and pulls the trigger. The classmate collapses. Blood speckles William head to toe, staining the leather of his new shoes a splotchy red. He puts them on anyway, not bothering to wipe them clean. On his walk home, he tosses his old shoes over a fence.

The stains are what undo him. Them and the gun, which confirms the story his bloody shoes had already told. The police take William into custody, where a stone-faced officer questions him for an hour. Most of his questions concern what happened and why, but near the end of their interview he asks the boy something different.

"Son, if you could do it all over again, would you do anything differently?"

William thinks about it for some time. Finally, he responds.

"I would have cleaned my shoes."

Consider William's reply. There is regret imbedded in his statement, but it is of a purely intellectual sort. He regrets his actions because they led to him being caught, not because they caused the death of an innocent human being. In that respect, the boy couldn't care less. He is capable of regret, an intellectual response, but not *remorse*, an emotional one. Perry's story highlights this distinction. We are all familiar with the concept of mental retardation, but children can also suffer from emotional retardation, in which their capacity for empathy is stunted or missing entirely. And while mental retardation is often the result of genetic conditions, emotional retardation is almost exclusively learned. Just as a child raised by wolves never learns how to speak, a child raised without love never learns to form the emotional bonds necessary to empathize with other people.

Over the past few decades, we have blamed this problem on a large and shifting cast of bogeymen. Poverty, single parenthood, television, heavy metal music, video games: each has at some point faced the ignominious spotlight cast by the media as a rogue and a villain, the blood of uncountable children on its hands. And in truth, it's unlikely that any of these factors serve to decrease problem behaviour in children. Being poor means more financial stress in the home, fewer opportunities for children to go to good schools or participate in extracurricular programs, and greater odds of living in a violent neighbourhood bereft of strong role models. Single parenthood doubles the burden placed on the mother (or father) and reduces the amount of time children can interact with them — somebody's got to pay the bills, after all, and it's a rare parent who can work productively and attend to their kid's needs at the same time. And there is evidence that an overexposure to violent media can to a certain extent inoculate children to its horrors, making them, if not more violent, then at least less repulsed by the concept of violence. Yet all of these factors pale in comparison to the true root cause of emotional malnourishment: relational poverty. Not to be confused with poverty of the socioeconomic sort, relational poverty refers to a lack of supportive adults in a child's life. Though a family may be well-off financially, their children can still suffer from emotional impoverishment if they have limited contact with parents, grandparents, and other friendly faces.

Children have in them a great capacity for resilience, but it is predicated upon the attention and support they receive from the adults around them. Parents act as a kind of psychological immune system, allowing children to deal with modest threats without suffering any long-term harm. Strip a child of this protection, and the smallest upset in her life — the emotional equivalent of a common cold — becomes a serious threat. Toxic stress is only toxic if children lack the means to combat it, just as a disease is only dangerous if a person lacks the necessary antibodies. Except with toxic stress, the antibodies are not internal. They come from outside of the child, delivered by the affection of parents, aunts, grandfathers, teachers, neighbours, and friends.

Parents are the conduits through which toxic stress must pass. This idea is both liberating and terrifying. On the one hand, it is comforting to know that a parent's loving presence can supersede most any external hardship their children may encounter. Poverty, violence, mourning, disaster: all can be endured if the affected child has the support of his or her caregiver. But such responsibility puts a tremendous amount of pressure on parents. In the midst of a crisis, a hectored mom can add yet another worry to what is likely already a long and daunting list: don't let stress trickle down to the children.

Still, Perry's assertion isn't something to fear. Good parenting doesn't require a degree or tons of cash or a rigid adherence to any set rules. To quote Lennon and McCartney, all you need is love (though effort and a bit of common sense don't hurt either). Happily, love is something that just about every parent has in abundant supply.

Bonding

In the grand sweep of human history, there is perhaps no force more powerful than the bond between parent and child. If you're a parent, you've probably experienced it firsthand. The need to protect, nurture, and guide one's offspring is deep, profound, and overwhelming, capable of circumventing even the most primal urges of self-preservation. Stories abound of mothers and fathers temporarily endowed with almost superhuman strength, speed, and endurance when their children are in peril, allowing them to lift up the back ends of cars with their bare hands and fight off violent criminals twice their size. Apocryphal and exaggerated many of these claims may be, but there is a grain of truth buried within them. From an evolutionary standpoint, it's not hard to envision why this would be. Any sexually reproducing organism that made no effort to protect its offspring would be far less likely to extend its lineage to subsequent generations than one who defends its children tirelessly, even if doing so costs the organism its life. Though our genetic imperative is to survive, an even greater imperative is to preserve our genetic lineage, and our children are the vessels in which this lineage resides. As far as our genes are concerned, child trumps parent every time.

The parent-child bond and the forces that forge it form the crux of attachment theory, which we discussed in a previous chapter. We often think of the parent-infant bond as something originating from the minds of mothers, but proponents of attachment theory argue that the infant has a part to play as well. Mothers may set the tone, but their children respond accordingly. As a result, we have the three major classes of attachment behaviour (or four, if you subscribe to the Main and Solomon school of attachment theory),[36] each of which corresponds to a different type of parenting behaviour. Type B children are called securely attached, comfortable with short separations from their parents but eager to see them return. Their parents are consistent, supportive, and attentive to their children's needs. Type A children are called avoidant, and true to their name, they tend to ignore their parents even when feeling insecure. Their parents are often inattentive, having never paid much heed to their cries, causing children to seek comfort in themselves rather than waste energy calling for their caregivers in vain. Type C children are called reactive/ambivalent, and they display a consistent yet curiously contradictory pattern of behaviour: though extremely agitated by short separations from their caregivers, they derive no comfort from them upon their return. Type C children cling to their parents while thrashing and crying, seemingly unsure whether they want to be comforted or left alone. This paradoxical reaction is the result of inconsistent caregiving; parents of Type C children may come running at their child's first whimper in one instance only to let them cry unattended for hours in the next.

When attachment theory was first created, its conclusions were drawn solely from observation. Dr. Bowlby, the theory's founder, knew maternal behaviour altered child attachment strategy because he'd seen it do so, but he didn't know why. At the time, the question seemed almost irrelevant. The important thing was to observe the cause and effect relationship between parent and child; the engine driving it was a mysterious biochemical transaction, relied upon but not understood. Gradually, this has begun to change. Researchers have started mapping the neuro-endocrine responses of new mothers to pregnancy, lactation, and childbirth, and have already found a vast network of hormonal signals responsible for "priming" mothers for motherhood. The epigenetic changes dutifully observed by Meaney and company do not flow unidirectionally from mother to child through mom's nursing behaviour, as was once assumed. The child, simply by being born, triggers a number of profound changes in a mother's brain, not the least of which being a surge of oxytocin production.

Oxytocin is a hormone responsible for our sense of cama-raderie, our capacity for empathy, and our ability to bond with other humans. Not surprisingly, it is released in copious amounts during and immediately after childbirth. One can hardly blame mothers for providing themselves with a little chemical compen-sation, given the gruelling nature of childbirth (it's called "going into labour" for a reason), but after the birth is over and the new baby has been swaddled and handed squalling to mom, oxyto-cin's work is only just beginning. It floats through the mother's bloodstream at elevated levels for months, its ebb and flow inti-mately tied to lactation. Each time a baby feeds, mom gets a fresh dose, a Pavlovian encouragement to keep it up. Oxytocin is the reason why a new mother will often report a profound sense of kinship with her children when breastfeeding; her brain is bribing her with tiny hits of bliss. It's a cynical way of looking at things, perhaps, but such crude tactics are hardly limited to childbirth. Just about everything we do is the result of biochemical bribery or threat. We keep our bodies nourished, hydrated, and rested, and our brains reward us with dollops of dopamine. We procreate, and our thankful genes reward us with an even bigger burst of the stuff. We come across a fire or a steep ledge or a predator and our brain reprimands us before we do something foolish. "Don't touch it," our cerebellum warns, "or you'll be sorry." Should the memory of past pain not suffice and we prove ourselves in need of another lesson — by touching the fire or tottering gleefully over the ledge or prodding the large and irascible predator with a stick — the brain is all too willing to deliver. Pain is a warning, alerting us to a potential problem we must attend to ("Hey! You're bleeding!"), but it's also a threat. "Smarten up," it growls, "or you'll get another."

Therefore, it should come as no surprise that when we engage in something as evolutionarily beneficial as motherhood our brains praise our noble behaviour with a burst of mood-enhancing hormones. Oxytocin is one of them. Dopamine is another. Though both are pleasurable chemicals, oxytocin and dopamine have distinct characters, and thus serve different purposes. Oxytocin, as mentioned above, promotes bonding and empathy — feelings that, though pleasant, emphasize the importance of connecting with others. Dopamine is far more self-absorbed. It is the id molecule, hedonism concentrated into a few choice atoms and released in tiny, intoxicating doses. Which is not to say dopamine works solely to selfish ends; mothers get a taste of it simply by looking upon their child's smiling face. Their varying characters make oxytocin and dopamine great partners in parental motivation. Oxytocin provides the softly harmonious sense of *rightness* about child-rearing, while dopamine offers ephemeral but potent moments of joy. Together, they comprise the parent-child bond studied by attachment theorists and are thus largely responsible for the continued existence of our species.

But sometimes these bonds loosen or break. The hormonal adhesives binding parent to child weaken, dissolved by competing chemicals that change the way a mother's brain responds to her infant's laughs, cries, and gurgles. A lot of things can derail mother-child attachment, but perhaps no force is as destructive and insidious in this regard as addiction.

Neural Solvents

No one would argue that drug addiction makes for better parenting. We've all heard horror stories of children living in squalid apartments, playing on a floor littered with syringes while their junky parents sprawl unconscious across the couch, of mothers leaving babies in trash cans, incapable of caring for them and afraid of putting them up for adoption lest the authorities cast a disapproving glance their way, of fathers murdering their children in a drug-fuelled rage. Such actions seem to us unconscionable, nefarious, and downright evil. How could a parent treat an innocent child that way? We resist the very thought of it, as if the idea itself was a rotten, repugnant, physical thing capable of dripping its slime onto the floors of our subconscious.

Mercifully, these are extreme examples, but addiction inarguably takes its toll on a person's ability to be a successful parent. Mothers addicted to cocaine are more hostile, are less emotionally engaged in maternal activities (e.g., feeding, bathing, and playing with their babies), and exhibit little to no pleasure in interacting with their children. It's as if their mothering gene had been switched off. Of course, we've learned enough about genes by now to realize that there is no mothering gene, just as there's no gene for depression or gene for addiction. Yet certain neural switches are being thrown, and certain connections rerouted, causing a dramatic shift in the way addict mothers view, interact with, and respond to their offspring.

Remember Marcy and Melissa, the twins we discussed in chapter 6?[37] Let's pay them another visit. Marcy, you'll recall, was ushered into a life of wealth and privilege while Melissa wallowed in emotional neglect. Now in adulthood, the two sisters have both become mothers.

Marcy's labour wasn't easy, but when she first laid eyes on her baby girl the pain and frustration and fear of the past 12 hours washed away. Her heart seemed to swell, infused with a love more primal and pure than anything she'd experienced before. It was like a drug, Marcy thought — though having never tried any substance stronger than a glass of wine, she could only guess that this was true. She named the girl Chloe.

The first few months were a challenge, and the sleepless nights and 3:00 a.m. feedings took their toll. Marcy was a driven woman, married to her career as much as her husband, and the endless days spent at home sometimes felt more like a prison sentence than a well-paid six-month maternity leave. She missed the bustle of the hospital, the patients and the dizzy chaos and the rush of adrenaline she felt whenever she stepped into an operating room and snapped latex gloves onto her steady, talented hands. Those hands felt wasted changing diapers and scrubbing baby spit-up off of bibs. Sometimes she sat on her bed and cried. But as the months passed Chloe became less of a helpless, mewling thing. She began to smile, to babble joyful gibberish, to trace the movement of Marcy's fingers with wonder. The tiniest giggle set Marcy's heart ablaze with maternal warmth. She watched her daughter grow with an unceasing sense of amazement and gratitude. Her body surged with affection for the little girl. She'd spent three months pining for her office and her operating theatre, but as her maternity leave drew to a close the thought of leaving Chloe made her miserable. The child was an endless fountain of comfort and joy.

While Marcy was delivering her first child, Melissa had just come home from the hospital with her third. The delivery had been a non-issue, a few hours, a few squirts of Demerol, and there you have it, another screaming mouth to feed, another pair of chubby little hands clawing greedily at her starving, threadbare chequebook. Melissa brought her baby — a girl she named Britney — home and went through the motions of motherhood. She fed her, changed her, bathed her on occasion, but the whole thing was joyless and dull. Drugs were what kept her going, and she popped, sniffed, or smoked them any chance she got. The exact substance didn't much matter; Melissa did whatever she could get her hands on.

The moments that followed these indulgences were sacred, her mounting bills and crappy job and wailing kids held at bay by a wall of inebriation. Then the high would fizzle and Melissa would trudge back to her duties, regarding her children with poorly disguised contempt.

The smiles and giggles and wide-eyed glances that bought Marcy such joy meant little to Melissa. Often she would just as soon have Britney sulk as smile. At least sulking was quiet. Laughter was better than her wretched wailing, but it still got on Melissa's nerves.

Each night after putting Britney to bed, Melissa got high, be it on pot, prescription pills, or simply cigarette after cigarette. Money was tight and drugs hard to come by, but she tried not to worry too much about it. She'd get more somehow. She always did. It was the only thing that mattered.

It's easy to cast Marcy as the benevolent, selfless mother and Melissa as the self-absorbed, self-destructive addict, but the distinction between the two women runs deeper than that. Marcy isn't entirely selfless — after all, caring for Chloe gives her joy, comfort, and a not unjustified sense of maternal pride. Without that burst of emotions, she would probably still do her duty as a primary caregiver, but would she be as good at it, or as dedicated to her daughter's happiness? Probably not. She might not be as neglectful to her children as Melissa — her greater financial means and more driven personality give her an additional leg up, to be sure — but if Marcy was deprived of her daily oxytocin-dopamine cocktail, or if Melissa was provided with one, the gulf separating the two mothers would likely shrink considerably.

The brain is a complex network of electrochemical impulses, a synaptic switchboard on a truly galactic scale. Billions of neurons forge trillions of connections with one another, allowing for more combinations of neural signals than there are stars in the Milky Way, and substantially more processing power than the fastest computer on earth. Imagine that each of these connections, when activated, gives off a flicker of light. These tiny lights fizzle and flash and coalesce, providing a bioluminescent map of brain activity. The more vigorously a neural region is being used, the brighter it shines, while underused regions remain dark.

Can you see it? Good. Let's take this concept and examine the phosphorescent cartography of Marcy and Melissa's brains. When Marcy sees Chloe smile or hears the sound of her laughter, Marcy's nucleus accumbens — the region of her brain associated with pleasure — lights up. Her dopamine receptors dazzle like flashbulbs, elevating her mood and forging a positive association between her and Chloe. Bolstered by her brain's neurochemical response, Marcy becomes more affectionate, attentive, and nurturing. This in turn makes Chloe a more interactive and curious baby, which sets Marcy's dopamine receptors glowing even brighter. Their synapses flash and sparkle in a glorious and highly synchronized display of neural fireworks. When mother and child interact, their nuclei accumbens display nearly identical patterns of activity — they light up in sync. They signal to one another, their brains and bodies engaged in what child development experts call a serve and return relationship. Chloe serves up a giggle or a smile and Marcy returns it, tickling Chloe's neurons and encouraging her cognitive development. Together the two of them play a kind of cerebral tennis, except the muscles being exercised are not calves and quads, but the nucleus accumbens and the cerebral cortex. And the more they play, the stronger the bond between them grows.

Meanwhile, Melissa's brain is a dim and listless thing. As far as her neurons are concerned, a smile from Britney is worth less than a candle in the wind. Her dopamine receptors fizzle. Try as she might, Britney can't trigger a single one. The fault is not with her; her mother's brain has been cruelly rewired. Cocaine has the reins now, and it is a savage and relentless master. The bursts of dopamine that should seal Melissa's relationship with her daughter come instead through outside substances. Her ability to feel happiness without chemical stimulation grows muted and weak. Melissa's brain only glows when she's taking a fresh hit, and with each snort, her light shines dimmer and dimmer.

Drug use erodes a mother's ability to derive pleasure from the very act of mothering. On a chemical level, parenting becomes a pursuit of diminishing returns. It's easy to call these mothers selfish — and perhaps selfishness does come into it, to a certain extent — but there is much more to the problem than that. The little things that compensate for the seemingly unending trials of motherhood — the warm maternal glow, the tiny joys imbued in a toddler's laughter — these pleasures no longer register. Drugs dissolve the bond between mother and child, and once that effortless, unconscious connection is gone, holding on becomes a deliberate and exhausting effort. Imagine devoting your every waking hour to a creature from which you derive no satisfaction, feel no love, and sense no fealty. Few addicts, admittedly, are this extreme, but the gradual numbing of maternal connection is a well-documented effect of substance abuse. Drugs (especially cocaine, though other narcotics are guilty as well) eat away at the bonds between mothers and children. They are neural solvents, dissolving warmth into want, happiness into hunger, love into cold, unfeeling sludge. Addict parents are often indifferent to, or even resentful of, their children's needs. Their parenting behaviour waffles between extremes: harsh, over-involved authoritarianism juxtaposed with excessively permissive indifference. On the latter pole, mothers occasionally invert the parent-child relationship, begging support from a child developmentally unequipped to take on the role of parent.

Sadly, growing up in this sort of environment has a palpable effect on children. Neglect, both emotional and physical, are distressingly commonplace in addicts' homes. And we know what emotional neglect hath wrought — think back to Bruce Perry's relational poverty, to Meaney's troubled low LG-ABN rats, to Sophie's sleepless nights. Children deprived of emotional and intellectual nourishment are cruelly denied the chance to grow and learn unfettered. Their dendritic gardens become parched and withered. Promise rots on the vine. Fussy infants become troubled toddlers become angry, sullen teens. Their love-starved brains lurch hungrily toward stimulus, anything to fire their rusty, underused dopamine receptors — alcohol, sex, cocaine, heroin, gambling. Booze and narcotics are the most popular choice, but the "what" of it is almost immaterial. The real issue is the why, and the why never changes.

Hungry Ghosts

Dr. Gabor Maté understands addiction. A veteran of Vancouver's poorest slums, Dr. Maté has worked on the city's troubled east side for over 20 years as a family doctor, medical coordinator, and most currently, staff physician for the Portland Hotel, a residence and drug treatment centre. His books explore the hidden side of ADHD, addiction, and toxic stress. And he is, by his own admission, an addict, though his addiction is of a refined and ostensibly benign sort: buying albums of classical music. Record shopping may sound more like a hobby than an addiction, but that is precisely Maté's point. Addiction is not broken junkies in alleys with track marks and rotting teeth, nor beer-bellied alcoholics slumped on couches and exhaling clouds of whiskey, nor rail-thin yellow-fingered women chain-smoking in filthy apartment kitchens. Addiction is simply a hole that can't be filled. It aches relentlessly, its bare expanse throbbing and cold and always hungry, and the addict can feel no respite until he throws something — anything — into the endless void forever swelling inside of him. The hole is a beast, and the beast must be fed. Heroin, booze, cigarettes, slot machines, sex, shoes, fast food, Pepsi, CDs, video games, television, and even work: addicts have tried to quell the beast with every one of them, but the beast is never sated, the hole never filled.

Addiction is treatable, but the cure is rarely absolute. The hole it bores into an addict's soul may shrink, its hunger dulled and subverted by professional treatment and familial support, but it never truly disappears. This makes understanding the origins of addictive behaviour all the more critical. If we can stop the offending factor before it takes shovel in hand and digs that gaping, bottomless, hungry hole into our neural tissue, then we don't have to worry about filling it in the first place.

Perhaps you're wondering why we have dwelled for so long on the mechanics of addiction. Your life is likely many degrees removed from hard drug users, and the ramifications of a heavy narcotics habit seem obvious. Street drugs don't do anybody much good, save criminals. But addiction makes an excellent case study for exploring the potential pitfalls of early child development.

Dr. Maté's book on the subject, entitled *In the Realm of Hungry Ghosts*, beautifully chronicles the development of addiction. It does so through deft portraits of addicts seeking treatment at his clinic, but also through a scientific exploration of how addiction, attachment, and infant stress response intersect.

We've discussed how a mother's interaction with her infant triggers a release of mood-enhancing hormones in her brain. Chief among them are oxytocin, which generates a sense of maternal warmth and nurturance, and dopamine, which provides a rush of pleasure. The same goes for infants. Parental interaction stimulates the development of key circuitry in the infant brain, among them the dopamine response system and the HPA axis responsible, as you know, for regulating our response to stress. Think of Meaney's rats: less licking and grooming resulted in poorly regulated, oversensitive stress response systems. The dopamine pleasure-reward system is no different. A lack of parental warmth leaves a child's dopamine receptors stunted and weak, and an outside stimulus becomes the only way he or she can jumpstart them.

The addict is a figure of great scorn in our society, often painted as lazy and entitled, sponging off the tax dollars of their more productive peers, deliberately pursuing inner pleasure at the expense of outer responsibility. The underlying assumption this picture presents is that addicts scout the many paths their lives could take, weigh the pros and cons of each venture, and consciously decide that addiction is the best way forward. In truth, they had very little say in the matter. Sure, even the lowliest junky has a certain theoretical autonomy, in that they are physically capable of not taking drugs, of seeking treatment, of building better lives for themselves, even if that "better life" is still pretty threadbare when compared to the way we live. After all, the majority of us have woken up every day and steadfastly chosen not to do heroin; why should it be any different for him?

Except it *is* different. The hole is a real thing, intangible but irrevocably there, yawning from the hearts and minds of every addict. Addiction may not be a disease in the bacterial sense of pneumonia, malaria, or yellow fever, nor the autoimmune sense of cancer, Crohn's disease, or lupus, but it is no less a disease than depression or schizophrenia. And we are far more forgiving of the depressed and schizophrenics in our society than we are of addicts. No one berates chronically depressed people if they fail to hold down jobs or contribute to the economy. And if a schizophrenic person tosses aside his medication and spirals into an abyss of paranoid rambling, he becomes a figure of pity rather than scorn, a casualty of an unfeeling society. But schizophrenia can be controlled through judicious use of medication, and depression can often be ameliorated by improving one's diet and exercise regime. How are they any different than addicts, who likewise suffer in part as a result of decisions they have made and continue to make?

Our intention here is not to offend, nor to imply that schizophrenic or chronically depressed people are responsible for their conditions. Quite the opposite. Depression, schizophrenia, and addiction are all diseases that an outside observer can only diagnose by noting the presence or absence of certain behaviours, and such conditions must invariably struggle to achieve or maintain a perceived legitimacy. No one questions that a cancer patient is truly sick, but depression has been written off as moping, and schizophrenia, in its milder forms, as a kind of wilful eccentricity. This is much less the case today. Addiction, however, has been unable to shed this dismissive attitude in spite of the fact that it, depression, and schizophrenia are all neurological conditions, and no one suffering from any of them ever asked to be so afflicted. The depressed man could eat better. The schizophrenic could take his medicine. The addict could seek treatment. Some people from each group do just that. But for too many others, their brain chemistry makes these ostensibly simple solutions difficult, if not impossible, to obtain. We do not choose addiction, depression, or schizophrenia; we inherit them. They come from an intersection of genetic and environmental influences, and they are far from the only conditions with such an origin.

Childhood spins the threads from which our lives are woven. We may choose the pattern, but the colour and the texture of the fibres are outside of our control.

Emotional Aegis

Addiction provides a poignant if extreme example of how deep, broad, and varied an infant's needs are. Another useful illustration of this idea comes from the esteemed American psychologist Abraham Maslow. Maslow developed his Hierarchy of Needs theory in 1943, in an academic paper he published entitled "A Theory of Human Motivation." When discussing human needs, Maslow envisioned a pyramid with five levels. The first, lowest, and widest need — the foundation of the pyramid — was a group of base, physiological necessities — things like food, water, and sleep. Directly above our physiological needs is safety, which comprises shelter, protection, and other physical kinds of security, but also financial and mental security — money for rent and a moral compass, respectively. Next is love — both platonic and romantic — and belonging, a sense of being cared for. Atop of love sits esteem. The respect of one's peers and a sense of confidence and accomplishment also dwell on this level. Lastly, self-actualization tops the pyramid. The most abstract of the hierarchy's layers, self-actualization is one's drive to reach their full potential, to live a life of true and lasting contentment. Unlike the other needs, which are feelings or physical things we can obtain, self-actualization is more about pursuit than achievement.

Maslow's pyramid is a marvellous and deeply intuitive concept, but it gets one critical thing wrong. The hierarchy of needs, simply by nature of being a hierarchy, suggests a linear progression from bottom to top. One must meet the lowest need before ascending to the next level, and so on until we reach the pyramid's self-actualized pinnacle. Maslow stated that we can pursue multiple levels simultaneously, but the bottom-up progression is nevertheless implied. Pyramids, after all, are never built from the top down or the middle out. The foundation is laid first, and the bricks are stacked one atop another until the very tip of the structure is in place.

But humans are not built; they are born. By the time the human zygote develops into an embryo — roughly a week after conception — it has already become a complex and highly interdependent network of cells. We come into being not from the bottom up, but outward in every direction at once. Children may occasionally be born feet-first, but they never *grow* that way. Our minds are no exception. It is true that depriving a child of his physiological needs — the sturdy foundation of Maslow's pyramid — will inevitably kill him, while depriving him of some of the hierarchy's higher strata may not. (Depriving a child of love, we feel, actually will kill them as inevitably as would denying them food or water. Without attachment, children cannot survive.) But while a child may not physically die from lack of self-esteem or security, they won't really live, either. The mechanisms necessary to their cognitive and physiological development will sputter and stall, deprived of their necessary fuel. The result will be a person who is not truly whole. They will have a drastically reduced mental capacity, or else become like young William from Bruce Perry's disturbing example of emotional retardation — cold-blooded, unfeeling, and sociopathic.

Our emotional and physical selves are not separate spheres that happen to overlap. They are one and the same. For years, it was assumed that emotional neglect could damage a child emotionally, but would do them no harm physically. Though the mind may rot, we argued, the body that houses it will remain fit as ever. We now know this to be utter folly. Mounting evidence has shown that adverse childhood experiences don't simply leave children vulnerable to depression, addiction, and other diseases of the mind. They increase the risk of conditions we once — foolishly, it must be said — believed the mind had nothing to do with. Diabetes. Heart disease. Obesity. Even cancer. The seeds of these dread diseases are planted at a young age, sown in the fertile soil of our minds. They spread beneath the topsoil of our cerebral cortices, taking root in the subconscious darkness of our cerebellums and hippocampi, growing patiently through adolescence and adulthood until, in our middle age or late in life, they burst forth, blossom, and bear their bitter fruit.

This concept, fearful though it may be, is also a cause for great hope. After all, if adult diseases like cancer and diabetes have their origins in our early caregiving environments, then our children are not shackled to disease or disorder by their genetic pedigrees. A wayward gene need not lead to heart disease or schizophrenia or cancer. New research continues to prove that a supportive, nurturing caregiving environment supersedes much of the genetic risk once thought to be inherent to these conditions. Certain diseases remain the purview of genes alone — cystic fibrosis, sadly, cannot be parented away — but many of the most ostensibly heritable and terrifying conditions can be overcome by a solid, supportive family. Sometimes the songs are true. Sometimes love really can conquer all. And good parenting, it seems, can break even the strongest of chains.

Chapter 10
ACE in the Hole

●───●

The trial determining the fate of Romanian dictator Nicolae Ceaușescu and his wife Elena began and ended on Christmas Day 1989. It was little more than a kangaroo court, a tribunal overseen by a rival political party and frothing with the backflow of 20 years of repression, forced austerity, and violence. In a span of two hours, the Ceaușescus were tried, convicted, dragged to a nearby courtyard, and executed by firing squad. The execution itself was so hastily arranged that the camera crew responsible for recording the trial didn't even have the chance to film it; by the time they made it out of the courtroom and into the yard with their gear in tow, the Ceaușescus were already dead, their bullet-ridden bodies covered by sheets of canvas.

During the early days of his reign, Ceaușescu was actually — by the admittedly shoddy standards of the Soviet Union — progressive, maintaining an open relationship with the capitalist West, easing censorship of the press, and opposing the 1968 invasion of Czechoslovakia. But as the years rolled on, Romania's relatively open society gradually and insidiously clamped shut, a political Venus flytrap closing around its unwitting populous. Harsh new laws were written, restricting Romanians' access to abortions, divorce, and dissent. Mothers were encouraged to have — or rather, strong-armed into having — as many children as possible. Five was the bare minimum, 10 a government-sanctioned goal to strive for. Censorship became commonplace. The streets ran thick with snitches; it was estimated that at the height of Ceauşescu's paranoia, one in four Romanians was a paid informant.

To counter the new, darker image of his increasingly repressive regime, Ceauşescu flooded Romania with communist propaganda and erected a cult of personality modelled after the Chinese and North Korean regimes. However, Ceauşescu's ties with the West remained strong, fostering a relationship that was not always beneficial. The dictator soon learned the dark side of capitalism, as his country became mired in 13 billion dollars of debt.

It was the debt that broke his government. Desperate to repay, Ceauşescu enacted absurdly strict austerity measures, effectively choking the life from the Romanian countryside. Farmers and factory workers saw their goods shipped off to appease foreign creditors, while they scraped by with a pittance. Food, gasoline, and electricity were ruthlessly rationed, leaving many families starving in the dark, as grocery store shelves stood empty and power stations faced rolling blackouts. Ceauşescu's austerity measures allowed him to aggressively attack Romania's debt, but it did so at the expense of his image, which had already begun to crack beneath the strain of public scrutiny.

Ceauşescu paid his debt, both to the western powers and, in a bloody and more primal currency, to the Romanian people. Less than two months after he balanced Romania's budget, the country revolted, and Nicolae Ceauşescu found himself impeached, derided, and standing before a firing squad. He left in his wake a legacy of corruption, poverty, and bureaucratic mismanagement. Few Romanians flourished under Ceauşescu's rule, though perhaps no group suffered more greatly by his hand than Romania's orphans.

By outlawing abortion and encouraging Romanian women to have as many children as possible while providing no means for them to support themselves economically, Ceaușescu created an influx of orphans. Lacking the financial ability to provide for the ever-swelling numbers of abandoned or parentless infants, the government swept them into public orphanages and, essentially, forgot about them.

As the Soviet Empire crumbled, the Western world was allowed its first unadulterated glimpse of life under communist rule. The horrors the media witnessed were varied in nature and distressing in their frequency, yet one could argue that, in sheer visceral repugnance, the Romanian orphanages trumped them all. Children sprawled across soiled mattresses in dank, windowless rooms, their legs chained to bedposts. Violent tremors wracked their bodies from hunger and the cold. The orphanages were criminally understaffed, and the few workers who were there offered the children no warmth or affection. Orphans were fed flavourless gruel from oversized bottles, clothed in little more than rags, and washed with hoses and cold water. Illness plagued them mercilessly; lung infections, intestinal inflammation, and skin disorders were the norm. Sexual abuse was distressingly commonplace. No one spoke to these children, played with them, or touched them with affection. No one learned their names or taught them to speak or treated them like human beings. Romanian criminals received more warmth than they did.

The neglect the Romanian orphans suffered in their dank and fetid prisons took its toll. Their growth was stunted, both mentally and physically. Their motor skills were unrefined and they exhibited classic signs of self-comfort: trembling, rocking back and forth, and compulsively repeating physical ticks and gestures. They met each developmental milestone months or years behind their more nurtured peers, or failed to reach them at all.

With Ceauşescu's nefarious orphanages in the media spotlight, the maltreated orphans became a *cause célèbre* for activists, critics of communism, and well-meaning middle-class families. Thousands of children were adopted by households throughout the world. Sadly, many of the orphans were beyond help. Members of this unfortunate majority, referred to by the blunted euphemism "non-recoverables," had simply spent too long in emotional and physical isolation. Their once arable neural soil, left untended, had eroded, leaving a parched and barren expanse of dust and clay. This "point of no return" for intellectual development occurs distressingly early in life. Two years is all it takes to irrevocably stunt a child's developmental potential. But even among the orphans fortunate enough to have been adopted before this deadline, that first emotionally starved year can often leave a lasting and costly mark.

A 1998 study helmed by psychiatrist Michael Rutter observed the development of three groups of children: Romanian orphans who had been adopted by British families before they were six months old; Romanian orphans who had been adopted by British families between the ages of six and 24 months; and children born in Britain who had been adopted but never experienced anything close to the neglect or brutality of the Romanian orphanages. The British-born group served as a control; Rutter wasn't particularly interested in their outcomes for their own sakes, but only as a benchmark to which he could compare the two Romanian groups.

Upon arriving in Britain, both groups of Romanian orphans were at a considerable developmental disadvantage. Orphans adopted within six months of being born had an average IQ of 76; those adopted between 6 and 24 months scored slightly lower, with an average of 48. Considering 100 represents average intelligence in any population, both numbers represent a level well below normal, unimpaired cognitive function.

Years later, after the children in each group reached four years of age, Rutter retested them. The results were encouraging. The orphans adopted before they were six months old had completely caught up to their British-born peers, scoring an average IQ of 115 versus 117 for British-born adoptees. The last vestiges of their cognitive delay had disappeared, and their IQs were just as high as the adoptees who had never been submitted to abuse and neglect — as high, indeed, as that of the general British population. Orphans adopted between the ages of 6 and 24 months fared well too, though the traces of their cognitive delay never left them entirely. At four years old, the group's average IQ was 96. Those are pretty impressive gains — 48 to 96, doubling their scores in just a few years' time — but they remain 20 points shy of their group's average. And this gap, however valiantly narrowed during those early years of frantic neural growth, would never completely disappear. Rutter performed a follow-up study when the children reached age 11, and the same trends were evident: Romanian children adopted within the first six months of their lives were no different than children adopted from within Britain, while Romanian children adopted later in infancy lagged behind by about 20 IQ points.

The six-month window corresponds perfectly to another physiological distinction between Romanian orphans: the stress response system. A Canadian study performed in 2001 observed daily cortisol levels in three groups of children analogous to those in Rutter's study: Romanian orphans adopted when they were four months old, Romanian orphans adopted at eight months old, and Canadian-born children adopted at four months old. To simplify things, we will call them the early adoption group, the late adoption group, and the Canadian-born group, respectively.

All participants in the study had been in their adopted homes for at least six years. Researchers collected a series of saliva samples over three non-consecutive days and measured the levels of cortisol present in each one. As we discussed last chapter, cortisol is the end product of the stress response system. Its main task is distributing extra energy to the heart, brain, and major muscle groups, allowing us the burst of speed, strength, and cognitive response necessary to face an imminent threat. Though helpful in short bursts, chronically elevated levels of cortisol continue drawing energy away from the parts of our body that, while not immediately useful in the face of imminent danger, are nevertheless necessary for our long-term survival: tasks such as digestion, immune system response, and the productions of gametes, or sex cells. When cortisol levels remain high, our body becomes locked in a perpetual state of war, maintaining an excessively large standing army at the expense of vital peacetime projects. Steroid soldiers march endlessly through our bloodstream while fields go untilled and factories lie dormant.[38]

When the Romanian orphans first came to their adopted homes, their cortisol levels were dangerously high. Their tiny bodies had been bombarded by severely toxic levels of stress unmitigated by any kind of supportive adult caregiver. With their living situations dire and no one to comfort them, they existed in a perpetual state of anxiety, fear, and hunger of both a physical and emotional sort.

Among the early adoption group, this hyper-responsive state eventually faded, as the amount of cortisol present in their systems dropped to the same level as found in their Canadian-born peers. The late adoption group was not so fortunate. Even six years after being adopted, their saliva contained cortisol at levels significantly higher than the early adoption and Canadian-born groups.

The results of the Canadian study line up neatly with Rutter's. In each case, the early-adopted Romanian orphan group blended into the Canadian-born control group, while the late-adopted Romanians lagged behind. Even the timeframes were similar in each case. Rutter divided early- and late-adopted groups at the six-month mark, while the Canadian study used less than four months and more than eight months to make the same division. Though the Canadian study includes a gap in ages as a result, the break still pivots neatly around the six-month period, with a buffer of two months on either side. Might there, then, be a connection between the two variables?

It seems plausible. Stress diverts resources away from the body's more far-sighted developmental tasks. And that first year is a hectic time for a child's brain, as synapses flare to life one after another and dendrites sprout up like weeds after a thunderstorm. Brain growth in humans is front-loaded; roughly 90 percent of the neurons we possess are generated within the first three years of our lives. By the time a child is a toddler, her brain is already three-quarters of its adult size. Every second in that critical timeframe bursts with activity. Yet humans are nothing if not flexible, and even children deprived of their first six months of highly productive brain growth can eventually close the gap between themselves and their more fortunate, uninterrupted peers. Considering the relentless pace of neural development, this comeback is truly remarkable, a testament to the phenomenal plasticity of the infant brain. Yet even the most pliant material can only be stretched so far. After six months of no affection, attention, or neural stimulation, the brain's once forgiving, pliant folds begin to stiffen up permanently. Change becomes more difficult. After a year, over a third of the young mind's potential for accelerated growth has been squandered. Neurons slow their development as the architecture of the brain begins to weaken. Sprouting dendrites starts to seem like a waste of effort. At that point, adoption can only partially undo the damage done to the child's stimulus-starved brain. By the time the brain realizes it has moved to a new, far more nurturing environment, many of its neurons have already called it quits.

But stress offsets more than just neural development. It is as much a physiological response as a mental response, and the HPA axis' warning cry echoes across every corner of the body. Virtually no system is left unaffected; cells are either marshalled into service or subjected to temporary austerity measures, their supplies rationed to better support the troops on the ground. In a healthy body, these sanctions are lifted as soon as the threat is gone, and the cells engaged in the heat of the conflict return to regular civilian duty. But if the siren cries too often, its warning shrill and unrelenting, those cells have more and more trouble relaxing after the passing of each threat. Austerity measures remain in partial effect, depriving the non-combatant cells of the supplies they need to perform their duties effectively. The body becomes locked in a cold war with a mysterious and largely unseen enemy, an invisible threat looming perpetually overhead. Cells, overtaxed and underfed, put less effort into their jobs or stop working altogether. Some even turn mutinous, inciting an autoimmune disorder, the physiological equivalent of treason. In this state of endless red alert, mind and body suffer alike — the two, after all, are really one and the same.

ACE

The enormous and pioneering ACE (Adverse Childhood Experiences) study, an ongoing project responsible for bridging the gulf in medical knowledge between childhood stress and adult sickness, sprouted from humble and unlikely roots. Dr. Vincent Felitti, the study's founder and principal investigator, was simply trying to help people lose weight.

Felitti heads the Department of Preventative Medicine for Kaiser Permanente, a managed care consortium based in Oakland, California. In the 1980s, he helped develop a radical new weight-loss program specializing in extreme cases. The program was an initial success, but it was marred by a vexing and recurring problem. Just when patients were starting to really lose weight and come within sight of their stated goals, they would quit.

"That really drove us nuts," said Felitti. Especially since the patients who quit were almost always doing well, becoming fitter, healthier, and by their own admission feeling better. Quitting made no sense. A few likely left the program for practical reasons — perhaps they moved out of the region or were no longer able to dedicate the necessary time and energy — but far more were driven away by something deeper. The question was, what could it be?

Desperate to reduce his program's rate of attrition, Felitti interviewed each patient who decided to quit. By his own admission, he didn't really know what he was looking for, or what questions to ask. "I did basically a social worker's time-line interview, asking 'what did you weigh when you were born, when you were in kindergarten, sixth grade, if a woman when you began to menstruate,' etcetera ..." Felitti was groping in the dark, hoping his fumbling hands might happen upon an answer.

Somewhere well into a long day of exhaustively detailed interviews, Felitti misspoke. While sitting across from a middle-aged, heavy-set woman, Felitti had meant to ask the question as he'd written it — "How old were you when you became sexually active?" — but instead, perhaps hypnotized by the parallel structure of the many weight-based questions, asked, "How much did you weigh when you first became sexually active?"

"Forty pounds," the woman blurted. "It was with my father." That declaration made, she broke down sobbing.

Felitti was stunned. This was the second case of incest he had come across in 24 years of practice, and it scurried into the light when he had least expected it, during an interview about weight loss. Ten days later, under very similar circumstances, he came across his third. Then his fourth, fifth, and sixth. Soon his tenth, fiftieth, hundredth. After recruiting five other interviewers and speaking to 286 patients determined to quit his program despite their success, Felitti found that *55 percent of them* reported a history of childhood sexual abuse.

Fifty-five percent is not a statistical blip. Fifty-five percent is a majority. Upon reviewing the data, Felitti's initial response was one of self-doubt. "I remember strongly feeling this really can't be true. People would know. Someone would've told me in medical school." Yet the data was undeniable.

Felitti presented his findings to the Centers for Disease Control in Atlanta. They were unconvinced by Felitti's modest sample size and fairly casual research methods, but encouraged him to pursue the link in a larger and more epidemiologically sound study. Luckily, Felitti had the resources to do just that. Kaiser Permanente's Department of Preventive Medicine, which Felitti headed, provided comprehensive biomedical, psychological, and social evaluation to 56,000 patients a year. And because of the clinic's proactive, questionnaire-based treatment plan, gathering the family history and current medical data of each patient was simple. However, in order to take on a project of such magnitude, Felitti needed more than patients and records and a medical facility. He needed a partner. It didn't take long for him to find one in Dr. Robert Anda.

Dr. Anda's interests lay slightly outside of the medical mainstream. In an era when genes and germs were increasingly considered the origin of all illness, Anda focused on the psychosocial causes of poor health. He lamented the fact that modern medicine seemed to ignore the "lower" functions of the brain — its emotional and unconscious responses — in favour of the "higher," more abstract-thinking cerebral cortex. Anda felt such a preference was needlessly divisive. The brain is not simply a connection of isolated parts; it is a network of highly synchronized chemical impulses. And just as the higher and lower brain are one, so too are the brain and body. When he learned about Felitti's proposed study and the link it sought to discover between childhood trauma and adult illness, he was immediately onboard.

Like Felitti, Anda felt betrayed by his medical background, as if he had deliberately been left in the dark on an enormous and critical aspect of epidemiology. "This was stunning to me," he said of the ACE study results. "Nobody taught me that in medical school. I felt like I should have known that. I felt stupid. I felt horrible. Why didn't I know this? Because nobody ever taught me to ask about it. We should know this about everybody we encounter in health and human services." Anda saw this omission as a terrible weakness in medical teaching, and he and Felitti sought, through their studies, to correct it.

Felitti and Anda developed a strong and highly productive working relationship. Together, the two researchers devised a study model with which they could observe, tabulate, and analyze the relationship between patients' past trauma and present illness. They recruited over 17,000 members of the Kaiser Permanente Health Plan, all of whom live in the relatively affluent San Diego County. Each participant filled out an exhaustive questionnaire chronicling their medical histories, family background, and any cases of childhood trauma. The definition of "childhood trauma" was not left vague. It needed robust, rigidly defined contours to sustain the crushing weight of scientific scrutiny. Thus Felitti and Anda sheathed their theory in a protective epistemological carapace called the Adverse Childhood Experiences score.

An Adverse Childhood Experience is very much what it sounds like: an incident in childhood traumatic enough to have long-term ramifications on a child's physical and mental health. Felitti and Anda identified 10 types of ACEs, which they divided into three groups. The first group, household dysfunction, was the biggest, comprising five of the 10 ACEs: substance abuse, divorce, mental illness, having a battered mother, and criminal behaviour. The second group, abuse, was subdivided into psychological, physical, and sexual varieties. The third group, neglect, could be either emotional or physical. The presence of any one of these ACEs in a person's childhood added one point to their ACE score. How often the ACE occurred didn't matter; once was enough to earn you a point, and the same ACE, even if it occurred every day, could accrue no additional points. A person's score, therefore, could be as low as zero and as high as 10.

The ACE study's participants, it should be noted, were not by and large underprivileged people. Most of them lived in nice neighbourhoods and came from solidly middle-class backgrounds. Only 6 percent of them had not completed high school, while almost 40 percent were college or university graduates. Both Felitti and Anda, while giving separate presentations on the findings of the ACE study, stressed that these people were not outliers drudged up from the fringes of society, track marks darkening their arms and matted grey beards covering crooked yellow smiles. They were our friends and neighbours, our teachers and plumbers and shopkeepers, our mothers and sisters and sons.

Among the participants of Felitti and Anda's study, *only 33 percent* received an ACE score of zero, meaning they had experienced none of the 10 adverse childhood experiences mentioned on the questionnaire. That means two-thirds of the population of the ACE study experienced at least one adverse childhood experience while growing up. Twenty-six percent of participants had an ACE score of one, 16 percent a score of two, 10 percent three, and 16 percent four or more.

And where one ACE occurred, more were likely to follow. Felitti and Anda noted a phenomenon they called clustering, where having one ACE dramatically increased a person's odds of having another. The severity of this increase varied from ACE to ACE. For instance, if your father beat your mother while you were a child, awarding you the highly dubious honour of a "battered mother" ACE, you also have a 95 percent chance of having experienced one other ACE, an 82 percent chance of having two additional ACEs, and a 52 percent chance of having *five or more additional ACEs*, giving you an ACE score of between 6 and 10. Put simply, one in every two children whose mother was abused will also, in their childhood, have experienced over five additional forms of abuse, neglect, or household dysfunction. Though terribly upsetting, there is a cold logic to this finding; very rarely does dad hit mom in an otherwise happy, loving, and well-adjusted home.

But ACEs are more than simply checkmarks on a scorecard. Their presence correlates to an alarming array of diseases, conditions, and maladies. Compared to individuals with ACE scores of zero, those who scored four or more were 300 percent more likely to have had a sexually transmitted disease, 500 percent more likely to suffer from alcoholism, 900 percent more likely to be intravenous drug users (meaning they regularly inject drugs like heroin into their bloodstreams), and a staggering *1,700 percent more likely* to have attempted suicide as teenagers.

Nor were the links limited to behavioural disorders like drug addiction, depression, and alcoholism, which we have come to more readily associate with troubled upbringings. ACEs, it seemed, were highly versatile saboteurs, gleefully throwing wrenches into any system they came across. The breadth and severity of their influence is jaw-dropping. Having two ACEs, as opposed to zero, doubles your chances of suffering from autoimmune disorders like rheumatoid arthritis. Each ACE a person has increases their risk of liver disease by 20 to 60 percent, heart disease by 30 to 70 percent, and drug abuse by 100 to 300 percent. A person with six or more ACEs is 300 percent more likely to contract lung cancer than a person with none, and will contract the disease an average of 13 years younger.

As the ACE study continues apace, other researchers have taken up Felitti and Anda's mantle, confirming their results and even adding new disorders to the tally. Researchers working outside the ACE study banner have linked early childhood adversity to increased risk of diabetes, hypertension, asthma, and many different cancers, as well as confirming much of Felitti and Anda's previous research. One of the largest of these studies was helmed by Dr. Lital Keinan-Boker, a professor at the University of Haifa in Israel. Dr. Keinan-Boker believed that traumatic experiences, particularly those that involved reduced access to basic resources like food and shelter, increased a person's risk of contracting cancer later in life. To prove it, she needed access to a large data set of people, a significant portion of whom had experienced trauma. And in living memory, one could scarcely fathom a more traumatic occurrence than the Holocaust.

Ideally, Keinan-Boker wanted to compare medical histories of thousands of Holocaust survivors to people of a similar ethnic and socioeconomic background who were lucky enough to have escaped the groping hand of the Third Reich. The trouble was, such data could not be easily obtained. Keinan-Boker didn't have the resources necessary to track down, contact, and retrieve medical histories from thousands of Holocaust survivors. She had to work with what she had available to her.

Luckily, Israel keeps fairly comprehensive medical records, and as a faculty member of a prominent Israeli university, Keinan-Boker had access to them. She compiled medical data on over 300,000 Jewish citizens who emigrated from Europe to Israel during the 20th century, dividing the cohort into two groups. The first contained only Jews who had left Europe before or during the height of the Second World War. This was the non-exposed group, as Keinan-Boker reasoned that any Jew capable of emigrating from Europe while the continent roiled under Hitler's rule could not likely have been interred in a concentration camp. The second group — the exposed, as she called them — emigrated after the war was over. The medical data did not explicitly state whether or not an individual had lived in a concentration camp, but any Jew who spent the entire war under Hitler's rule, Keinan-Boker reasoned, was almost certainly subject to physical and emotional hardship of some kind. Even if they'd gone undiscovered, the anxiety of living under the filthy shadow of Hitler's deplorable Final Solution would certainly have had longstanding psychological — and physiological — implications.

When comparing the two groups, Keinan-Boker found cancer rates to be significantly higher in the exposed group. This fact alone confirmed her hypothesis, but subdividing the groups based on their ages yielded even more interesting results. In every age bracket, exposed Jews (those who lived in Europe throughout the war) were more likely than their non-exposed peers (those who emigrated) to contract cancer. However, the relative risk of exposure varied depending on a person's age. Among men born between 1920 and 1924, exposure to European living conditions during the height of Hitler's anti-Semitic fervour increased one's risk of cancer by 17 percent. In women born of the same period, the increase was 30 percent. For men and women born between 1935 and 1939 — the period immediately before the war — the risk was 37 percent and 55 percent respectively. An increase compared to those who were already adults when war broke out, if not a terribly dramatic one. But among men and women born during the outbreak of the Second World War, between 1939 and 1945, exposure increased cancer risk by *250 percent and*

133 percent, respectively. Jewish men born and raised in war-torn Europe were more than three times as likely — and women twice as likely — to develop cancer in adulthood as Jews born in similar conditions but spirited away to the safety of Israel.

Why the spike? Think back to another Nazi atrocity, the Dutch Hunger Winter. Those who lived through the ordeal as adults recovered, by and large, after their food supply returned. But among those still in their mothers' wombs, the effect of the famine was far more long-reaching, affecting not just them, but their children and grandchildren.

The Holocaust devastated everyone it touched. Yet the adults who suffered through its terror, hunger, and inhuman cruelty had, at least, the small respite of a sturdy physiological and neurological framework, set in times of relative peace and durable enough to withstand even the most egregious of conditions. Their minds and bodies, ravaged though they were by terror and torture and imprisonment, were still fully developed, and thus capable of fixing much of the damage wrought by their egregious mistreatment. The building may have been razed by deprivation, malice, and despair, but the foundation beneath it remained solid.

The cohort born into the Holocaust never had the same chance. Their tiny bodies faced hardship before they'd so much as drawn their first breath. Once they were born, fear and hunger defined their lives. Their earliest memories consisted of weeping mothers, skeletal men with sunken eyes, jackbooted soldiers with cold stares and savage smiles. Their parents were (understandably) less able to buffer their young children's exposure to the stressors all around them. In short, their young children's ACE scores were off the charts. Their neurological foundations were bashed, shattered, and trodden upon before the synaptic cement had even dried. With damaged foundations, even the hardiest building will find it difficult to stand.

The High Cost of Cortisol

As enlightening, fruitful, and remarkably consistent as the ACE studies and their ilk have been in describing the link between childhood adversity and adult illness, they are unable to provide any real explanation as to how the former causes the latter. As retrospective observational studies, they lack the tools necessary to bridge the chasm between correlation and causation. They can prove unequivocally that adverse childhood experiences are connected to an increased risk of heart disease, cancer, depression, drug abuse, suicide, autoimmune disorders, and liver disease, but they can't say for sure that those experiences *caused* them. Indeed, the ACE study still gets flak for its backward-looking, self-reporting design. Felitti and Anda take their participants on their word, a practice that is actually more reliable than you might think. It simply requires a lot of attention to detail. Felitti found that surveys yielded far more open and honest responses than face-to-face interviews, and the sacrosanct confidentiality of their medical records made participants much less hesitant to open up. Yet for all their planning, Felitti and Anda's study remains, in some ways, limited.

However, the ACE study hasn't occurred in a vacuum. Outside research bolsters Felitti and Anda's claim by producing culprits that could, conceivably, be responsible for converting childhood stress into adult disease. The prime suspect is cortisol, and the evidence against the accused steroid is damning. We've already mentioned a few of the many studies showing that stress leads to a prolonged elevation of cortisol levels in the bloodstream — the orphans of Romania are perhaps the most extreme example — so we know that adverse childhood experiences are sure to produce a lot of it. But cortisol is like salt, or iron, or even water — vital in proper quantities, but deadly in excess. We need cortisol to make sure our HPA axis maintains its proper alignment, but keep too much of it around for too long and it becomes nasty stuff indeed.

In unchecked amounts, cortisol increases the risk of diabetes, hyperthyroidism, and obesity. It reduces bone density, leaving you vulnerable to osteoporosis. It increases the level of lipids in your blood, raising your cholesterol and weakening your heart's ability to pump blood through your body. It deregulates digestion, promoting your risk of gastrointestinal disease and allowing digestive acid to eat away at your stomach lining, causing ulcers. It shrinks connective tissue, lowering your muscle tone and exposing your joints to the ravages of arthritis. It suppresses your immune system, leaving you vulnerable to barbarian hordes of invading bacteria. It bores its way into the hippocampus, damaging your short-term memory and putting you at risk of developing Alzheimer's. But it does not limit its neurological meddling to the hippocampus. Though we are as yet unsure of the exact mechanisms at play, elevated cortisol levels have been linked to panic disorders, depression, alcoholism, obsessive compulsive disorder, suicide, and other mental disorders.

In short, cortisol can and does cause many of the problems seen in dizzying numbers among adults with high ACE scores. Again, we must stress that correlation is not causation. However, if we know that a) cortisol causes these problems, b) people with high ACE scores are more likely to have these problems, and c) early childhood stress (as caused by ACEs) leads to sustained above-average levels of cortisol in the bloodstream, then the connection between ACEs and cortisol, if not yet scientifically proven, at least merits contemplation and further study.

With such an exhaustive and egregious list of offences, you may wonder why we've deigned to suffer cortisol to gallivant unimpeded through our bloodstreams as long as we have. The short answer is we really have no choice. At desirable levels, cortisol is a key component in the network of transmitters, receptors, and feedback loops responsible for keeping us alive.

Indeed, having too *little* cortisol is almost as bad as having too much. This seemingly paradoxical notion forms the crux of Drs. Gregory Miller and Edith Chen's theory on the mechanisms that translate young trauma into old disease.

Chen and Miller are professors of clinical psychology at Northwestern University in Evanston, Illinois. They're also husband and wife. Together, they've blazed trails beyond those first laid by Anda and Felitti, venturing past the forest of correlation and into the murky, theoretical mires of causality. They've charted their journey with great detail, gradually mapping the path that leads childhood trauma to adult disease. The link, they argue, is all about inflammation.

From a layman's viewpoint, it seems like a bold and bizarre claim. We tend to associate inflammation with symptoms that are temporary, irritating, and often cosmetic. Conditions like headaches and black eyes and acne. These hardly seem like the bitter, caustic roots from which cancer, heart disease, and diabetes stem. But inflammation is not limited to puffy eyes and swollen ankles, or to more serious but still well-known inflammatory diseases like bronchitis and meningitis. Indeed, inflammation isn't even always a problem. Like so many diseases, chronic inflammation is the result of a very good thing gone bad.

When properly regulated, inflammation is a critical part of our immune system's response to injury or infection. By engorging a wounded or infected area with fluid, our body provides a protective cushion of blood or pus or plasma. Simultaneously, the increased blood flow promotes healing and increases the presence of white blood cells, which keep invading bacteria at bay. This is a very useful thing in the event of injury. However, inflammation is fairly energy intensive, which is why cortisol — the HPA axis' first responder to stress — acts as an anti-inflammatory agent. In an attack, the body's first priority is short-term survival, and cortisol reacts accordingly, depleting our glucose stores in order to fuel the brain, heart, and major muscle groups and putting our many support systems, including our immune system, on hold. Once the immediate threat has been dealt with, cortisol dials itself down through a negative feedback loop, allowing the immune system to go about repairing any tissue injured in the stress-inducing fight-or-flight.

But if cortisol reduces inflammation and toxic stress causes a surplus of cortisol, then how can disease caused by toxic stress be the result of chronic inflammation? Should the opposite not be true? Shouldn't toxic stress cause, if anything, an impotent and ineffective immune system response? The answer is no, and there are two major reasons why not.

The first is, admittedly, nitpicky. Toxic stress doesn't *always* cause a surplus of cortisol. Sometimes it actually causes a deficiency. Scientists have yet to parse the exact causes of this distinction, but it has been observed in a number of conditions, most vexingly post-traumatic stress disorder (PTSD). Sufferers of PTSD are disproportionally likely to have a cortisol imbalance, but while some studies find it to be a surplus, others instead see a deficit. Excessively high doses of cortisol can indeed cause any number of physiological disorders, but the true cost of toxic stress isn't surplus or deficiency, but imbalance. An engine won't run if it doesn't have enough power, but if it gets too much power and overheats, the result is, from a certain angle, the same.[39] Too much or too little, the engine doesn't run.

This leads to our second answer, which is the explanation favoured by Chen and Miller. To discuss it, however, we need to understand how the immune system works.

The Front Lines

When a part of the body is bruised, scraped, cut, punctured, burned, poisoned, or beset by roving bands of malicious bacteria, viruses, or parasites, it sends an urgent message to the immune system requesting help. Think of it as your finger, shin, or kidney dialing 911. The immune system, receiving the body's urgent call for assistance, dispatches leukocytes (more commonly known as white blood cells) to the affected area.

Leukocytes are not a homogenous group of cells, but a general class of microscopic entities responsible for healing injuries and protecting your body from invasion. We tend to use the term "white blood cells" as if it referred to a highly specific job — the bacteria police, say — but leukocytes are more like first responders, a group of support personnel with unique skill sets and responsibilities, but a common goal. Just as 911 often dispatches police officers, paramedics, and firefighters to an emergency, the immune system sends a full corps of white blood cells[40] to deal with whatever problems the scene of the injury presents them with. Some produce antibodies, which latch onto harmful bacteria and mark them for extermination. Some carry out that extermination. Some reconstruct damaged cells and promote healing. And some release protein molecules called cytokines that inflame the injured tissue. By causing inflammation, white blood cells dilate the surrounding capillaries, improving blood flow and allowing leukocyte reinforcements quicker and less impeded access to the affected area.

The leukocytes responsible for inflammation are called macrophages, tiny amorphous cells whose other task is devouring and deconstructing bacteria. Macrophages will continue to release "pro-inflammatory" cytokines until the brain tells them to stop. Because white blood cells are independent agents capable of moving about the body, one cannot communicate with them through the nervous system. They are itinerant cells, and the nervous system is our body's landline. Without a fixed address, leukocytes must communicate in a different manner. They speak a language of hormones transmitted by the body's endocrine system, a network of glands that secrete their chemical missives and send them, often via the bloodstream, to their intended targets. And when the body needs to tell its white blood cells to stop producing cytokines, what hormone does it turn to? Our good friend cortisol.

Mobilized by the adrenal glands and triggered by a cascade of hormonal telegraphs flowing along the HPA axis, cortisol swarms white blood cells and binds with their glucocorticoid receptors, shutting down the production of cytokines. Once cortisol levels drop, the white blood cells resume the production of cytokine and inflammation continues apace until the wound is healed. However, if white blood cells are constantly beleaguered by cortisol, their glucocorticoid receptors grow callused and dull. After too much wear and tear, the receptors lose the ability to bind with cortisol, locking the affected white blood cells in the ON position.

At first blush, this seems like a fairly short-term problem. Individual cells break down all the time. Even the comparatively long-lived macrophages don't last more than a few months. Even if an entire fleet of white blood cells becomes trapped in inflammation overdrive, the next generation should take over for their deranged forbearers and resume a more balanced course of action, right?

Unfortunately not. Just as infancy is a time of unparalleled neural plasticity, so too does it chart the life course of the body's regulatory functions, including the immune system. Changes in hormone levels, sculpted in early childhood by stress, eventually crystallize into lifelong physiological behaviours. Stress might make the initial imprints, but what force holds them in place for 20 or 40 or 50 years? The evidence increasingly points to epigenetics.

Some of this evidence we've seen already. Think back to Szyf and Meaney, the Montreal researchers whose studies examined the effects of maternal licking and grooming behaviour on the stress response of infant rats. Invariably, rats who received above-average licking, grooming, and arched-back nursing (LG-ABN) from their mothers had efficient, well-balanced responses to stress. Their bodies responded normally in the face of danger, but when the threat departed so too did their hammering hearts, high blood pressure, and elevated levels of cortisol. They were also more confident than typical rodents, less fazed by novel environments, and unafraid to explore their surroundings. Meanwhile, rats whose mothers licked and groomed them less frequently grew into trembling, craven adults. Cortisol flooded their bodies at the slightest threat and skulked around their bloodstreams long after it was no longer needed.

Aside from their behavioural differences, rats born of low and high licking and grooming mothers also exhibited different patterns of epigenetic imprinting. Significantly, low LG-ABN rats developed methyl tags on their glucocorticoid receptor genes. Glucocorticoid receptors are the switches that allow cortisol to shut down inflammation. But receptors, like everything else in the body, undergo continuous wear and tear. In order to secure a steady supply of new and well-functioning parts, the genes that make them need to be switched on and running. But if those genes are methylated, and hence unable to produce receptors, then our white blood cells lose the ability to cut off the flow of pro-inflammatory cytokines. More cytokines means more inflammation, and more inflammation means a host of trouble in the years to come.

Though confirmed ad nauseam in rodent studies, stress-induced epigenetic change has been scarcely documented in humans. The reason for this is not that we've looked for it and failed to find anything, but that our ability to look is compromised by the highly invasive nature of the search. We're sad to say that the rodent participants in Meaney and Szyf's studies are not allowed a relaxed and well-earned retirement upon completion of their duties. Their service ends beneath a scalpel blade.

The trouble lies in the nature of epigenetic change. When researchers study an organism's genes, a single cell is all they require. In many cases, the type of cell doesn't even matter. A hair, a flake of skin, or a drop of blood will suffice. Even a cotton swab rubbed against the inside of one's cheek can collect enough cellular material to effectively genotype an individual. After all, every cell in our body is genetically identical.[41] Chart one cell's genome and you have a reliable genetic roadmap of every neuron, leukocyte, and skin cell in your body.

The same cannot be said of the epigenome. A brain cell and a liver cell may be genetically identical, but epigenetically, they are completely different. In fact, epigenetics is the *reason* that they're different. When sperm and egg meet to form the initial cell from which we are formed, every tool in our newly acquired chromosomal toolbox is polished and ready to go. But as our nascent bodies become more complex, individual cells begin to specialize. They keep the tools they need to do their jobs available and lock the rest away, lest their tiny workspace become unduly cluttered. Epigenetic tags are the locks that keep these unused tools in place. Without them, every cell would be doing every job all at once, and nothing would end up actually getting accomplished.

The more cells divide and grow and specialize, the more varied and idiosyncratic each individual epigenome becomes. In order to verify an epigenetic change in a specific cell, you need unimpeded access to the cell in question. Looking for signs of epigenetic change in a blood sample means little if the epigenome you're interested in is located in the brain.

Meaney and Szyf found a way around this. They wanted to confirm that the epigenetic changes impacting their rats were occurring in a similar manner in humans. Since live humans were out of the question, they had to resort to dead ones. The two researchers recruited — or perhaps acquired would be a better term — 36 cadavers, 24 of which belonged to individuals who committed suicide. Of the suicide group, 12 had experienced physical and emotional abuse in childhood and 12 had not. Meaney and Szyf divided the suicide group accordingly, into abused and non-abused subgroups. The remaining 12 participants formed their own group, which acted as a control. These individuals died sudden, accidental deaths, and had no history of abuse, childhood trauma, or major mood disorders.

Meaney and Szyf took a sample of each participant's hippocampus — a long, narrow section of the midbrain strongly affected by stress — and checked the patterns of methylation present on their glucocorticoid receptor genes. In rats, an upbringing devoid of licking and grooming is akin to emotional abuse. Rat pups that are infrequently licked and groomed by their mothers develop physiological problems and temperaments roughly analogous to human children subject to emotional abuse and neglect, and both groups have similar issues with overactive stress response systems. It stood to reason, then, that under-stimulated rats and abused humans would show similar patterns of methylation on their glucocorticoid receptor genes, which are an important part of regulating stress response.

As it turned out, that was very much the case. Compared to the control group, who died in accidents and showed no signs of depression or other emotional problems, members of the abused suicide cohort displayed four times as much methylation of their glucocorticoid receptor genes.[42] The non-abused suicides, meanwhile, showed only slightly more methylation than the control group, proving that the emotional tumult preceding suicide was not the culprit. Childhood abuse alone caused the unique epigenetic pattern.

These results, though accrued through tragedy, allow us an incredible step forward in our understanding of human development. It wasn't just that the glucocorticoid genes of rats and humans were both methylated, but that they were methylated *in exactly the same places*. The connection, thought to exist for many years now, can finally be seen.

The Trouble with Inflammation

Stress in childhood sets in motion a vicious cycle of inflammation, illness, and self-destructive behaviour. Exposure to toxic stress tweaks a child's stress response system, causing an influx of cortisol and shorting out their immune systems. Eventually, this maladaptive response gets embedded in our genes and held in place by epigenetic markings. These physiological changes, wrought by early childhood stress, beget emotional and behavioural changes. Children poisoned by toxic stress are often mistrustful and impulsive, prone to perceiving threat or anger in situations where it doesn't exist, and quicker to respond in kind. Their brains shift and change, their corticolimbic circuitry rewired into patterns more conducive to suspicion and aggression and less conducive to communication and forming meaningful social relationships. This, understandably, shapes the way they behave, the people they associate with, and how others perceive them. They are more likely to smoke, drink, pop, snort, shoot, and ingest their drug or drugs of choice. They participate in, suffer from, and bear witness to more violent behaviour. They eat to excess, don't exercise, and become obese in greater numbers than their well-adjusted peers. These behaviours don't just beget violence, addiction, and crime. They beget cortisol. The corrosive hormone floods their veins, further taxing their already underproductive glucocorticoid receptors. Inflammation continues apace, and their tissues function in a state of constant damage control. The swelling never ceases, the tissue never heals.

Inflammation leads to high blood pressure, increased fatty deposits, and a buildup of plaque in arteries, all of which increase a person's risk of suffering a heart attack or stroke. It interferes with glucose levels and promotes the development of diabetes. It weakens muscle, softens bone, and corrupts neurons.

The more active an immune system is, the worse its discretion becomes. White blood cells, after years of endless struggle, suffer from a cellular equivalent of PTSD. They begin to see threats where they don't exist, turning on the body and causing any number of autoimmune disorders. More frustrating still, they lose sight of legitimate threats they should be attacking. Inflamed tissue is weak and prone to damage, and damaged cells are particularly likely to become cancerous. Inflammation throws the immune system into chaos, providing cancer with an opportunity to mutate and breed undetected. Our white blood cells, busy with the emergency response of fighting infection and repairing tissue, lose the ability to spot and respond to cancer's subtler, more insidious threat. And once tumours have begun to take root, a steady supply of blood flow to and from the inflamed area allows them to migrate easily to other parts of the body.

Putting the Puzzle Together

The evidence is clear. Parenting matters. The events that occur during children's first few years echo down the corridors of their lives, resonating in every chamber of their being and reverberating in generations to come. Famine, fear, abuse, and neglect cast long shadows across the lives of the afflicted, while the light of love, kindness, and support cuts through the deepest gloom.

The mechanisms driving these interactions are complex, and we've done our best to explain some difficult biological and psychological concepts. And much about the human body, particularly the murky electrochemical depths of the mind, remains only partially understood even to the scientists who have devoted their lives to studying them.

Researchers from across disciplines and around the globe are working tirelessly to assemble the grand epidemiological puzzle of child development, but the task is not an easy one. We've only just traced the edges, studiously linking one piece to the next and establishing that the puzzle's disparate sections — genes, methyl tags, parent-child attachment, early environment — are really connected. Yet the hardest work still remains. Within the borders of our multidisciplinary puzzle sits a great dark void. Intrepid scientists have placed a few small clusters here and there, hinting at a bigger image, but the main task remains far from complete. Pieces lie in disarray around the table, and we fear some may be missing entirely, stuck behind a couch cushion or swept accidentally into the trash. But the researchers keep at it, picking up two pieces and pressing them together experimentally to see if they connect. Often they don't; but every once in a while our studious puzzle solvers find a match.

Dr. Felitti touched obesity to abuse accidentally and let out a gasp of shock when they linked. Van IJzendoorn and Bakermans-Kranenburg united disorganized attachment and unresolved loss after frightening behaviour didn't fit, despite how neatly their tongue-and-groove appeared, at first glance, to match. Meaney and Szyf merged rodent maternal grooming with rat pup stress response, then amended epigenetics to the cluster.

Dutifully they toil, heads bent to the task, conferring and trading pieces and occasionally stepping away from their seat to observe other parts of the board. With your nose mere inches from the table, it's easy to get absorbed in the task, to consider your small cluster of variables to comprise their own isolated nucleus, but take a few steps away from the table and the truth becomes clear: everything's connected.

Conclusions

"*There can be no keener revelation of a society's soul than the way it treats its children.*"
— NELSON MANDELA

Chapter 11

Returning to the Realm of Relationships

———————————————————————

We've ventured far afield over the last 10 chapters, tracing the strange and exotic fringes of scientific study, crossing the borders of academic disciplines with impunity, and documenting the many wonders and curios unearthed by the great intellectual explorers currently charting the mysterious and largely unknown lands of child development. We hope you've enjoyed the journey, but the time has come to return home to our families, light a fire in the hearth, pour ourselves a glass of red wine, and reflect on the many wondrous things we've seen.

From the outset, we stressed that this was not, in the strictest sense, a parenting book. We have no interest in dictating your behaviour, and can provide no 10 Easy Steps or Foolproof Formula for Parenting Success. Our aim was, and is, to inform, not command. We sought to answer the *whys* and *hows* implicitly whispered in the wake of conventional parenting advice, to pull back the curtain and reveal the mechanics of child development, the high-reactive genes and epigenetic tags and neural wiring behind the glossy tips on parent-infant bonding.

After writing an entire book expounding upon the irreducible complexity of child development, we could not in good conscience boil parenting down to a few pithy rules. With so many complex, interdependent components, such a multitude of variables and eccentricities, a one-size-fits-all approach to parenting is clearly wrongheaded. But that doesn't mean that parenting is nothing more than an exercise in blind luck in the face of chaos. It simply means that you can't go out and buy a guidebook telling you how to parent your child; you have to write the book yourself. Sound daunting? It's not, really. After all, you're going to get a lot of help writing it. Not from professionals or parenting experts, but from your child.

Even before they can talk or even say a few words, babies communicate their needs. Crying and temper tantrums are the most obvious examples, but infants also show pleasure, happiness, and affection through smiles, laughter, wide-eyed focus, and furtive attempts to grab or touch. Understanding and responding to these signals is called sensitivity, and it is arguably the most important skill in a parent's repertoire.

Patricia Crittenden, attachment theorist and developer of the Dynamic Maturational Model of attachment discussed in an earlier chapter, emphasizes the importance of parental sensitivity, which she defines as "any pattern of behaviour that pleases the infant, increases its comfort and attentiveness, and reduces its distress." Sensitivity is not a specific behaviour, but a state of adaptability. Not a set action, but an engaged and dynamic interaction between parent and child, a positive feedback loop that nourishes both parties. Good parenting isn't just good for the child — it's good for the parent, too.

Fostering Sensitivity

The parent-child bond begins early in life. Its first links are forged while the child is still in the womb. At that stage it may seem that parents can do little to foster their child's develop-ment besides paying attention to the food they eat, the air they breathe, and the stress they face on a daily basis, but there are important steps they can take beyond that. Learn about par-enting. Talk to other parents you know about their experiences. Gather a support network of friends, family, and professionals. Avoid overburdening yourself or taking on too much responsi-bility at work or home.

Once the child is born, take time to recover. This is no easy task with a newborn at home, but it can be accomplished with a little foresight, deft planning, and a supportive circle of family and friends. Don't be afraid to ask for help, as this is one time in your life when people will be particularly willing to lend a hand. Child-rearing has long been a communal endeavour, and many societies — particularly pre-industrial ones — understand the importance of rearing not just one's own child, but all the chil-dren in one's community. After all, they are the ones who will one day harvest your food, make your goods, and protect your village from warring tribes and predators.

Of course, though a child can never have too much extra-familial support, yours is still the role of primary caregiver, with all the privileges and responsibilities that entails. Respond to your child's cries quickly and consistently. Pay attention to milestones and give your child the opportunity to meet them. Language skills are important from an early age, as are fine and gross motor skills and sensory perception. There are many books available that provide detailed breakdowns of children's stages of growth and exercises and games that help develop these skills. However, the most important thing is to stay alert to your child's likes and dislikes, and not to get discouraged if he falls a month or two behind his prescribed developmental itinerary. Children aren't clockwork beings, and any milestone they will reach is, at best, only an approximation.

Watch your child closely to see what activities really capture his attention. Once you find some that work, do them. But don't *overdo* them. Newborns dive headfirst into a world that is, to them, strange and loud and bright and entirely new. Sights and sounds and smells and tastes and textures crowd them at every turn. They need time to experience, explore, and engage with these novel sensations, but they also need time to lie back and process them. Pushing a child too hard can actually slow down their learning, as their brains become mired in a backflow of excess information and lack the neural infrastructure necessary to deal with it all. If your baby seems tired or disengaged, let him rest.

Perhaps the trickiest part is learning your child's tastes. Though they can seem, to an outside observer, pretty interchangeable in their early months, babies really do have distinct tastes, personalities, and preferences. They simply lack the ability to tell you about them directly. Despite this roadblock, babies can make their preferences clear. You just need to get to know them a little bit first. Try things like massaging your infant, carrying them on walks, or ample face-to-face time on your lap. Until they learn to grasp and explore objects, toys aren't really necessary. Nothing pleases an infant more than direct interaction with a parent.

When the child is around six months old, the more complex flavours of their personalities begin to emerge. You can leave them be a little more, attend to their cries less immediately, and give them opportunities to entertain and to soothe themselves. If things are going well and your parent-child relationship is successfully strengthening, your child should be able to maintain an alert, calmly focused state for increasingly long periods of time.

A strong parent-child relationship pays dividends in a child's intellectual and emotional development throughout her entire life. What's more, it calibrates her burgeoning stress response system. Remember that, for at least the first six months of a child's life, parents are the only defence from, and source of, toxic stress. Such responsibility is both daunting and liberating. It puts the onus on parents to provide for, interact with, and care about their children, but so too does it rob the genetic and socioeconomic determinists of their power. Genes and poverty and divorce and job stress may all make parenting harder than it would otherwise be, but they alone do not have the power to hurt your child; they have to get through you first.[43]

Stress and Support

Making a child from scratch — *truly* from scratch, handpicking each nucleotide and individually wiring each neuron — is impossible, and perhaps always will be. Luckily, humans come equipped with a prefabricated child mix — a sort of genetic Bisquick, if you'll indulge our admittedly bizarre image — called gametes, or sex cells. Simply combine sperm and egg and the mixture is ready to cook.

The obvious extension of this metaphor would be bake for nine months in a mother's amniotic oven and remove a risen, fully developed baby. But the process is neither that tidy nor that controlled. People don't have a "cooking" period and a "done" period. People are always cooking. The process contains periods of greater activity, of course, and displays a general slowing trend as individuals age. But it never truly stops. Environmental effects are dynamic and cumulative and all too often out of our control. We cannot help the families we are born into, the genes we inherit, or the unforeseen obstacles that blindside us on the road of life. Other factors can be controlled to a certain degree — our finances, our lifestyles, our diets, our jobs, etc. — but exert their own force on us as well, necessitating a certain amount of give and take. Only a fortunate few of us have the time, energy, and financial means necessary to shape our lives into their precise, ideal form, to quit our jobs on a whim or buffer ourselves from the slightest stress.

These same restraints influence the way we raise our children. We often don't have time to make the home-cooked meals we want to make, or the luxury of a full-time stay-at-home parent, or the financial means to provide an elite education or plethora of extracurricular activities. These are all nice things if you have access to them, but fortunately they are not necessities. Far from it. The most important ingredient in child development is, fortuitously, one that every mother and father has in abundant supply: love.

Sounds quaint, doesn't it? When we say love, we're not simply referring to some lazy platitude, but to the physical and emotional manifestations of that emotion. Emotional availability. Attentiveness. Encouragement. Effort. Paying attention. Taking time together. Trying to adapt to your child's changing tastes, needs, and interests. These are the tools of the successful parent's trade, and every mother and father has a full set at their disposal. And even if you have trouble keeping up with the Joneses, if you lack the newest and flashiest equipment, those humble tools in your standard-issue parenting toolbox are all you need to build a healthy, happy, well-adjusted child.

However, though these basic parenting tools are available to everyone, the skill and drive necessary to effectively use them are less universally accessible. In 2010, my research team performed a substantial meta-analysis examining the effect of socioeconomic status on children's behavioural and intellectual development — in short, if and how low income, single-parenthood, minimal parental education, and other factors associated with poverty affected the way children learned and grew.

A meta-analysis is a large-scale study in which the results of numerous smaller studies are collected, analyzed, and synthesized, distilling their many angles, perspectives, and nuances into a single comprehensive report. Beginning with a pool of over 250,000 academic articles, we sent our data through a rigorous screening process, filtering out redundancies and irrelevancies until we were left with a highly concentrated serum of 33 papers representing, in effect, every bit of research performed on our particular topic that we could combine statistically. Though time-consuming and complex, meta-analyses allow researchers the most inclusive and up-to-date perspective possible on a given subject, which was precisely what we were after.

Our analysis did suggest a modest correlation between low socioeconomic status and child behavioural problems, but the connection was mostly superficial. Beneath the gritty veneer of poverty lay deeper and more complex causes of disparity. Children of poor families attend worse schools, have fewer books at home, receive less attention from parents who often work longer or more erratic hours while being unable to afford quality childcare, live in rougher areas of town, have fewer strong and positive role models, and witness more abuse, neglect, alcoholism, drug abuse, and violence than do children from more socioeconomically advantaged homes. All of these factors do, statistically speaking, contribute to poorer developmental outcomes. But the biggest contributors, by a wide margin, were emotional support and stress. Socioeconomically disadvantaged people tend to have less of the former and more of the latter, and suffer disproportionately as a result. But while poorer mothers may face these added challenges in greater numbers, they are by no means guaranteed to do so, nor are mothers from more privileged backgrounds guaranteed to successfully avoid them.

Think of parents as the vehicle that drives their children from infancy to adolescence. Qualities such as love, emotional support, commitment, and guidance provide the necessary mechanical components: the engine, drive train, transmission, and so forth. Such parts are vital if you want a car that runs, but they can't get you anywhere on their own. A car also needs gas. Even the most tricked-out sports car on earth can't so much as tour the block without it.

If love is the parent's engine, what constitutes parenting petrol? Support. Not from parents, but *for* parents. Wealthy mothers are more likely than poor mothers to be able to "afford" this gas, as the statistics are often on their side. But like real gasoline, mothers need access to fueling stations in order to fill up, and an emotionally isolated, traumatized, or depressed mother from any socioeconomic background risks running on an empty tank. Nor do all cars get the same mileage, and that expensive Ferrari may very well burn through a tank a lot quicker than a more modest Toyota Corolla. Likewise, a well-to-do mother may have high-sensitive genes that make her more vulnerable to depression and an upbringing emotionally cold enough to exacerbate them, while a low-income mother, despite her financial setbacks, might be better genetically or emotionally equipped for the job.

Scientific evidence confirms what many of us — myself included — have seen in our day-to-day lives. Stress erodes parental quality, but support for parents is the windbreak that halts this process. Though intangible, support is a commodity, and parents need a source they can draw on in order to provide support for their children in turn. You can't give what you don't have, and one of the most common and pervasive problems in "troubled" homes is simply a scarcity of this humble yet all-important resource.

The Return of Resilience

Sophie sits on the couch, the TV bathing her in soft, multi-coloured light. Its volume is turned to a low whisper and its screen flashes images in vain; Sophie pays it no mind. Her focus is on the two-year-old girl asleep in her lap. Elizabeth's small face is lit with a beatific smile. Sophie runs her fingers gently over the crown of her tiny head, eliciting soft, sleepy coos of contentment.

The road back from postpartum depression has been a rough one, but Sophie walks it with great resolve. Her husband's support is endless and unwavering, and co-workers regularly pop by or call to see how she's doing. She took a one-year sabbatical with the school board's blessing and has gradually become better at putting her own needs second only to those of her daughter. The impulse to people please hovers at the fringes of her consciousness, a sinister voice muttering words of discontentment and anxiety, but Sophie has gotten better at tuning it out.

We began this book by talking about resilience, the intangible quality that allows some children to transcend difficult circumstances and succeed in the face of troubled upbringings. But as Sophie's story has shown, resilience is never free; it always comes at a price, and the cost is often steep. Our society values resilience. It is the crux of the American Dream, the engine driving our rags-to-riches narrative arcs. It provides a path upward for children of lesser means, raised in impoverished, neglectful, or even abusive homes, an all-important foothold with which they can drag themselves, inch by inch, into better circumstances. It is a way to keep society fair. But it isn't the only way. It isn't even the best way.

Why do we need resilience? Why can't we have a world where success can come without it? It wouldn't require major structural changes to our economic system or a fundamental redistribution of wealth. It would simply mean providing help to those who need it, when they need it. Doing so would pay dividends not just to parents, but to entire societies. It may sound crass, but children are a kind of social capital. They are investments. A down payment of love and support, bolstered by hard work and a bit of luck, will allow these investments to mature into intelligent, productive, emotionally sound, and socially responsible adults. Skimp on the supply, meanwhile, and the end product will suffer. And just as one must invest in infrastructure in order to have a prosperous society, so too must one invest in its children. They are, after all, the ones who will build and maintain that infrastructure, invent new technologies, heal our ill and injured, and ultimately run our countries. People make a society, not buildings or machines. It only makes sense that we provide the emotional capital they need to flourish.

All You Need Is Love

Much of this book has dealt with the interplay between genes, the environment, and the regulatory body called the epigenome that brokers developmental deals between them. Our goal was — and is — to emphasize the importance of these factors, declaring the supremacy of none of them but instead mapping, through discussion of the latest scientific discoveries, their intertwining influences. Yet our solutions, such as they are, cannot take a similarly nonpartisan approach. When attempting to impact child development, necessity dictates that we favour one side over the other.

In the grand and complex calculation of your existence, the genetic side of the equation is fixed. Your genes don't change, and even your comparatively malleable epigenome is, at present, outside the reach of contemporary medicine. Our focus must remain on the equation's other half: the environment. Here we can make changes, and though the equation's genetic side may remain intractable, its solution can nevertheless benefit from our input.

In an age when every disease from cancer to depression to obesity seems etched at conception into the core of our beings, it is easy to despair, to throw down our oars and set adrift on the currents of genetic determinism to whatever shore our genes choose, be it white sand or trash-strewn dirt. We must reject this impulse. Cycles of violence, addiction, depression, and illness are all too common in our society, but they are not unbreakable; the prophecies that generate them are more often than not self-fulfilling. If a child is told that depression, addiction, violence, or other hardships will form a significant part of his life, the child will operate under that assumption. Its message will colour the way they act, think, and are treated by those around them, which will only reinforce what they've already known about themselves and further entrench them in their abusive or impoverished "destiny."

The message need not be overt; in fact, it seldom is. Rarely are children outright told that they will bear the addictions, abuses, and mental conditions of their parents for the rest of their lives. The suggestion comes to them implicitly through the attitudes and actions of their guardians and peers. Children aren't dumb. They absorb information, intuit meaning, and *mould themselves to expectation* with remarkable skill. That's a scary thought, considering how tumultuous, threatening, and unpredictable the world can be. But as we've already stated, the environment can't reach young children directly. It must first pass through their parents.

Mind you, children interact with their environment from a very early age, and the older they get the less control over their absorption of information parents retain. They will move through life like a powerful electromagnet, attracting truths and mistruths and opinions and observations everywhere they turn. They'll get them from their peers and teachers, from aunts and uncles and family friends, from neighbours and people they see on the street, from billboards and graffiti, from television and radio and the Internet. You can't stop children from acquiring this information, but you can control the way they absorb it. When we say that all the stress that children feel first passes through their parents, we don't mean that they are physically incapable of feeling stress, but that stress can only really dig in its talons if it goes through parents first. Hence the three-tiered stress model offered by the Harvard Center on the Developing Child, a think tank and research group dedicated to educating the public on the dangers of toxic stress. We mentioned this model in chapter 9. Stress isn't the problem. Stress unmitigated by support is.

But what do we mean when we say support? What is it that successful parents provide to their children? Is it attention? Encouragement? Discipline? Education? To a certain extent, yes. But what really matters is relationships. Children need to forge tangible emotional connections to their adult caregivers. The precise nature of these connections will vary from child to child, though of course there will — and should — be some overlap.

Children should never feel alone. Neither should parents. Relationships help on both counts. The more connected we are, the more emotional braces running from person to person, the harder it is to tip us over. This is as true of a community as it is of a family.

Esteemed psychologist Donald Winnicott once stated that there is no such thing as a baby — only a baby and someone else. A bizarre and existential claim, perhaps, but he doesn't mean that a baby is not a tangible entity, or that it somehow exists solely in the minds of its parents. Rather, he means that babies do not become distinct individuals immediately after birth. They wade into personhood gradually, buoyed by the calm and protective waters of family. Long after the umbilical cord is cut, a second, far stronger cord remains. This second cord is the subject of attachment theory, of epigenetic inheritance, of the nature/nurture debate. It is spun from love and kinship, those ethereal fibres, and extends backward through the gener-ations and outward through family, community, country, and, ultimately, the entire planet. We weave relationships from this fibre, and it is a resilient and versatile fabric. From it we can make blankets to keep us warm, tents to keep the rain off of our heads, hot air balloons to lift us to the heavens, and parachutes to save us if we fall.

So listen to your children. And don't fear parenting. It's a complicated process, sure, if you concentrate on the details, a network of intersecting variables and difficult scientific precepts. But at its core, simple truths do, miraculously, hold true. No child ever floundered because they were raised in a warm, nurturing home. Strong positive parent-infant relationships are a panacea capable of staving off the most sinister diseases in childhood and adulthood. Alcoholism, obesity, heart disease, depression, and cancer all stumble before them. These relationships can, and will, stitch together even the most tattered of family environments.

Just give them time.

Acknowledgements

This book would not have been possible without the amazing research completed by dozens of gifted scientists working in psychology, nursing, community health, neuroscience, and medicine, including Miriam Stewart, Thomas and Chess, Gregory Miller, Edith Chen, Robert Anda, Vincent Felitti, Sara Jaffee, Stephen Suomi, Michael Meaney, Moshe Szyf, Lital Keinan-Boker, Marinus Van IJzendoorn, Marian Bakermans-Kranenburg, Patricia Crittenden, Mary Main, John Bowlby, W. Thomas Boyce, Gabor Maté, Donald Winnicott, Bruce Ellis, Marilyn Essex, Christian Caldji, Bruce Perry, Francis Champagne, Ian Weaver, M. Champoux, Judit Gervai, Arie Kaffman, Joan Kaufman, James Li, Mary Ainsworth, Michael Rutter, Emmy Werner, Ruth S. Smith, Marian Diamond, Janet Hopson, Eva Jablonka, Marion J. Lamb, Matt Ridley, David Moore, Lise Eliot, Po Bronson, Ashley Merryman, Richard Francis, Robin Karr-Morse, Meredith S. Wiley, Lane Strathearn, Jane Drummond, Janice Lander, Carmen Gill, Linda Mayes, Nancy Suchman, Clyde Hertzman, Ron Barr, J. Douglas Willms, Fraser Mustard, Dan Offord, Karen Benzies, Tiffany Field, Lynne Murray, Peter Cooper,

Sandra Graham-Berman, Karlen Lyons-Ruth, Peter Fonagy, P.O. Svanberg, Cheryl Tatano-Beck, Kathryn Barnard, Georgina Sumner, Anita Spietz, Bryan Kolb, Bruce McEwan, Leanne Whiteside-Mansell, David Olds, Jay Belsky, Anita Kozyrskyj, and Linda Duffett-Leger.

I also owe a debt of gratitude to many funders, including Norlien Foundation, Alberta Children's Hospital Foundation, New Brunswick Health Research Foundation, Alberta Centre for Child, Family, and Community Health Research, Canadian Institutes of Health Research, Peter Lougheed Foundation, Atlantic Health Sciences Corporation, Faculties of Nursing at University of New Brunswick and the University of Calgary, Canada Research Chairs, Canadian Foundation for Innovation, and CIHR Institute of Neuroscience, Mental Health, and Addiction. Thanks as well to the many, many staff and students who have worked on the projects funded by these sources over the years.

So many organizations have contributed to my understanding of the issues covered in *Scientific Parenting*, including Calgary Public Health (Elizabeth Palmquist, Donna Wallace), Calgary Urban Project Society (Carlene Donnelly, Dean Schroeder), Toronto Public Health (Mary Lou Walker), Peel Public Health (Claudette Bennett, Anne Fenwick, Judy Buchan), New Brunswick Department of Health (Claudette Landry, Sarah Aldous, Ken Ross), Sykes Telecare (Alan Bechervaise, Jim Murphy), Infant Mental Health Promotion — Toronto Sick Kids (Chaya Kulkarni), Alberta Family Wellness Initiative (Paula Tyler, Michelle Gagnon), Alberta Association of Infant Mental Health (Carole Ann Hapschyn), World Association of Infant Mental Health, International Association for the Study of Attachment, Society for Research on Child Development, International Society for Infant Studies, and Frameworks Institute.

Finally, thanks to my family for putting up with my constant refrains about the importance of parenting — especially my adored husband, Dean Mullin, and my precious boys, Maxwell and Jackson. I have learned so much from all of you! I look forward to the surprises to come.

Nicole Letourneau

In addition to the many scientists, organizations, and funders Nicole mentioned, I would like to thank the entire UNB Child Studies team for welcoming me into their group and showing me the ropes as a young and largely clueless English major. I'd also like to thank my wife, Chantal, for her unfailing support and encouragement.

Justin Joschko

Notes

1. We are referring only to the third-person narratives used to illustrate certain principles. Stories regarding scientific studies and historical events are true.

2. At this point in history, the term "genes" referred merely to an abstract idea. The term was coined in 1909 by Danish botanist Wilhelm Johannsen, and DNA was only properly discovered in the 1940s, but the concept of a molecular unit of inheritance had already existed for many years prior to either of these events. Darwin himself championed the theory of gemmules, microscopic particles responsible for passing traits to subsequent generations, in 1868.

3. These are, of course, generalizations, ignoring geographic variation and the general heterogeneity of the scientific community, but the broad trends serve to illustrate the combative aspects of nature and nurture, and the notion that embracing either one was an all-or-nothing proposal.

4. Okay, we made this one up.

5. A congenital condition where the lower vertebrae do not fully fuse, allowing the spine to protrude partway through the gap. It can cause weakness or outright paralysis of the lower limbs.

6. CFTR stands for Cystic Fibrosis Transmembrane Conductance Regulator, a protein responsible for transporting ions between cells. It is coded for by a gene of the same name, which we are referring to here.

7. Think back to our example of cystic fibrosis in the last section, for example: evidence is accumulating to suggest that the severity of CF symptoms is determined by genes other than the CFTR gene. This suggests significant gene interactions in the presentation of even the easiest to identify genetic diseases.

8. New research has begun to indicate that introns might not be as "junky" as first thought. Though our understanding of their function remains spotty at best, scientists speculate that they may have a hand in controlling our development and regulating the transcription of other genes.

9. Proteins are created by the following sequence: DNA is transcribed into RNA, which is translated into amino acids, which form polypeptide chains, which then form proteins. While the end product of a gene is usually a protein, this is not always the case. On occasion, a gene merely codes for an RNA product, and the progression stops there.

10. This can make things rather confusing, which is why we have adopted the conventions suggested by the Human Genome Nomenclature Committee; from here on in, an alphanumeric symbol referring to a gene will be italicized (*DRD4*), while the same symbol referring to a gene product (in this case the receptor) will be written in standard, unitalicized characters (DRD4).

11. Recent research has actually downgraded the similarity to 95 percent, though this change is not yet universally acknowledged.

12. Certain conditions cause people to be born with too many or too few chromosomes, often with devastating effects. Perhaps the most well-known example of this is Down's syndrome, which occurs when a child inherits three sets of chromosome 21 rather than two. Strangely, having an extra chromosome can be as bad, or worse, as having one fewer than normal.

13. Or a partner of the same sex and opt for in vitro fertilization or surrogacy. It's all good.

14. Occasionally, a person is born with different-coloured eyes, or eyes where multiple colours coexist within the same iris. However, this condition — called heterochromia — is not a common occurrence (though one of the authors of this book has it, coincidentally) and does not speak to the typical rules of inheritance.

15. We are oversimplifying here in the interest of providing a straightforward example. Eye colour is actually the product of multiple genes.

16. In genetic nomenclature, an allele is assigned a single letter. The dominant version of the allele is written as a capital letter (B in our example), and the recessive allele with the same letter, only lower case (b). Which letter the writer chooses is unimportant, so long as he makes it clear which allele he is referring to.

17. Those that do are referred to as "Mendelian traits."

18. *5-HTTLPR* is actually not a gene. Rather, it is a section of the serotonin transporter gene *SLC6A4*. It sits on the promoter region of *SLC6A4*, making it responsible for determining how often the gene is coded. Calling it a gene in and of itself is technically inaccurate, but as the studies presented in this book deal exclusively with the *5-HTT* region, and treat it as if it were a gene, we have continued with that convention in order to simplify things.

19. For those interested in understanding the logic behind these names, they refer to the mutation which caused the split between the two alleles in the first place. Where the original "val" gene codes for the amino acid valine, the mutated "met" allele codes for a different amino acid, called methionine. Alleles are traditionally named after what makes them different from one another, which makes telling variations of individual polymorphisms apart fairly easy, but leads to tricky inconsistencies in nomenclature when discussing multiple genes (7-repeat and non-7-repeat versus l/l and s/s, for instance).

20. Only two children had rare met/met genotype, and they were removed from the study, as they were too small a cohort to

study as their own group, and rolling them into the val/met group would have skewed the data.

21. Complicating matters, zygosity can also refer to the allelic makeup of an individual gene. A person with two copies of the same allele is homozygous for that gene, and a person with two different alleles is heterozygous. We are unsure why the different terms use inconsistent suffixes — *ous* for one and *otic* for the other. The terms *monozygous* and *dizygous* are sometimes used, but they are not the standard. Sometimes scientific nomenclature seems deliberately confusing.

22. Perhaps more than any other, this study contributed to my recognition of the need for this book. It helps parents understand that the small, positive things they do with their children can count in big ways.

23. In doing Strange Situation procedures in my (Nicole's) lab, we were satisfied with as little as 30 seconds of separation.

24. Within reason, of course. Macaques set free in the tundra of Nunavut or the merciless, sizzling wastes of Death Valley would likely not last long. But then again, bereft of technology or a long tradition of survival in such extreme conditions, neither would humans.

25. This is a particularly nasty example of contradictory nomenclature within genomics. In Boyce's theory of Biological Sensitivity to Context, low reactivity refers to children who are minimally affected by the quality of their environment — dandelion children, as he calls them. But in Kim-Cohen's study, having a low-reactive *MAO-A* allele means you are actually more sensitive to environmental influence; a child with a

low-reactive *MAO-A* would be, according to Boyce's theory, high-reactive. Confusing, I know.

26. Gestaltism is a psychological theory dealing principally with the way the brain organizes and processes data. Gestalt psychologists often use optical illusions as examples of how the brain synthesises its perceptions, and the gestalt closure test is an extension of this practice. Children are presented with an incomplete picture, usually a series of black shapes, and are asked to fill in the blanks — using the white space to reconstruct the outline of an object, in spite of that object not being concretely presented. This may sound awfully abstract for a five-year-old, but such tricks are actually quite intuitive. Perhaps the most popular example is an image of a black vase on a white background that, upon further inspection, also resembles two white faces separated by a black background.

27. "Coding" refers to the process wherein a gene instructs the cell it resides in to make a protein.

28. The term epigenetics makes use of the Greek prefix "epi," meaning "above." Thus the epigenome is above the genome, both metaphorically as a controlling factor and, in the case of molecules clinging to our DNA, literally.

29. Some methyl tags may remain from the sex cells, but how and to what extent is not yet totally understood. We know certain traits can be passed down epigenetically, but cannot say for sure how often these influences are passed along with the genes directly and how often the genes in question are re-methylated by environmental factors.

30. Gene transcription is the process of converting a DNA sequence into an RNA sequence, the first step in the protein development process. Converting that RNA sequence into a polypeptide chain (the amino acid sequence that eventually becomes a protein) is called translation. The gene "transcribes" its message onto a more disposable medium, the RNA, which is then "translated" from a nucleotide sequence into a different language, one of amino acids.

31. The more technical term for this diversity is "potential." In biological parlance, a cell's potential refers to its ability to replicate the function of other cells. The zygote's first few cells — commonly known as stem cells — are totipotent, as they can become any cell in the human body. The blastula's stratified cells — the ectoderm, mesoderm, and endoderm — are pluripotent, capable of becoming a wide swath of cells, but limited in choice to one of three major families. Specialized cells — such as a liver cell, say — are unipotent, as they have the potential to become only one type of cell.

32. Phenotype simply means the end result of development. Your genotype consists solely of your DNA, while your phenotype also accounts for any epigenetic or environmental influences that caused you to become who you are.

33. Recent studies of the Dutch Hunger Winter cohort have unearthed a gene called *IGF2* (short for insulin-like growth factor) that is less methylated in the offspring of those affected by the Hunger Winter than in the general Dutch population. The gene has not, however, been linked to any of the conditions associated with the Hunger Winter cohort, so the odds of it being a silver bullet for obesity,

cancer, or any other health concerns are, unfortunately, quite slim.

34. Compared to the relatively straightforward licking and grooming, "arched-back nursing" may sound arbitrary, but it actually makes a big difference to infant rats. Mothers who arch their backs while nursing their young make their teats more accessible, allowing the pups greater access and more time to spend feeding. Nursing is an excellent bonding exercise in mammals, making arched-back nursing a gesture of comfort and support on par with the more obvious licking and grooming.

35. The actual gene in question is the glucocorticoid receptor gene, which features prominently in the body's ability to produce and respond to the stress hormone cortisol. Calling it the "stress response gene" is oversimplifying things a bit, perhaps, but we did so anyway for the sake of readability.

36. Discussed in greater detail in a previous chapter.

37. Marcy and Melissa's story was used to examine the concept of Biological Sensitivity to Context. The fictional twins were separated shortly after birth. Marcy went to an affluent and doting couple while Melissa remained with her impoverished and flighty birth mother. Marcy, enriched by her privileged upbringing, thrived, ultimately becoming a neurosurgeon. Melissa, resentful of her mother's emotional distance and poverty, rebelled, took a lot of drugs, and got pregnant before graduating high school.

38. Chronic stress can also result in a blunted cortisol response. That is, the HPA system, like an engine in overdrive,

eventually downshifts when it can't accelerate or maintain a
high speed.

39. This is called cortisol or HPA axis blunting.

40. We will spare you the full litany of tongue-twisting names, as
knowing which leukocyte performs which task isn't necessary
to understanding how the immune system works as a whole.
Simply bear in mind that we use the terms "leukocyte" and
"white blood cell" interchangeably, and that they may refer to
any cell under that banner.

41. Aside, of course, from any mutations that may have occurred
within a cell — and our cells do not suffer mutations gladly,
maintaining a strict and merciless regimen of tracking them
down and purging them from our DNA.

42. In truth, the findings are slightly more complicated. Meaney
and Szyf couldn't simply peer through a microscope and
count the methyl tags on each patient's GR gene. Instead,
they look at the prevalence of the gene's products in the surrounding tissue. As you may recall, DNA produces RNA,
which produces the polypeptide chains used to build proteins. Unlike DNA, which coils into tight, protective strands
of chromatin, RNA floats freely through our bodies, and is
thus far easier to collect and count. The more RNA of a given
gene is present in a tissue, the more actively that gene is functioning and the less methylated it is, allowing us an accurate
picture of a gene's pattern of methylation.

43. There are, of course, exceptions in extreme cases. For instance,
cystic fibrosis is caused by a child inheriting two copies of a
certain recessive allele. The best parents in the world cannot

change that fact, and it would be grossly unfair to pin the blame for their child's condition on them. However, even in such a case, strong, supportive parenting could conceivably help to alleviate some of the disorder's symptoms.

Bibliography

Anda, Robert F., Alexander Butchart, Vincent J. Felitti, and David W. Brown. "Building a Framework for Global Surveillance of the Public Health Implications of Adverse Childhood Experiences." *American Journal of Preventive Medicine* 39, no. 1 (2010): 93.

Bakermans-Kranenburg, Marian J., and Marinus H. Van IJzendoorn. "Gene–Environment Interaction of the Dopamine D4 Receptor (DRD4) and Observed Maternal Insensitivity Predicting Externalizing Behavior in Preschoolers."*Developmental Psychobiology* 48, no. 5 (2006): 406–409.

Bakermans-Kranenburg, Marian J., and Marinus H. Van IJzendoorn. "Research Review: Genetic Vulnerability or Differential Susceptibility in Child Development: The Case of Attachment." *Journal of Child Psychology and Psychiatry* 48, no. 12 (2007): 1160–1173.

Bakermans-Kranenburg, Marian J., Marinus H. Van IJzendoorn, Judi Mesman, Lenneke R.A. Alink, and Femmie Juffer. "Effects of an Attachment-Based Intervention on Daily Cortisol Moderated by Dopamine Receptor D4: A Randomized

Control Trial on 1- to 3-Year-Olds Screened for External-izing Behavior." *Development and Psychopathology* 20, no. 3 (2008): 805–820.

Bakermans-Kranenburg, Marian J., Marinus H. Van IJzen-doorn, Femke TA Pijlman, Judi Mesman, and Femmie Juffer. "Experimental Evidence for Differential Susceptibil-ity: Dopamine D4 Receptor Polymorphism (DRD4 VNTR) Moderates Intervention Effects on Toddlers' Externalizing Behavior in a Randomized Controlled Trial." *Developmental Psychology* 44, no. 1 (2008): 293.

Barr, C.S., T.K. Newman, M.L. Becker, C.C. Parker, M. Cham-poux, K.P. Lesch, D. Goldman, S.J. Suomi, and J.D. Higley. "The Utility of the Non-human Primate Model for Studying Gene by Environment Interactions in Behavioral Research." *Genes, Brain and Behavior* 2, no. 6 (2003): 336–340.

Barr, C.S., T.K. Newman, M.L. Becker, M. Champoux, K.P. Lesch, S.J. Suomi, D. Goldman, and J.D. Higley. "Serotonin Transporter Gene Variation Is Associated with Alcohol Sensitivity in Rhesus Macaques Exposed to Early-Life Stress." *Alcoholism: Clinical and Experimental Research* 27, no. 5 (2006): 812–817.

Bath, Kevin G., and Francis S. Lee. "Variant BDNF (Val66Met) Impact on Brain Structure and Function." *Cognitive, Affective, & Behavioral Neuroscience* 6, no. 1 (2006): 79–85.

Beckett, Celia, Barbara Maughan, Michael Rutter, Jenny Castle, Emma Colvert, Christine Groothues, Jana Kreppner, Suzanne Stevens, Thomas G. O'Connor, and Edmund J.S. Sonuga-Barke. "Do the Effects of Early Severe Deprivation on Cognition Persist into Early Adolescence? Findings from the English and Romanian Adoptees Study." *Child Development* 77, no. 3 (2006): 696–711.

Belsky, Jay. "Theory Testing, Effect-Size Evaluation, and Dif-ferential Susceptibility to Rearing Influence: The Case of

Mothering and Attachment." *Child Development* 68, no. 4 (2006): 598–600.

Bennett, A.J., K.P. Lesch, A. Heils, J.C. Long, J.G. Lorenz, S.E. Shoaf, M. Champoux, S.J. Suomi, M.V. Linnoila, and J.D. Higley. "Early Experience and Serotonin Transporter Gene Variation Interact to Influence Primate CNS Function." *Molecular Psychiatry* 7, no. 1 (2002): 118–122.

Bowlby, John. *Attachment and Loss: Volume II: Separation, Anxiety and Anger*. London: The Hogarth Press and the Institute of Psycho-Analysis, 1973.

Boyce, W. Thomas, Margaret Chesney, Abbey Alkon, Jeanne M. Tschann, Sally Adams, Beth Chesterman, Frances Cohen, Pamela Kaiser, Susan Folkman, and Diane Wara. "Psychobiologic Reactivity to Stress and Childhood Respiratory Illnesses: Results of Two Prospective Studies." *Psychosomatic Medicine* 57, no. 5 (1995): 411–422.

Boyce, W. Thomas, and Bruce J. Ellis. "Biological Sensitivity to Context: I. An Evolutionary-Developmental Theory of the Origins and Functions of Stress Reactivity." *Development and Psychopathology* 17, no. 2 (2005): 271–301.

Brody, Gene H., Steven R.H. Beach, Robert A. Philibert, Yi-fu Chen, Man-Kit Lei, Velma McBride Murry, and Anita C. Brown. "Parenting Moderates a Genetic Vulnerability Factor in Longitudinal Increases in Youths' Substance Use." *Journal of Consulting and Clinical Psychology* 77, no. 1 (2009): 1.

Bronson, P., and A. Merryman. *Nurtureshock: New Thinking about Children*. New York: Twelve, 2009.

Caldji, Christian, Josie Diorio, and Michael J. Meaney. "Variations in Maternal Care Alter GABAA Receptor Subunit Expression in Brain Regions Associated with Fear." *Neuropsychopharmacology* 28, no. 11 (2003): 1950–1959.

Caldji, Christian, Josie Diorio, Hymie Anisman, and Michael J. Meaney. "Maternal Behavior Regulates Benzodiazepine/ GABAA Receptor Subunit Expression in Brain Regions Associated with Fear in BALB/c and C57BL/6 Mice." *Neuropsychopharmacology* 29, no. 7 (2004): 1344–1352.

Campbell, Susan B., Daniel S. Shaw, and Miles Gilliom. "Early Externalizing Behavior Problems: Toddlers and Preschoolers at Risk for Later Maladjustment." *Development and Psychopathology* 12, no. 3 (2000): 467–488.

Cattaert, Daniel, Jean-Paul Delbecque, Donald H. Edwards, and Fadi A. Issa. "Social Interactions Determine Postural Network Sensitivity to 5-HT." *The Journal of Neuroscience* 30, no. 16 (2010): 5603–5616.

Champagne, Frances A., Ian C.G. Weaver, Josie Diorio, Sergiy Dymov, Moshe Szyf, and Michael J. Meaney. "Maternal Care Associated with Methylation of the Estrogen Receptor-α1b Promoter and Estrogen Receptor-α Expression in the Medial Preoptic Area of Female Offspring." *Endocrinology* 147, no. 6 (2006): 2909–2915.

Champoux, Maribeth, Allyson Bennett, Courtney Shannon, J. Dee Higley, Klaus Peter Lesch, and Stephen J. Suomi. "Serotonin Transporter Gene Polymorphism, Differential Early Rearing, and Behavior in Rhesus Monkey Neonates." *Molecular Psychiatry* 7, no. 10 (2002): 1058–1063.

Charmandari, Evangelia, Tomoshige, Kino, and George P. Chrousos. "Glucocorticoids and Their Actions: An Introduction." *Annals of the New York Academy of Sciences* 1024, no. 1 (2004): 1–8.

Charney, E. "Behavior Genetics and Post Genomics." *Behavioral and Brain Sciences* 35, no. 5 (2012): 331–358.

Chen, Edith, Gregory E. Miller, Michael S. Kobor, and Steve W. Cole. "Maternal Warmth Buffers the Effects of Low Early-Life Socioeconomic Status on Pro-inflammatory Signaling in Adulthood." *Molecular Psychiatry* 16, no. 7 (2010): 729–737.

Cirulli, Francesca, Alessandra Berry, and Enrico Alleva. "Early Disruption of the Mother–Infant Relationship: Effects on Brain Plasticity and Implications for Psychopathology." *Neuroscience & Biobehavioral Reviews* 27, no. 1 (2003): 73–82.

Cirulli, Francesca, Nadia Francia, Alessandra Berry, Luigi Aloe, Enrico Alleva, and Stephen J. Suomi. "Early Life Stress as a Risk Factor for Mental Health: Role of Neurotrophins from Rodents to Non-human Primates." *Neuroscience & Biobehavioral Reviews* 33, no. 4 (2009): 573–585.

Collins, W. Andrew, Eleanor E. Maccoby, Laurence Steinberg, E. Mavis Hetherington, and Marc H. Bornstein. "Contemporary Research on Parenting: The Case for Nature and Nurture." *American Psychologist* 55, no. 2 (2000): 218.

Dawkins, Richard. *The Greatest Show on Earth: The Evidence for Evolution.* London: Transworld Digital, 2009.

Diamond, Marian, Marian Cleeves Diamond, and Janet Hopson. *Magic Trees of the Mind: How to Nurture Your Child's Intelligence, Creativity, and Healthy Emotions from Birth Through Adolescence.* New York: Plume Books, 1999.

Dobbs, D. "Orchid Children." *The Atlantic Monthly* (2009): 60–68.

Dreber, Anna, Coren L. Apicella, Dan T.A. Eisenberg, Justin R. Garcia, Richard S. Zamore, J. Koji Lum, and Benjamin Campbell. "The 7R Polymorphism in the Dopamine Receptor D4 Gene (*DRD4*) Is Associated with Financial Risk Taking in Men." *Evolution and Human Behavior* 30, no. 2 (2009): 85–92.

Eisenberg, Nancy, Amanda Cumberland, Tracy L. Spinrad, Richard A. Fabes, Stephanie A. Shepard, Mark Reiser, Bridget C. Murphy, Sandra H. Losoya, and Ivanna K. Guthrie. "The Relations of Regulation and Emotionality to Children's Externalizing and Internalizing Problem Behavior." *Child Development* 72, no. 4 (2001): 1112–1134.

Eliot, Lise. *What's Going On in There?: How the Brain and Mind Develop in the First Five Years of Life.* New York: Bantam, 2000.

Ellis, Bruce J., Marilyn J. Essex, and W. Thomas Boyce. "Biological Sensitivity to Context: II. Empirical Explorations of an Evolutionary-Developmental Theory." *Development and Psychopathology* 17, no. 2 (2005): 303–328.

Essex, Marilyn J., W. Thomas Boyce, Clyde Hertzman, Lucia L. Lam, Jeffrey M. Armstrong, Sarah Neumann, and Michael S. Kobor. "Epigenetic Vestiges of Early Developmental Adversity: Childhood Stress Exposure and DNA Methylation in Adolescence." *Child Development* (2011).

Felitti, Vincent J., Robert F. Anda, Dale Nordenberg, David F. Williamson, Alison M. Spitz, Valerie Edwards, Mary P. Koss, and James S. Marks. "Relationship of Childhood Abuse and Household Dysfunction to Many of the Leading Causes of Death in Adults." *American Journal of Preventive Medicine* 14, no. 4 (1998): 245–258.

Felitti, Vincent J. "The Relation Between Adverse Childhood Experiences and Adult Health: Turning Gold into Lead." *Perm J* 6, no. 1 (2002): 44–47.

Fisher, Lianne, Elinor W. Ames, Kim Chisholm, and Lynn Savoie. "Problems Reported by Parents of Romanian Orphans Adopted to British Columbia." *International Journal of Behavioral Development* 20, no. 1 (1997): 67–82.

Foley, Debra L., Lindon J. Eaves, Brandon Wormley, Judy L. Silberg, Hermine H. Maes, Jonathan Kuhn, and Brien Riley. "Childhood Adversity, Monoamine Oxidase a Genotype, and Risk for Conduct Disorder." *Archives of General Psychiatry* 61, no. 7 (2004): 738.

Francis, Darlene D., Josie Diorio, Dong Liu, and Michael J. Meaney. "Nongenomic Transmission Across Generations of Maternal Behavior and Stress Responses in the Rat." *Science* 286, no. 5442 (1999): 1155–1158.

Francis, Darlene D., Josie Diorio, Paul M. Plotsky, and Michael J. Meaney. "Environmental Enrichment Reverses the Effects of Maternal Separation on Stress Reactivity." *The Journal of Neuroscience* 22, no. 18 (2002): 7840–7843.

Francis, Richard C. *Epigenetics: The Ultimate Mystery of Inheritance*. New York: W.W. Norton, 2011.

Frigerio, Alessandra, Elisa Ceppi, Marianna Rusconi, Roberto Giorda, Maria Elisabetta Raggi, and Pasco Fearon. "The Role Played by the Interaction Between Genetic Factors and Attachment in the Stress Response in Infancy." *Journal of Child Psychology and Psychiatry* 50, no. 12 (2009): 1513–1522.

Garmezy, Norman, ed. "Stress, Coping, and Development in Children." In *Seminar on Stress and Coping in Children, 1979, Ctr for Advanced Study in the Behavioral Sciences, Stanford, CA, US*. Johns Hopkins University Press, 1983.

Gervai, Judit, Zsofia Nemoda, Krisztina Lakatos, Zsolt Ronai, Ildiko Toth, Krisztina Ney, and Maria Sasvari-Szekely. "Transmission Disequilibrium Tests Confirm the Link Between DRD4 Gene Polymorphism and Infant Attachment." *American Journal of Medical Genetics Part B: Neuropsychiatric Genetics* 132, no. 1 (2004): 126–130.

Gervai, Judit, Alexa Novak, Krisztina Lakatos, Ildiko Toth, Ildiko Danis, Zsolt Ronai, Zsofia Nemoda, et al. "Infant Genotype May Moderate Sensitivity to Maternal Affective Communications: Attachment Disorganization, Quality of Care, and the DRD4 Polymorphism." *Social Neuroscience* 2, no. 3–4 (2007): 307–319.

Gunnar, Megan R., Sara J. Morison, Kim Chisholm, and Michelle Schuder. "Salivary Cortisol Levels in Children Adopted from Romanian Orphanages." *Development and Psychopathology* 13, no. 3 (2001): 611–628.

Haberstick, Brett C., Jeffrey M. Lessem, Christian J. Hopfer, Andrew Smolen, Marissa A. Ehringer, David Timberlake, and John

K. Hewitt. "Monoamine Oxidase A (MAOA) and Antisocial Behaviors in the Presence of Childhood and Adolescent Maltreatment." *American Journal of Medical Genetics Part B: Neuropsychiatric Genetics* 135, no. 1 (2005): 59–64.

Haggerty, Robert J., Lonnie R. Sherrod, Norman Garmezy, and Michael Rutter. *Stress, Risk, and Resilience in Children and Adolescents: Processes, Mechanisms, and Interventions.* Cambridge: Cambridge University Press, 1994.

Hesse, Erik, and Mary Main. "Frightened, Threatening, and Dissociative Parental Behavior in Low-Risk Samples: Description, Discussion, and Interpretations." *Development and Psychopathology* 18, no. 2 (2006): 309–343.

Higley, J.D., S.J. Suomi, and M. Linnoila. "A Nonhuman Primate Model of Type II Excessive Alcohol Consumption? Part 1. Low Cerebrospinal Fluid 5-Hydroxyindoleacetic Acid Concentrations and Diminished Social Competence Correlate with Excessive Alcohol Consumption." *Alcoholism: Clinical and Experimental Research* 20, no. 4 (2006): 629–642.

Hinshaw, Stephen P. "On the Distinction Between Attentional Deficits/Hyperactivity and Conduct Problems/Aggression in Child Psychopathology." *Psychological Bulletin* 101, no. 3 (1987): 443.

Jablonka, Eva, and Marion J. Lamb. *Evolution in Four Dimensions: Genetic, Epigenetic, Behavioral, and Symbolic Variation in the History of Life.* Cambridge, MA: MIT Press, 2005.

Jaffee, Sara R., Avshalom Caspi, Terrie E. Moffitt, Kenneth A. Dodge, Michael Rutter, Alan Taylor, and Lucy A. Tully. "Nature × Nurture: Genetic Vulnerabilities Interact with Physical Maltreatment to Promote Conduct Problems." *Development and Psychopathology* 17, no. 1 (2005): 67–84.

Kaffman, Arie, and Michael J. Meaney. "Neurodevelopmental Sequelae of Postnatal Maternal Care in Rodents: Clinical and Research Implications of Molecular Insights." *Journal of Child Psychology and Psychiatry* 48, no. 3–4 (2007): 224–244.

Karr-Morse, Robin. *Scared Sick: The Role of Childhood Trauma in Adult Disease.* New York: Basic Books, 2012.

Kaufman, Joan, Bao-Zhu Yang, Heather Douglas-Palumberi, Shadi Houshyar, Deborah Lipschitz, John H. Krystal, and Joel Gelernter. "Social Supports and Serotonin Transporter Gene Moderate Depression in Maltreated Children." *Proceedings of the National Academy of Sciences of the United States of America* 101, no. 49 (2004): 17316–17321.

Kaufman, Joan, Bao-Zhu Yang, Heather Douglas-Palumberi, Damion Grasso, Deborah Lipschitz, Shadi Houshyar, John H. Krystal, and Joel Gelernter. "Brain-Derived Neurotrophic Factor–5-HTTLPR Gene Interactions and Environmental Modifiers of Depression in Children." *Biological Psychiatry* 59, no. 8 (2006): 673–680.

Keating, Daniel P., ed. *Nature and Nurture in Early Child Development.* Cambridge, MA: Cambridge University Press, 2010.

Keinan-Boker, Lital, Neomi Vin-Raviv, Irena Liphshitz, Shai Linn, and Micha Barchana. "Cancer Incidence in Israeli Jewish Survivors of World War II." *Journal of the National Cancer Institute* 101, no. 21 (2009): 1489–1500.

Kim-Cohen, Julia, Avshalom Caspi, Alan Taylor, Benjamin Williams, Rhiannon Newcombe, Ian W. Craig, and Terrie E. Moffitt. "MAOA, Maltreatment, and Gene–Environment Interaction Predicting Children's Mental Health: New Evidence and a Meta-analysis." *Molecular Psychiatry* 11, no. 10 (2006): 903–913.

Kreek, Mary Jeanne, David A. Nielsen, Eduardo R. Butelman, and K. Steven LaForge. "Genetic Influences on Impulsivity, Risk Taking, Stress Responsivity and Vulnerability to Drug Abuse and Addiction." *Nature Neuroscience* 8, no. 11 (2005): 1450–1457.

Lakatos, K., I. Toth, Z. Nemoda, K. Ney, M. Sasvari-Szekely, and J. Gervai. "Dopamine D4 Receptor (DRD4) Gene Polymorphism Is Associated with Attachment Disorganization in Infants." *Molecular Psychiatry* 5, no. 6 (2000): 633.

Lerman, Caryn, Neil Caporaso, David Main, Janet Audrain, Neal R. Boyd, Elise D. Bowman, and Peter G. Shields. "Depression and Self-Medication with Nicotine: The Modifying Influence of the Dopamine D4 Receptor Gene." *Health Psychology* 17, no. 1 (1998): 56.

Letourneau, N., L. Duffett-Leger, L. Levac, B. Watson, and K. Young (2011). Socioeconomic Status and Child Development: A Meta-Analysis. *Journal of Emotional and Behavioral Disorders.* Published online before print, December 15, 2011, doi: 10.1177/1063426611421007.

Letourneau, N.L., C.B. Fedick, and J.D. Willms. "Mothering and Domestic Violence: A Longitudinal Analysis." *Journal of Family Violence* 22, no. 8 (2007): 649–659.

Letourneau, Nicole, Gerald F. Giesbrecht, Francois P. Bernier, and Justin Joschko. "How Do Interactions Between Early Caregiving Environment and Genes Influence Health and Behavior?" *Biological Research for Nursing* (2012).

Li, James J., and Steve S. Lee. "Association of Positive and Negative Parenting Behavior with Childhood ADHD: Interactions with Offspring Monoamine Oxidase A (MAO-A) Genotype." *Journal of Abnormal Child Psychology* 40, no. 2 (2012): 165–175.

Luijk, Maartje P.C.M., Glenn I. Roisman, John D. Haltigan, Henning Tiemeier, Cathryn Booth-LaForce, Marinus H. Van IJzendoorn, Jay Belsky, et al. "Dopaminergic, Serotonergic, and Oxytonergic Candidate Genes Associated with Infant Attachment Security and Disorganization? In Search of Main and Interaction Effects." *Journal of Child Psychology and Psychiatry* 52, no. 12 (2011): 1295–1307.

Mainemer, Henry, Lorraine C. Gilman, and Elinor W. Ames. "Parenting Stress in Families Adopting Children from Romanian Orphanages." *Journal of Family Issues* 19, no. 2 (1998): 164–180.

Marcovitch, Sharon, Susan Goldberg, Amanda Gold, Jane Washington, Christine Wasson, Karla Krekewich, and Mark Handley-Derry. "Determinants of Behavioural Problems in Romanian Children Adopted in Ontario." *International Journal of Behavioral Development* 20, no. 1 (1997): 17–31.

Maté, Gabor. *In the Realm of Hungry Ghosts: Close Encounters with Addiction.* Toronto: Knopf Canada, 2008.

Maté, Gabor. *When the Body Says No: Understanding the Stress–Disease Connection.* Hoboken, NJ: Wiley, 2011.

McCormack, K., M.M. Sanchez, M. Bardi, and D. Maestripieri. "Maternal Care Patterns and Behavioral Development of Rhesus Macaque Abused Infants in the First 6 Months of Life." *Developmental Psychobiology* 48, no. 7 (2006): 537–550.

McCormack, K., T.K. Newman, J.D. Higley, D. Maestripieri, and M.M. Sanchez. "Serotonin Transporter Gene Variation, Infant Abuse, and Responsiveness to Stress in Rhesus Macaque Mothers and Infants." *Hormones and Behavior* 55, no. 4 (2009): 538–547.

McCormick, J.A., V. Lyons, M.D. Jacobson, J. Noble, J. Diorio, M. Nyirenda, S. Weaver, et al. "5'-heterogeneity of Glucocorticoid Receptor Messenger RNA Is Tissue Specific: Differential Regulation of Variant Transcripts by Early-Life Events." *Molecular Endocrinology* 14, no. 4 (2000): 506–517.

McDermott, Rose, Dustin Tingley, Jonathan Cowden, Giovanni Frazzetto, and Dominic D.P. Johnson. "Monoamine Oxidase A Gene (MAOA) Predicts Behavioral Aggression Following Provocation." *Proceedings of the National Academy of Sciences* 106, no. 7 (2009): 2118–2123.

Meaney, Michael J., Josie Diorio, Darlene Francis, Shelley Weaver, Joyce Yau, Karen Chapman, and Jonathan R. Seckl. "Postnatal Handling Increases the Expression of cAMP-inducible Transcription Factors in the Rat Hippocampus: The Effects of Thyroid Hormones and Serotonin." *The Journal of Neuroscience* 20, no. 10 (2000): 3926–3935.

Meaney, Michael J. "Maternal Care, Gene Expression, and the Transmission of Individual Differences in Stress Reactivity Across Generations." *Neuroscience* 24 (2001).

Meaney, Michael J., and Moshe Szyf. "Maternal Care as a Model for Experience-dependent Chromatin Plasticity?" *TRENDS in Neurosciences* 28, no. 9 (2005): 456–463.

Miller, Gregory E., and Edith Chen. "Harsh Family Climate in Early Life Presages the Emergence of a Proinflammatory Phenotype in Adolescence." *Psychological Science* 21, no. 6 (2010): 848–856.

Miller, Gregory E., Margie E. Lachman, Edith Chen, Tara L. Gruenewald, Arun S. Karlamangla, and Teresa E. Seeman. "Pathways to Resilience: Maternal Nurturance as a Buffer Against the Effects of Childhood Poverty on Metabolic Syndrome at Midlife." *Psychological Science* 22, no. 12 (2011): 1591–1599.

Miller, Gregory E., Edith Chen, and Karen J. Parker. "Psychological Stress in Childhood and Susceptibility to the Chronic Diseases of Aging: Moving Toward a Model of Behavioral and Biological Mechanisms." *Psychological Bulletin* 137, no. 6 (2011): 959.

Moore, David. *The Dependent Gene: The Fallacy of "Nature Vs. Nurture."* New York: Holt Paperbacks, 2003.

National Scientific Council on the Developing Child. *Young Children Develop in an Environment of Relationships. Working Paper No. 1.* Retrieved from *www.developingchild.net*.

Perry, Bruce D. "Incubated in Terror: Neurodevelopmental Factors in the 'Cycle of Violence.'" *Children in a Violent Society* (1997): 124–148.

Ridley, Matt. *The Agile Gene: How Nature Turns on Nurture.*
New York: Harper Perennial, 2004.

Rutter, Michael. "Developmental Catch-up, and Deficit, Following Adoption after Severe Global Early Privation." *Journal of
Child Psychology and Psychiatry* 39, no. 4 (1998): 465–476.

Rutter, Michael. *Genes and Behavior: Nature–Nurture Interplay
Explained.* Malden, MA: Blackwell, 2008.

Sabatini, Michael J., Philip Ebert, David A. Lewis, Pat Levitt, Judy
L. Cameron, and Károly Mirnics. "Amygdala Gene Expression
Correlates of Social Behavior in Monkeys Experiencing
Maternal Separation." *The Journal of Neuroscience* 27, no. 12
(2007): 3295–3304.

Schmidt, Louis A., Nathan A. Fox, Kenneth H. Rubin, Stella
Hu, and Dean H. Hamer. "Molecular Genetics of Shyness
and Aggression in Preschoolers." *Personality and Individual
Differences* 33, no. 2 (2002): 227–238.

Shah, Prachi E., Peter Fonagy, and Lane Strathearn. "Is Attachment Transmitted Across Generations? The Plot Thickens."
Clinical Child Psychology and Psychiatry 15, no. 3 (2010):
329–345.

Shannon, Courtney, Maribeth Champoux, and Stephen J. Suomi.
"Rearing Condition and Plasma Cortisol in Rhesus Monkey
Infants." *American Journal of Primatology* 46, no. 4 (1998):
311–321.

Shelton, Katherine H., Gordon T. Harold, Tom A. Fowler,
Frances J. Rice, Michael C. Neale, Anita Thapar, and
Marianne B.M. van den Bree. "Parent–Child Relations,
Conduct Problems and Cigarette Use in Adolescence:
Examining the Role of Genetic and Environmental Factors
on Patterns of Behavior." *Journal of Youth and Adolescence*
37, no. 10 (2008): 1216–1228.

Shonkoff, Jack P., Andrew S. Garner, Benjamin S. Siegel, Mary I.
Dobbins, Marian F. Earls, Laura McGuinn, John Pascoe, and

David L. Wood. "The Lifelong Effects of Early Childhood Adversity and Toxic Stress." *Pediatrics* 129, no. 1 (2012): e232–e246.

Siegel, Daniel J. *The Developing Mind: Toward a Neurobiology of Interpersonal Experience.* New York: Guilford Press, 1999.

Siegel, Daniel J., and Mary Hartzell. *Parenting from the Inside Out: How a Deeper Self-understanding Can Help You Raise Children Who Thrive.* J.P. Tarcher, 2004.

Smith, Mark A., Su-Yong Kim, Helga J.J. Van Oers, and Seymour Levine. "Maternal Deprivation and Stress Induce Immediate Early Genes in the Infant Rat Brain." *Endocrinology* 138, no. 11 (1997): 4622–4628.

Spangler, Gottfried, Monika Johann, Zsolt Ronai, and Peter Zimmermann. "Genetic and Environmental Influence on Attachment Disorganization." *Journal of Child Psychology and Psychiatry* 50, no. 8 (2009): 952–961.

Strathearn, Lane, and Linda C. Mayes. "Cocaine Addiction in Mothers." *Annals of the New York Academy of Sciences* 1187, no. 1 (2010): 172–183.

Strathearn, L. "Maternal Neglect: Oxytocin, Dopamine and the Neurobiology of Attachment." *Journal of Neuroendocrinology* 23, no. 11 (2011): 1054–1065.

Suomi, Stephen J. "Gene–Environment Interactions and the Neurobiology of Social Conflict." *Annals of the New York Academy of Sciences* 1008, no. 1 (2003): 132–139.

Szyf, Moshe, Ian C.G. Weaver, Francis A. Champagne, Josie Diorio, and Michael J. Meaney. "Maternal Programming of Steroid Receptor Expression and Phenotype Through DNA Methylation in the Rat." *Frontiers in Neuroendocrinology* 26, no. 3–4 (2005): 139–162.

Tochigi, Mamoru, Hiroyuki Hibino, Takeshi Otowa, Chieko Kato, Tetsuya Marui, Toshiyuki Ohtani, Tadashi Umekage, Nobumasa Kato, and Tsukasa Sasaki. "Association Between

Dopamine D4 Receptor (DRD4) Exon III Polymorphism and Neuroticism in the Japanese Population." *Neuroscience Letters* 398, no. 3 (2006): 333–336.

Van IJzendoorn, Marinus H., and Marian J. Bakermans-Kranenburg. "Disorganized Attachment in Early Childhood: Meta-analysis of Precursors, Concomitants, and Sequelae." *Development and Psychopathology* 11 (1999): 225–249.

Van IJzendoorn, Marinus H., and Marian J. Bakermans-Kranenburg. "DRD4 7-Repeat Polymorphism Moderates the Association Between Maternal Unresolved Loss or Trauma and Infant Disorganization." *Attachment & Human Development* 8, no. 4 (2006): 291–307.

Van Tol, Hubert H.M., Caren M. Wu, Hong-Chang Guan, Koichi Ohara, James R. Bunzow, Olivier Civelli, James Kennedy, Philip Seeman, Hyman B. Niznik, and Vera Jovanovic. "Multiple Dopamine D4 Receptor Variants in the Human Population." (1992): 149–152.

Waters, E., and M. Valenzuela. "Explaining Disorganized Attachment: Clues from Research on Mild-to-Moderately Undernourished Children in Chile." *Attachment Disorganization* (1999): 265–290.

Weaver, I.C., Patricia La Plante, Shelley Weaver, Angel Parent, Shakti Sharma, Josie Diorio, Karen E. Chapman, Jonathan R. Seckl, Moshe Szyf, and Michael J. Meaney. "Early Environmental Regulation of Hippocampal Glucocorticoid Receptor Gene Expression: Characterization of Intracellular Mediators and Potential Genomic Target Sites." *Molecular and Cellular Endocrinology* 185, no. 1–2 (2001): 205.

Weaver, Ian C.G., Nadia Cervoni, Frances A. Champagne, Ana C. D'Alessio, Shakti Sharma, Jonathan R. Seckl, Sergiy Dymov, Moshe Szyf, and Michael J. Meaney. "Epigenetic Programming by Maternal Behavior." *Nature Neuroscience* 7, no. 8 (2004): 847–854.

Weaver, Ian C.G., Frances A. Champagne, Shelley E. Brown, Sergiy Dymov, Shakti Sharma, Michael J. Meaney, and Moshe Szyf. "Reversal of Maternal Programming of Stress Resp-onses in Adult Offspring Through Methyl Supplementation: Altering Epigenetic Marking Later in Life." *The Journal of Neuroscience* 25, no. 47 (2005): 11045–11054.

Werner, Emmy E., and Ruth S. Smith. *Overcoming the Odds: High Risk Children from Birth to Adulthood*. Ithaca, NY: Cornell University Press, 1992.

Index

Of Related Interest

Raising Boys in a New Kind of World
Michael Reist
978-1-459700437
$24.99

From video games to the Internet, technology is having a profound effect on today's boys. Author Michael Reist writes from the front lines. As a classroom teacher for more than thirty years and the father of three boys, he is in an ideal position to provide practical advice on how to communicate with boys and how to identify their problems.

Children Come First
Mediation, Not Litigation When Marriage Ends
Howard H. Irving
978-1-554887958
$24.99

For three decades Dr. Howard H. Irving has championed the use of divorce mediation outside the adversarial court system to save couples and their children the bitterness of winner-takes-all custody battles. Here, he calls on his vast experience of mediating more than two thousand cases to help couples contemplating divorce.

Dads Under Construction
Adventures in Fatherhood
Neil Campbell
978-1-550029666
$19.99

Many men today feel set adrift from the notion of themselves as "father." Times have changed, and the old, familiar, traditional models of parenting no longer work. Society has not yet evolved a strong and workable new model of parenting, or, in particular, of fathering. Dr. Neil Campbell believes the answer to the question "What is an involved father?" can be found within the experiences and stories of our own lives. In this book, he takes us into his life, first as a son, then as a father, sharing some of the profound insights he learned along the way.

Available at your favourite bookseller